THE COMPLETE INDEX TO

Fine Print

1975–1990

2003

· · · ·

PRO ARTE LIBRI

SAN FRANCISCO

· · · ·

OAK KNOLL PRESS

NEW CASTLE

Published by
Oak Knoll Press
310 Delaware Street
New Castle
Delaware 19720, USA

and

Pro Arte Libri
P.O. Box 193397
San Francisco
California 94119 USA

Title: The Complete Index to *Fine Print*, 1975–1990
Editor: Sandra Kirshenbaum

Copyright © 2003 by Sandra D. Kirshenbaum
All rights reserved

Library of Congress Cataloging-in-Publication Data

The complete index to Fine print, 1975–1990
   p.   cm.
Publication of Fine Print ceased in 1990 with v. 16, no. 3; this is v. 16, no. 4.
ISBN 1-58456-096-7
1. Fine print (San Francisco, Calif.)—Indexes
2. Printing—periodicals—Indexes
Z119.F55 2003
016.6862—dc21   2002034558

No part of this book may be reproduced in any manner without the express written consent of the publisher, except in the case of brief excerpts in critical reviews and articles. All inquiries should be addressed to: Oak Knoll Press, 310 Delaware St., New Castle, DE 19720. Web: http://www.oakknoll.com

This work was printed in the United States of America on 60# archival, acid-free paper meeting the requirements of the American Standard for Permanence of Printed Library Materials.

A SHORT HISTORY

Fine Print began life in 1975 as an eight-page "Newsletter for the Arts of the Book". Its initial purpose was to present bibliographic descriptions of finely printed books (i.e. letterpress) along with reports on allied arts like hand bookbinding, calligraphy, and papermaking. Over the years it grew, both in physical size and in quality, and the title was changed to "review" rather than "newsletter." Then, at the time Hermann Zapf designed its tenth anniversary cover, he honored *Fine Print* by changing the subtitle from "*A*" to "*The* Review for the Arts of the Book."

At first we had each issue totally redesigned by a different graphic artist or printer. This lent a kind of pleasing unpredictability to the magazine, but soon became too burdensome to maintain.

Beginning in 1981, we settled into a comfortable yet lively design by Linnea Gentry using Spectrum, the compact type designed by Jan van Krimpen. To maintain the graphic excitement of *FP*, we initiated the practice of choosing a different outstanding graphic artist to design the cover of each issue.

Meanwhile, both articles and reviews of the various book arts continued to increase in sophistication. *Fine Print* became the international medium for exploring the intellectual content of books in relation to their graphical, historical, and craft aspects. It garnered a modest circulation on every continent, and in all the great national libraries. Despite these successes, publication of *Fine Print* had to cease with volume 16, number 3.

This then, *The Complete Index to Fine Print*, is our final issue, volume 16, number 4.

HOW TO USE THIS INDEX

The Complete Index to Fine Print is organized into three sections:

Pages 157–167
THE MASTER TABLES OF CONTENTS

In addition to the two regular indexes, for easy access and an overview of the contents of *Fine Print*, a chronological Table of Contents lists major articles and features such as Book Arts profiles, Book Arts Reporter, Exhibition Reviews, The Featured Bookbinding, and On Type. Also listed here is the name of the Issue Designer (1975-1981) and later, the Cover Designer, which changed with each issue.

Pages 169–202
THE NAMES INDEX

All authors, reviewers, press names, and proprietors. Press names are followed by the proprietors' names in parentheses, and the names of proprietors have their press names following unless eponymous (same name). Included are individual typographers and printers, calligraphers, papermakers, bookbinders, and other practitioners of the book arts, as well as authors of reference books reviews, fine press book reviews, and of articles in the magazine.

Pages 203–230
THE SUBJECTS INDEX

A list of subjects from abar marbling to Year of the Reader. Included are many different types of book arts equipment and techniques, past and present, as well as topics of book-historical interest, such as illuminated manuscripts and the Gutenberg 42-line Bible.

* * * * * * *

However, there are names in the Subjects Index; among them: papermills; a long list of type designs, by name; metal typefoundries and digital typefoundries by name.

* * * * * * *

Our numbering system follows; it is based on four issues per year.

Example: 88:4.186–188il+*il*

88 is the year, 1988.

4 is the issue number (1, 2, 3, 4).

186–188 are page numbers.

il after the page number means there is an illustration in the article or review.

+*il* means an illustration is on another page.

* * * * * * *

We sincerely hope you will find this index to be a guide to the florescence of fine printing and all the book arts in the last quarter of the twentieth century.

ACKNOWLEDGEMENTS

Our very special thanks go to Elmer L. Andersen, former governor of Minnesota and to Rob Rulon-Miller, noted antiquarian bookseller of St. Paul, whose generosity made possible the printing and production of *The Complete Index to Fine Print*.

Never to be forgotten is the inspiration that came from the founding editors, Linnea Gentry, George F. Ritchie, and the late D. Steven Corey, who led us on the true paths of fine printing, type and typography, and book history, as did E. M. Ginger, who became our Managing Editor, putting us on a firm schedule, bringing order and timeliness to the production of the journal, and taking a major role in editing.

The following associate and contributing editors greatly enriched and enlivened our pages:

TYPE AND TYPOGRAPHY: Principally Charles Bigelow and Kris Holmes, Paul Hayden Duensing, and Linnea Gentry. Others who contributed to the excellence of our coverage in this field were Robert Bringhurst and E. M. Ginger.

BOOKBINDING: Susan Spring Wilson, W. Thomas Taylor, Joanne Sonnichsen.

CONTRIBUTING EDITORS: William Bright, Linnea Gentry, Mark C. Livingston, Leigh McLellan, Kathleen Walkup, Robert Bringhurst, Betsy Davids, Crispin Elsted, Doris Grumbach, Alastair Johnston, Will Powers, Charles Seluzicki, Monica Strauss, and Don M. Moy. Consulting editors were George F. Ritchie and Abe Lerner.

* * * * * * * * *

OFFICE STAFF: Early on the scene were Melody Sumner, our first employee and the late Adele Zoger, who volunteered to be our mail clerk, "just because I like the magazine." Over the years, other office staff included Deborah Bruce, Calendar Editor and Director of Advertising; Carla Fabrizio, Circulation Director; Alan Hillesheim, Director of Development; Liz Sizensky, formerly Associate Publisher; Barbara Golden; Marie Carluccio and Mary Farr, Art Directors.

LEGAL ADVISOR: Alan Freeland, who guided us whenever a question arose about copyrights and permissions.

ACCOUNTING: Leah Wolff, who kept us straight with the Internal Revenue Service and gave us wise financial advice.

We thank the Pro Arte Libri Board of Directors for its wisdom and their patience when we were uncommunicative: Anne Anninger, Monica Strauss, J. Curtiss Taylor, Leah Wolff, and the late Decherd Turner who always supported us in time of need. Major donors were Joyce L. Wilson and Beatrice W. Kirshenbaum, as well as Robert McCamant of the Sheridan Beach Press in Chicago.

We give thanks and admiration to our wonderful "coterie" of article authors and reviewers whose knowledge and creativity enlivened *Fine Print*'s pages, and without whom the publication would never have reached the high level of esteem that it enjoyed.

Special thanks go to our *Complete Index* design and production managers, Will Powers and Cheryl Miller, and to our very talented photographer and cover designer, Jonathan Clark.

ARCHIVAL MATERIALS OF *FINE PRINT*

The archive materials of *Fine Print* (correspondence, illustrations, etc.) are at The Bancroft Library of the University of California, Berkeley. To view the Finding Aids for the Fine Print Archives:

Go to:
http://library.berkeley.edu

Next:
Select UC Berkeley Manuscript and Archival Collections.

Then:
Select Bancroft Library finding aids (top of right column). This will provide the list of posted finding aids.

Next:
Scroll down the list to the desired entry, select it, and view the whole document. A search box on the screen enables the viewer to find key words in the finding aids.

1975–1990 TABLES OF CONTENTS

VOLUME 1, NUMBER 1, JANUARY 1975
    Issue design: Andrew Hoyem   75:1.8
Open Letter from the Editors   75:1.1
Valenti Angelo   D. Steven Corey   75:1.2–3
Copyright for Type Designs?   75:1.6
Scene at the Book Fair [Los Angeles, 1974]   75:1.6
Jackson Burke Collection   75:1.7
Strauss Collection at Auction   75:1.7

VOLUME 1, NUMBER 2, APRIL 1975
    Issue design: Andrew Hoyem   75:2.20
Type ornament: Linnea Gentry   75:2.20
The Western Book Exhibit of 1975: A Review   Clifford Burke   75:2.9
The American Printing History Association   Linnea Gentry   75:2.10
Plantin Press Retrospective   Michael R. Thompson   75:2.11
Relief Etching: Claire Van Vliet and Keith Achepohl   75:2.16–17
Dorothy Abbe and William A. Dwiggins   75:2.18–19

VOLUME 1, NUMBER 3, JULY 1975
    Issue design: Andrew Hoyem   75:3.32
On William Everson as Printer   Linnea Gentry   75:3.21–22
Caslon Old and New   Albert Sperisen   75:3.22–25*il*
The Fifty Books of the Year [American Institute of Graphic Arts]
    exhibition review by Linnea Gentry   75:3.28–29

VOLUME 1, NUMBER 4, OCTOBER 1975
    Issue design: Andrew Hoyem   75:4.44
Wilder Bentley Remembers Porter Garnett   edited by D. Steven Corey   75:4.33–35
Ancient Spanish Ballads: A Rediscovery   Sandra Kirshenbaum   75:4.37*il*

VOLUME 2, NUMBER 1, JANUARY 1976
    Issue design: Michael and Winifred Bixler   76:1.16
Philip Smith: Artist of the Book   Eugenie Candau   76:1.1–5*il*
Charles Meunier and the French Bookbinders   Nancy Zinn   76:1.5–6+*il*
News of European Presses: Gwasg Gregynog; The Shakespeare Head Press   76:1.7

VOLUME 2, NUMBER 2, APRIL 1976
    Issue design: Linnea Gentry   76:2.20
Making Paper by Hand at the Hayle Mill in England   Simon Barcham Green   76:2.17–20*il*
Acquiring Handmade Paper: A Printer's View   Jonathan Clark   76:2.21–23

VOLUME 2, NUMBER 3, JULY 1976
    Issue design: Wesley B. Tanner   76:3.49
The Nightowl at Ten [The Press of the Nightowl]   Dwight Agner   76:3.37–40

VOLUME 2, NUMBER 4, OCTOBER 1976
    Issue design: Maria Poythress Epes   76:4.78
The Book as an Aesthetic Object: Part I   David Greenhood   76:4.57–60
The Artist and the Word: The Word Show at La Mamelle Gallery   Fred Martin   76:4.68–69
Rudolf Koch, 1876–1934   Linnea Gentry   76:4.69–70*il*

The Complete Index to *Fine Print*

VOLUME 3, NUMBER 1, JANUARY 1977
    Issue design: Jack Werner Stauffacher   77:1.23
Balancing the Books: Notes on Two Different Worlds of Bookbinding   Philip Smith   77:1.1–4
The Book as an Aesthetic Object: Part II   David Greenhood   77:1.4–6
Eishiro Abe: Japanese Papermaker   D. Steven Corey   77:1.15–16
Goudy Scripps Oldstyle   77:1.23*il*

VOLUME 3, NUMBER 2, APRIL 1977
    Issue design: Dwight Agner   77:2.38
German Expressionist Art and the Illustrated Book   Breon Mitchell   77:2.25–28+*il*
Some Thoughts on Expressionism   Claire Van Vliet   77:2.31–32+*il*
Sorting Handmade Paper — The Fatal Mistake   Edo G. Loeber   77:2.39–40
Fleischmann Antiqua [by Joan Michal Fleischman]   Linnea Gentry   77:2.42.*il*

VOLUME 3, NUMBER 3, JULY 1977
    Issue design: Stephen Harvard   77:3.58
Calligraphy for the Typographic Book   Stephen Harvard   77:3.49–52+*il*
Scribes and the Book   Lance Hidy   77:3.52–55*il*
Civilité   D. Steven Corey   77:3.71+*il*

VOLUME 3, NUMBER 4, OCTOBER 1977
    Issue design: Will Powers   77:4.86
Twinrocker: Collaboration in Custom Papermaking   Kathryn Clark   77:4.77–81*il*
The AIGA [American Institute of Graphic Arts] 1976 Book Show   review by Abe Lerner   77:4.93–94
David Kindersley and Computerized Composition   Charles A. Bigelow   77:4.98–100
A Lover of Washi [Asao Shimura]   77:4.100–101

VOLUME 4, NUMBER 1, JANUARY 1978
    Issue design: Kim Merker   78:1.13
Harry Duncan & The Cummington Press   Mary L. Richmond   78:1.1–4+*il*
Harry Duncan, Maker of Books   interview by Kay Amert & Kim Merker   78:1.4–6*il*
A Checklist of Books Printed by Harry Duncan   78:1.9–10
Bookbinding: An Island Renaissance [Ireland and the British Isles]   Margaret Simmons   78:1.14

VOLUME 4, NUMBER 2, APRIL 1978
    Issue design: George F. Ritchie   78:2.46
Hand Bookbinding Today: An International Art   exhibition review by Colin Franklin   78:2.33–34+*il*
"Hand Bookbinding Today, An International Art," San Francisco Museum of Modern Art,
    Illustrative Supplement   (insert: color illustrated pamphlet)
Private Type Faces — Part I   Paul Hayden Duensing   78:2.46–48*il*

VOLUME 4, NUMBER 3, JULY 1978
    Issue design: Ronald Gordon   78:3.80
On Wood Engraving   Barry Moser   78:3.65–69*il*
Pochoir Illustration   Frances Butler   78:3.70–73*il*
From Reckoning to Writing Systems [Denise Schmandt-Besserat's theory]   78:3.78–79*il*
The Work of William Matthews and Edgar Mansfield [bookbinders]   Philip Smith   78:3.79–80
Private Type Faces — Part II   Paul Hayden Duensing   78:3.86–90*il*

VOLUME 4, NUMBER 4, OCTOBER 1978
    Issue design: Carol Goldenberg   78:4.111
Observations on Islamic Calligraphy   Mohamed U. Zakariya   78:4.97–102+*il*
The Gutenberg Bible Makes News Again   Abe Lerner   78:4.102+
Pursuit of the Ideal: The Uncial Letters of Victor Hammer   David Farrell   78:4.121–123*il*

VOLUME 5, NUMBER 1, JANUARY 1979
    Issue design: Linnea Gentry   79:1.18+*il*
Jack Werner Stauffacher, Typographer   A. M. Johnston   79:1.1–6*il*
The Featured Bookbindings   Deborah Evetts   79:1.18, 24*il*
Galliard [type by Matthew Carter]   review by Charles A. Bigelow   79:1.27–30*il*

1975–1990 TABLES OF CONTENTS

VOLUME 5, NUMBER 2, APRIL 1979
    Issue design: Barry Moser, with banner by Sheila Waters   79:2.65
Sheila Waters and Under Milkwood *[calligraphic book]*
    review by Ashton Nichols   79:2.33–39*il*
The Featured Bookbinding   Peter Waters   79:2.38–39*il*
Printing at Oxford   Wesley B. Tanner   79:2.40–41
Calligrapher's Choice   exhibition review by James E. Sutherland   79:2.45

VOLUME 5, NUMBER 3, JULY 1979
    Issue design: Scott Walker, with calligraphy by Tim Girvin   79:3.71
The Five Books of J. G. Lubbock   Colin Franklin   79:3.69–71+*il*
Five Fine Printers [Bigus, Everson, Hoyem, Stauffacher, Wilson]
    exhibition review by W. Thomas Taylor   79:3.84–85
The Featured Bookbinding   Bernard C. Middleton   79:3.86+*il*
After All, What Does "Functional Typography" Mean?
    reprint of 1953 article by G. W. Ovink   79:3.92–96
Postscript after Twenty-five Years   G. W. Ovink   79:3.96

VOLUME 5, NUMBER 4, OCTOBER 1979
    Cover and issue design: Adrian Wilson   79:4.126
A Panoply of Printers' Marks, 1975 to 1980
    collected and edited by Mark Livingston   79:4.102–109*il*
Printers' Choice: A Selection of American Press Books 1968–1978
    review by Abe Lerner   79:4.119
Hans Eduard Meier's Syntax-Antiqua   Sumner Stone   79:4.120–123*il*
The Featured Bookbinding   Philip Smith   79:4.124–126*il*
Stanley Morison & D.B. Updike: Selected Correspondence [excerpt]
    David McKittrick, ed.   79:4.130–134

VOLUME 6, NUMBER 1, JANUARY 1980
    Cover design: Mark Livingston   80:1.3
    Issue design: Linnea Gentry   80:1.3
American Book Arts Magazines, 1903–1961   Joseph Blumenthal   80:1.4–9
The Featured Bookbinding   Sally Lou Smith   80:1.10–11*il*
A Visit to Bianca Tallone in Torino   Richard-Gabriel Rummonds   80:1.13+
ITC *Zapf Chancery*   review by Kris Holmes   80:1.26–30*il*

VOLUME 6, NUMBER 2, APRIL 1980
    Cover design: Carol Blinn   80:2.39
    Issue design: Linnea Gentry   80:2.39
The Papermaking Craft in Japan: Past, Contemporary, and Future
    Timothy Barrett   80:2.40–44*il*
Seventy from the Seventies [contemporary fine books]
    exhibition review by August Heckscher   80:2.45–46
Type and Technology [three exhibitions]: Matthew Carter; Adrian Frutiger; ITC
    review by Charles Bigelow   80:2.45
The Featured Bookbinding   Carolyn Coman and Nancy Southworth   80:2.58–59*il*
Gérard Charrière Bindings at the Princeton Graphic Arts Collection
    exhibition review by Dale Roylance   80:2.60–61+*il*
Buying Metal Type Abroad   Paul Hayden Duensing   80:2.67–68

The Complete Index to *Fine Print*

VOLUME 6, NUMBER 3, JULY 1980
    Cover design: Kris Holmes   80:3.75
    Issue design: Linnea Gentry   80:3.75
Craft Printing — A Philosophy and Technique   Clifford Burke   80:3.76–81
The Carl Purington Rollins Symposium at Yale University   David Pankow   80:3.82–83+
The Featured Bookbinding   Donald Glaister   80:3.84–85*il*
Trade Roots: 1920–1950 [book design]   exhibition review by Charles Farrell   80:3.92–94*il*
The Tradition of Fine Bookbinding in the Twentieth Century
    exhibition review by Donald Etherington & Ellen McCrady   80:3.94–95+
Hiero-Rhode Italic   Paul Duensing   80:3.101–102*il*
Gerard Unger, Type Design and Lettering   Charles Bigelow   80:3.102–103*il*

VOLUME 6, NUMBER 4, OCTOBER 1980
    Cover design: Frances C. Butler   80:4.107
    Issue design: Linnea Gentry   80:4.107
Experiments in Superannuated Color Printing Techniques   Frances C. Butler   80:4.108–112
American Fine Printing, 1820–1880   exhibition review by Ruth Fine   80:4.113
Elmer Adler and the Pynson Printers   exhibition review by James E. Sutherland   80:4.113+
A Memoir of the Janus Press, Summer 1979   Barbara Luck   80:4.115–117*il*
The Featured Bookbinding   Julie Beinecke Stackpole   80:4.118–119+*il*
Diotima of Gudrun Zapf-von Hesse   Paul Hayden Duensing   80:4.134–135*il*

VOLUME 7, NUMBER 1, JANUARY 1981
    Cover design: Czeslaw Jan Grycz, with drawings by Barry Moser   81:1.3
    Issue design: Linnea Gentry   81:1.3
On Illustrating Dante   Barry Moser   81:1.4–8*il*
The Featured Bookbinding   Bruce Schnabel and Harvey Redding   81:1.10–11*il*
Juan Pascoe and his Taller Martín Pescador   William Bright   81:1.12–13+
The Work of Berthold Wolpe   exhibition review by A. S. Osley   81:1.14–15
Donald Knuth's Tex & Metafont: *New Directions in Typesetting*   Donald Day   81:1.31–32*il*

VOLUME 7, NUMBER 2, APRIL 1981
    Cover design: Gerard Unger   81:2.71
    Issue design: Linnea Gentry   81:2.39
Raw Materials for Papermaking   Simon Barcham Green   81:2.40–43+*il*
Arno Werner, Master Bookbinder   exhibition review by James E. Walsh   81:2.44–45*il*
The Featured Bookbinding   by Denise Y. Lubett   81:2.46–47*il*
The Types of Jan van Krimpen (Part 1)   by Walter Tracy   81:2.51–56*il*
Rudolf Koch and the Offenbach Workshop: A Seminar   report by David Farrell   81:2.66–69*il*

VOLUME 7, NUMBER 3, JULY 1981
    Cover design: Christopher Weimann (marbling) and Sumner Stone (calligraphy)   81:3.95
    Issue design: Linnea Gentry   81:3.75
Traditional Paper Marbling: An American View   Don Guyot and Joan Knapp   81:3.76–78+
Suminagashi: Ink Floating   Karo Thom   81:3.79–81+*il*
The Featured Bookbinding   Betty Lou Chaika   81:3.82–83+*il*
Ward Ritchie: 76   D. Steven Corey   81:3.85+
The Types of Jan van Krimpen (Part 2)   Walter Tracy   81:3.99–102*il*
The Plain Wrapper Press: A Fifteen-Year Retrospective
    exhibition review by David Becker   81:3.104–105*il*

VOLUME 7, NUMBER 4, OCTOBER 1981
    Cover design: Sebastian Carter   81:4.115
    Issue design: Linnea Gentry   81:4.115
Successful Small Press Publishing Strategies:
    Graywolf and North Point Presses   Kathy Walkup   81:4.116+
    The Windhover Press   Leigh McLellan   81:4.116+
The Small Fine Press as Business   David R. Godine   81:4.118–120+
The Art of the Printed Book Conference in Omaha
    report by Sandra Kirshenbaum   81:4.132–135+
The Century Family [of types]   Paul Shaw   81:4.140–144*il*

VOLUME 8, NUMBER 1, JANUARY 1982

Cover design: Shelley Hoyt-Koch   82:1.3
Beginning with this issue the cover designers still change but the internal design by Linnea Gentry remains the same.
Edition Hand Bookbinders: A Survey and Resource List   Leigh McLellan   82:1.4–5+
The New Type Specimen Books, a Critical Review   Charles Bigelow   82:1.6–7+
Book Works: Sculptural Books by Twenty Artists   exhibition review by Philip Smith   82:1.11+
The Featured Bookbinding   Andrew Hoyem   82:1.12–13*il*
The Century Thumb-Nail Series: A Case History in Edition Bookbinding
   Sue Allen   82:1.15–18+*il*

VOLUME 8, NUMBER 2, APRIL 1982

Cover design: Max Caflisch   82:2.73
A Short List of Books About Ornament   Frances Butler   82:2.44–47+*il*
American Bard *by Walt Whitman: A Tale of Two Books:*
   The Limited Edition: Lime Kiln Press   Richard Bigus & Maureen Carey   82:2.53+
   The Trade Edition: Viking Press   Sandra Kirshenbaum   82:2.53+
The Featured Bookbinding   J. C. Sheehan   82:2.54+*il*
Ornament: Purpose and Play in Medieval Manuscripts   Linda L. Brownrigg   82:2.64–67+*il*
The Guild of Bookworkers: 75th Anniversary
   exhibition review by Decherd Turner   82:2.70

VOLUME 8, NUMBER 3, JULY 1982: ERIC GILL CENTENARY ISSUE

Cover design: Christopher Skelton   82:3.119
Eric Gill's Perpetua Type   James Mosley   82:3.90–91+*il*
The Artist & Book Production   Eric Gill   82:3.96–97+
Langley, a New Paper from Hayle Mill   Linnea Gentry   82:3.114

VOLUME 8, NUMBER 4, OCTOBER 1982

Cover design: William Stewart   82:4.157
The Rampant Lions Press: A Printing Workshop Through Five Decades
   exhibition review by John Dreyfus   82:4.125+
The Bookplates of James Hayes   Don Moy   82:4.126–127*il*
The Featured Bookbinding: A Cobden-Sanderson Bookbinding   Anthony Bliss   82:4.129+*il*
Calligraphy: More Than a Fad   Don Moy   82:4.132–135*il*
The Columbia Fine Printing Conference   report by Kathy Walkup   82:4.136–138+*il*
Natalie D'Arbeloff   Colin Franklin   82:4.151–152+*il*

VOLUME 9, NUMBER 1, JANUARY 1983

Cover design: Abe Lerner   83:1.35
Typefounding, Past and Future: The Oxford Conference
   report by Paul Hayden Duensing   83:1.4–5*il*
Robert Bridges, Poet-Typographer   Donald E. Stanford   83:1.7–9*il*
The Featured Bookbindings   W. Thomas Taylor   83:1.14–15*il*
The Book Art of Valenti Angelo: An Homage   Abe Lerner   83:1.26–29*il*
The First Printing Press in America   William Bright   83:1.33–35*il*

VOLUME 9, NUMBER 2, APRIL 1983

Cover design: Claire Van Vliet   83:2.43
The Romance of Wood Type   Stephen O. Saxe   83:2.45–49+*il*
The Designer Bookbinders   exhibition review by W. Thomas Taylor   83:2.59+*il*
The Featured Bookbinding   Don Etherington   83:2.60–61*il*
Edition Hand Bookbinders: Addendum [to January 1982 List]   83:2.60

The Complete Index to *Fine Print*

VOLUME 9, NUMBER 3, JULY 1983:
SPECIAL PAPER ISSUE
    Cover design: Wesley B. Tanner   83:3.125
Thoughts on Western Book Paper [Commentary by Six Contemporary Papermakers]
    83:3.92–101+*il*
Some Early American Mouldmakers   John Bidwell   83:3.104–105+*il*
The Featured Bookbinding   Angela James   83:3.108–109*il*
Paper Report: Mohawk Letterpress   Will Powers   83:3.110–112
BR [Bruce Rogers] Today: A Selection of His Books
    exhibition review by Stuart B. Schimmel   83:3.126–127*il*

VOLUME 9, NUMBER 4, OCTOBER 1983
    Cover design: Christopher Weimann (marbling) and Marie Carluccio   83:4.174
Techniques of Marbling in Early Indian Paintings   Christopher Weimann   83:4.134–137+*il*
An Investigation of the Interdependency of Paper Surface, Printing Process, and Printing Types
    Max Caflisch   83:4.138–142+*il*
Japan: International Paper Conference   report by Vera Freeman   83:4.159–161
American Craft Binders: William Matthews, 1882–1896   W. Thomas Taylor   83:4.162–163+*il*
Featured Bookbinding   Michael Wilcox   83:4.168–169+*il*
The Guild of Book Workers at the Metropolitan Museum of Art
    exhibition reviews by John P. Chalmers and W. Thomas Taylor   83:4.170–172*il*

VOLUME 10, NUMBER 1, JANUARY 1984
    Cover design: Lance Hidy   84:1.43
ATypI: Association Typographique Internationale, (1983) Seminar
    report by David Pankow   84:1.7–10
The Featured Bookbinding   Kirstin Tini Miura   84:1.15+*il*
The Rediscovery of a Type Design: Miklós Kis   Horst Heiderhoff   84:1.25–31*il*

VOLUME 10, NUMBER 2, APRIL 1984
    Cover design: Betsy Davids   84:2.86
The Yolla Bolly Press   84:2.57–60*il*
Graduate Book Arts Education — Two Approaches:
    Introduction   Sandra Kirshenbaum   84:2.73
    The University of Alabama Program   Gordon B. Neavill   84:2.74–77*il*
    The Mills College Program   Kathleen Walkup & Melody Sumner   84:2.79–81+*il*

VOLUME 10, NUMBER 3, JULY 1984
    Cover design: Sarah Chamberlain   84:3.135
Paper Report: More about Mohawk Letterpress   Mike Burton   84:3.99–100
    A Reply   Scott O. Petrequin, Mohawk Paper Co.   84:3.100
Continuous-Tone Lithography   Don Cushman   84:3.101
The 1984 Broadside Round-Up:
    Introduction   Charles Seluzicki   84:3.103
    Tiger Learns the Alphabet; Poor Tiger   original broadside by Mary Ann Hayden   84:3.103
        (insert: continuous-tone lithograph, printed by Don Cushman)
    Broadside Reviews   84:3.104–113*il*
The Featured Bookbinding   Hedi Kyle   84:3.114–115*il*
Renaissance Painting in Manuscripts: Treasures from the British Library
    exhibition review by Roger S. Wieck   84:3.116–117

VOLUME 10, NUMBER 4, OCTOBER 1984
    Cover design: Charles Skaggs   84:4.183
Bruce Rogers's Basic Principle of Book Design   Abe Lerner   84:4.150–153*il*
American Calligraphy Revisited, 1945–1965   Charles E. Skaggs   84:4.155–163+*il*
Book Typography of Hermann Zapf   Jerry Kelly and Kit Currie   84:4.164–167+*il*

VOLUME 11, NUMBER 1, JANUARY 1985
SPECIAL 10TH ANNIVERSARY ISSUE

Cover design: Hermann Zapf   85:1.1–2, 70
Graphic designs throughout issue on theme of "ten" by previous Fine Print designers [list]   85:1.1+il
A Decennary Letter from the Publisher   Sandra Kirshenbaum   85:1.3–10
Fine Printing and Trade Book Publishing: Conflict and Compromise   Scott Walker   85:1.11–14
Bookbinding: Perspective and Prescription   W. Thomas Taylor   85:1.15–19
Metal Type: Whither Ten Years Hence?   Paul Hayden Duensing   85:1.20–22
The Social Economy of the Book   Frances Butler   85:1.23–25
The Featured Bookbinding   John Franklin Mowery   85:1.26–27+il
August Heckscher, Printer   Joseph Blumenthal   85:1.28–31il
A Unique Handpress: Harold F. Smith's Har-ma Press   Roger Levenson   85:1.32–34il
A New Civilité [Zapf Civilité]   Paul Hayden Duensing   85:1.35–41il
James D. Hart's Engelhard Lecture on San Francisco Fine Printing   Craig D'Ooge   85:1.64–65
Anniversary Acknowledgments   Sandra Kirshenbaum   85:1.73

VOLUME 11, NUMBER 2, APRIL 1985

Cover design: Kathleen Walkup   85:2.128
Contemporary Fine Printing: Change and Tradition   exhibition review by Doug Wolf   85:2.82–83
The First Decade: An Exhibition of Work of Members of the New York Center for Book Arts
   review by Gary Frost   85:2.83–85
Fourth Biennial American Typecasting Fellowship Conference
   report by Paul Hayden Duensing   85:2.86–87
A Moon to Their Sun: Writing Mistresses of the Sixteenth and Seventeenth Centuries
   Robert Williams   85:2.88–98il
By Sovereign Maiden's Might: Notes on Women in Printing   Kathleen Walkup   85:2.100–104il
The Featured Bookbinding: James Joyce's Tales Told of Shem And Shaun
   Trevor Jones   85:2.119+il
John Howell — Books, San Francisco, 1912–1984   Jennifer S. Larson   85:2.128–129

VOLUME 11, NUMBER 3, JULY 1985

Cover design: Gunnlaugur SE Briem   85:3.138
The 1985 *Broadside Round-Up:*
   Introduction   Alastair Johnston   85:3.139–140
   Broadside Reviews   85:3.140–147+il
Terpsichore and Typography [the Isadora typeface]   Kris Holmes   85:3.148–152il
The Collegiate Press Conference at the University of Alabama
   report by Betsy Davids   85:3.153–155
Five Contemporary Printers: Further Notes on Women in Printing
   Kathleen Walkup   85:3.177–181il
The University of Iowa "Art and Craft of Bookbinding"
   exhibition review by Susan Spring Wilson   85:3.182–183
Stone Sheep [three European bookbinding exhibitions]   review by Philip Smith   85:3.184–185+

VOLUME 11, NUMBER 4, OCTOBER 1985
SPECIAL ITALIAN ISSUE

Cover design: Martino Mardersteig   85:4.194
Il Romanzo del Libro: Three Styles of Italian Bookmaking   Sandra Kirshenbaum   85:4.205–217il
   Alberto Tallone   85:4.205–208
   Giorgio Upiglio   85:4.212–215il
   Giovanni Mardersteig   85:4.208–212il
The Dante Types [Giovanni Mardersteig]   John Dreyfus   85:4.219–222il
An Exhibition of Tallone Books [Alberto Tallone]   review by John McBride   85:4.238+

The Complete Index to *Fine Print*

VOLUME 12, NUMBER 1, JANUARY 1986
SPECIAL ISSUE: NON-ROMAN LETTER FORMS
    Cover design: Glenn Goluska   86:1.4
The Punchcutter in the Tower of Babel   Paul Hayden Duensing   86:1.6–10*il*
Kings to Hold a Calligrapher's Inkstand: The Scribe in Muslim Society
    Annemarie Schimmel   86:1.11–17*il*
The Artist's Book in the Public Eye [1985 Conference]   report by Frances Butler   86:1.18–19
Acrophonic, Micrographic, Typographic: The Story of Hebrew Letters   Leila Avrin
    86:1.21–27*il*
The Featured Bookbinding   Betty Lou Chaika   86:1.46–52*il*

VOLUME 12, NUMBER 2, APRIL 1986
SPECIAL GERMAN ISSUE
    Guest Editor: Renate Raecke   86:2.65
    Cover design: Roswitha Quadflieg   86:2.109
Drei Deutsche Buchkünstler [Three German Book Artists]:
    Gotthard de Beauclair   Jerry Kelly with Margaret L. Ford   86:2.80–84*il*
    Roswitha Quadflieg [Raamin Presse]   Paul Raabe   86:2.84–85, 117*il*
    Otto Rohse   Bertold Hack   86:2.85–86+, 117*il*
Twentieth-Century Fine Printing in Germany   Walter Wilkes   86:2.87–99*il*
Influences on Book Design in the Federal Republic of Germany   Hans Peter Willberg
    86:2.100–102
Anna Simons: Calligrapher, Letterer, Teacher, and Type Designer   George Abrams
    86:2.103–107*il*
Treasure Houses of the Book Arts in Germany:
    Gutenberg Museum [Mainz]   Hans A. Halbey   86:2.110
    Klingspor Museum [Offenbach am Main]   Christian Scheffler   86:2.110–111
    Herzog August Bibliothek [Wolfenbu4ttel]   Paul Raabe   86:2.111–112
The VIth Annual ATypI Working Seminar, Hamburg 1985   Fernand Baudin   86:2.113–114
Christian Zwang, Bookbinder   Bertold Hack   86:2.116–117*il*

VOLUME 12, NUMBER 3, JULY 1986
    Cover design by Harry Duncan (with relief etching by Keith Achepohl)   86:3.180
An Illusive Image: Some Thoughts about Watermarking Handmade Papers
    Simon Barcham Green   86:3.136–143*il*
Notes on Frederic Warde and the True Story of His Arrighi Type
    Herbert H. Johnson   86:3.158–161*il*

VOLUME 12, NUMBER 4, OCTOBER 1986
    Cover design: Leigh McLellan   86:4.238
Old Books for New   Michael Gullick   86:4.204–208*il*
Parchment Making—Ancient and Modern   Benjamin Vorst   86:4.209–211+*il*
Searching for Gutenberg in the 1980s   Janet Ing   86:4.212–215+*il*
Cutting Anglo-Saxon Sorts   Stan Nelson   86:4.228–229*il*

VOLUME 13, NUMBER 1, JANUARY 1987
SPECIAL ISSUE: CZECHOSLOVAKIA AND THE BOOK
    Guest Editor: James Fraser   87:1.24
    Cover design: Jan Jiskra   87:1.24
A Word from the Guest Editor   James Fraser   87:1.15
The Beginnings of Modern Czech Book Art   Tomáš Vlček   87:1.16–19*il*
The Typography and Design of Czech Books between the Wars   Jan Rous   87:1.19–21+*il*
The Contemporary Renaissance of Fine Bookbinding in Czechoslovakia, 1973–1985
    Emil Minář   87:1.21–24+*il*
The Teaching of Illustration at the Academy of Applied Art in Prague
    Jiří Mikula   87:1.32–33*il*
Oldřich Menhart [type designer]   Paul Hayden Duensing   87:1.34–39*il*

VOLUME 13, NUMBER 2, APRIL 1987

Cover design: Dorothy Abbe (with W. A. Dwiggins stencil ornaments)   87:2.62

A Rejoinder and Extension to Herbert Johnson's Notes on Frederic Warde and The True Story of his Arrighi Type   John Dreyfus   87:2.69–73+il

The Featured Bookbinding: Edition Binding of a Vellum Book
Janice Mae Schopfer and Eleanore Ramsey   87:2.75–78+il

Northwest Artists' Books   exhibition review by Charles Seluzicki   87:2.79–81

William Addison Dwiggins:
  A Current Assessment   Steven Heller   87:2.82+il
  A Contemporary's View   Alexander Nesbitt   87:2.87–89il

VOLUME 13, NUMBER 3, JULY 1987

Cover design: Joseph Blumenthal   87:3.137

The Economics of Printing Limited Editions   Richard-Gabriel Rummonds   87:3.134–137

The First Simultaneous Book   Monica Strauss   87:3.139–140+il

Prose of the Transsiberian and of Little Jehanne of France
Blaise Cendrars and Sonia Delaunay   87:3.141–150 *(color foldout)*

Designing a New Greek Type [Lucida Greek]   Kris Holmes   87:3.162il

Bookbinding in the United States: Present and Potential   Joanne Sonnichsen   87:3.169–171

The 1987 Broadside Round-Up:
  Introduction   James Trissel   87:3.118–119
  Broadside Reviews   87:3.119–125il, 164–168il
  Growing Up   Susan E. King *(insert: original letterpress broadside)*

VOLUME 13, NUMBER 4, OCTOBER 1987

Cover design: Kay Amert   87:4.210

[Designing] a Novelist's Letters [Frank Norris]   Will Powers   87:4.196–200il

VOLUME 14, NUMBER 1, JANUARY 1988

Cover design: Will Powers   88:1.10

Bitwitched, Bothered, and Bewildered, Type 1987 [Type Directors Club]
report by Sandra Kirshenbaum   88:1.24–25+il, 39–41il

The Book as Theatre: The Cranach Press Hamlet
review by Adela Spindler Roatcap   88:1.26–33il

Owning [bookbinder] Philip Smith's Book Wall   Colin Franklin   88:1.34+

The Printed Poem/The Poem as Print: Twenty-four Broadsides Edited by Dana Gioia and Alastair Reid   review by Betsy Davids   88:1.38–39il

The New Seizin Press [Tomás Graves]   Frederick Reid   88:1.42–44

VOLUME 14, NUMBER 2, APRIL 1988

Cover design: John Randle   *88:2.93*

British Fine Printing Today: A Personal View of Seven Private Presses
Joshua Heller   88:2.57–67+il

Stones on the Riverbed: Jack Stauffacher's Typographic Art   Victoria Nelson   88:2.92–93

VOLUME 14, NUMBER 3, JULY 1988

Cover design: Georgia Deaver   88:3.119

Printing and the D P of the U [Divine Power of the Universe]
Walter Hamady   88:3.116–119+il

The Stone Family of Typefaces: New Voices for the Electronic Age
Sumner Stone   88:3.123–126il

Paint and Paint and Draw and Draw (calligraphic book) [Ben Shahn]
Suzanne Moore and Donald Glaister   88:3.137–141il

VOLUME 14, NUMBER 4, OCTOBER 1988

Cover design: Bonnie Pratt O'Connell   88:4.176

The Author as Printer   Lucia Berlin   88:4.160–162

Philosophies of Form in Seriffed Typefaces of Adrian Frutiger
Charles Bigelow   88:4.171–174il

The Complete Index to *Fine Print*

VOLUME 15, NUMBER 1, JANUARY 1989
    Cover design: Margery Cantor   89:1.34
The Featured Bookbinding: Full Metal Binding, The Single Hinge
    James Brockman   89:1.8–11*il*
Face to Face with the Daily News   Jeff Level   89:1.23–30+*il*
The Daily Reader [newspaper type specimens] insert (screenless lithography)

VOLUME 15, NUMBER 2, APRIL 1989
    Cover design: Richard Bigus and Steve Mott   89:2.60
Form, Pattern, & Texture in the Typographic Image   Charles Bigelow   89:2.75–82*il*
Creative Collaboration   Dana Gioia   89:2.83–86*il*

VOLUME 15, NUMBER 3, JULY 1989
    Cover design: Tree Swenson   89:3.113
The Featured Bookbinding   Claire van Vliet   89:3.114–118*il*
Granary Books: Purveyor of the Artful and Literary   Steven Clay   89:3.130–133
Whence [Nicolas] Jenson: A Search for the Origins of Roman Type
    Juliet Spohn Twomey   89:3.134–141*il*

VOLUME 15, NUMBER 4, OCTOBER 1989
SPECIAL ISSUE: PRINTING ARTS IN THE NETHERLANDS
    Guest Editor: Monica Strauss   89:4.214
    Cover design: Janine Huizenga   89:4.175
Letter from the Editor: Pro Arte Libri   Sandra Kirshenbaum   89:4.159–160
Dutch Book Design   Monica Strauss
    The Avant-Garde Tradition: Hendrik Werkman; Piet Zwart; Willem Sandberg
        89:4.176–184*il*
    The Contemporary Book [Boekie Woekie; Uitgeverij Philip Elchers; Ewald Spieker]
        89:4.185–186*il*
    Hendrik Nicolaas Werkman   exhibition review by Poltroon   89:4.177–178+*il*
    Drukkers in de Marge [private presses]   Jan Keijser   89:4.187–188
    Type Design in the Netherlands and the Influence of the Enschedé Foundry
        Huib van Krimpen   89:4.189–197*il*

VOLUME 16, NUMBER 1, SPRING 1990
    Cover design: Antonie Eichenberg (illustration by Fritz Eichenberg)   90:1.9
Typocrafters Trash Derby City [1989 Louisville, Kentucky conference]
    report by Dr. Hawley T. Tompkins (*pseud.*)   90:1.19–22
A Memoir of John Peters (1917–1989)   John Dreyfus   90:1.25–29*il*
The Featured Bookbinding   Sün Evrard   90:1.37–39*il*
A Celebration of Fritz Eichenberg   Steven Heller   90:1.43–45*il*

VOLUME 16, NUMBER 2, SUMMER 1990
    Cover design: Fernand Baudin   90:2.61
Using Letterforms in Bookbinding: A Typographer's View   Kay Amert   90:2.62–68+*il*
Twentieth-Century Contributions to the Jensonian Model [Nicolas Jenson]
    Paul Hayden Duensing   90:2.69–71*il*

VOLUME 16, NUMBER 3, AUTUMN 1990
    Cover design: Herbert Gutsch   90:3.143
The 1990 Broadside Round-Up:
    Classic   Martin Antonetti   90:3.104–108
    Typographic   Christine Taylor   90:3.109–111
    Primitive   Carolyn Robertson   90:3.111–114
    Polemic   David Lance Goines   90:3.114–117
Carol Twombly: Type Design and Other Sports   Margery Cantor   90:3.121–125+*il*
Book Arts in the USA: The Conference   report by Ruth McGurk   90:3.142–143*il*

INDEX BY NAMES

A

Abattoir Editions (Harry Duncan), 85:2.120, 89:3.131
    books from, 76:3.42, 48, 76:4.66, 77:4.82, 78:1.4+*il*, 8*il*, 78:2.38+*il*, 78:4.113, 84:1.41*il*, 89:2.85*il*
    checklist, 78:1.10
    FP cover design by, with Keith Achepohl, 86:3.180+(*cover*)
    press mark, 79:4.103*il*
    See also Cummington Press (Harry Duncan)
Abbe, Dorothy, 83:4.154
    FP cover design (honoring W. A. Dwiggins), 87:2.62+(*cover*)
    Püterschein-Hingham books, 75:2.18–19, 80:1.18–19*il*, 80:2.39, 87:2.89*il*
    See also Dwiggins, William Addison
Abbe, Press of Elfriede, 83:2.76–77*il*, 85:3.177
Abbott, Edwin, 82:1.12–13*il*, 19–21
Abe, Eishiro, 77:1.15–16, 80:2.39+(*cover*), 47
Abraham, Elizabeth (Dreadnaught Press), 78:4.104*il*, 107–108
Abrams, George, 86:4.235–236, 90:2.71*il*, 76–77
    On Type article, 86:2.103–107*il*
Achepohl, Keith, 75:2.17, 81:4.148, 85:1.50*il*, 54–55
    cover print by, 86:3.180+(*cover*)
Adagio Press (Leonard F. Bahr), 77:1.10, 84:1.5
    broadside by, 84:3.104
Adamic, Louis, 84:2.85
Adams, Ansel, 80:2.58–59*il*
Adams, John, 77:3.65
Adams, Léonie, 81:1.20
Addison House, 77:3.56+
Adler, Elmer, 80:2.60, 80:3.94+*il*, 94
    and Pynson Printers, 78:2.37, 80:1.6–7, 80:4.113+
Adloff, Jean Gabriel (Paradise Press), 89:4.173–174+*il*
Aesop, 76:2.34, 80:3.74*il*, 81:2.49*il*, 64*il*, 83:1.26*il*, 86:1.29+*il*
    illustration history of, 89:1.31*il*
    motifs transmission, 79:4.127–128, 85:2.123+*il*
Agee, James, 89:1.46–47
Agner, Dwight, 77:2.42, 86:2.123
    article by, 76:3.37–40
    FP issue design by, 77:2.38
    See also Press of the Nightowl
Agner, Margaret, 77:3.60+
Agricola, Georgius, 83:3.123
Aischylos, 86:4.200
Aldus Manutius (Aldine Press), 79:2.42, 43, 81:4.146, 82:1.8, 88:4.167–168, 90:2.76
    biography of, 90:1.34–36*il*
    books about, 80:2.63–65, 82:2.58*il*, 84:4.170–171, 85:1.68
    press mark of, 90:1.35*il*
    type design by, 87:1.47–50*il*
Aleš, Mikoláš, 87:1.16
Alexander, Charles (Black Mesa Press), 84:3.104
Alexander, J.J.G., 79:3.86
Alighieri, Dante. *See* Dante Alighieri
Aliquando Press (William Rueter), 76:2.29–30, 78:2.38+*il*, 86:2.72+*il*, 76, 89:2.57
    press mark, 79:4.103*il*
    See also Rueter, William
Allen, Greer (*reviewer*), 82:2.75, 82:4.139–140, 90:2.80–81
Allen, Lewis (*reviewer*), 77:1.20–21, 77:4.89–90, 82:1.21
Allen Press (Lewis and Dorothy Allen), 75:2.19, 76:2.36, 77:1.7, 79:2.45, 80:1.11–12, 85:1.69
    bibliography, 81:1.2, 82:1.27–29*il*
    press mark, 79:4.103*il*
Allen, Sue:
    article by, 82:1.15–18+*il*
    reviews by, 83:4.143, 85:1.42
Allen, Susan M. (Oldtown Press), 88:4.184–185
Allix, Susan (Willow Press), 87:2.91–93+*il*, 87:4.181–183, 88:1.5
Almond Tree and Nomadic Presses (collaboration), 87:4.192
Alpert, Michael (Theodore Press), 87:3.130+*il*, 89:3.114, 90:1.10–11+*il*
Altman, Benjamin and Deborah (Married Mettle Press), 88:2.55, 90:2.63*il*
Altschul, Charles (The New Overbrook Press), 85:1.30, 51–54+*il*
Amaranth Press (Linnea Gentry):
    books from, 76:4.71, 78:2.41+*il*, 85:3.172–173*il*
    press mark, 79:4.103*il*
Amaranth Press (Linnea Gentry and Will Powers), 76:4.71
Amert, Kay, 78:2.43
    articles by, 78:1.4–6, 90:2.62–68+*il*
    FP cover design by, 87:4.210+(*cover*)
    photograph of, 85:3.176*il*
    profile of, 85:3.179
    reviews by, 86:1.33–34, 87:1.14+, 88:1.21–23
    Seamark Press book, 78:2.42–43
Anachronic Editions (Meryl and Steven Chayt), 84:3.118–120, 87:4.213+*il*
Andersch, Martin, 89:1.15–17*il*
Anderson, Betty, 85:1.14, 85:3.138
Anderson, Donald, 81:4.136, 84:4.175–176
Anderson, Elizabeth, 84:3.108
Anderson, John:
    profiles of, 76:3.40, 81:3.87+*il*, 103*il*
    See also Pickering Press
Anderson, Marta (Crepuscular Press), 77:2.34, 80:4.123–124*il*
André, Edouard François (on bromeliads), 84:3.131–132
Andreä family (Frankfurt am Main), 85:2.79
Angelica Press (Dennis J. and Marilyn Grastorf):
    books from, 76:3.42–43, 77:2.34–35, 77:4.90, 78:2.42
    catalogue, 78:2.54
    press mark, 79:4.103*il*
Angelo, Valenti, 75:1.2–3, 77:3.73
    FP cover illustrations, 83:1.35+(*cover*)
    Golden Cross Press mark, 83:1.29+*il*
    press mark, 79:4.103+*il*
    review by, 76:3.44–45
    obituaries (1897–1982), 83:1.26–29*il*, 36–39*il*
Angiolieri, Cecco, 89:1.41–42
Annenberg, Maurice, 79:2.46
Annigoni, Pietro, 77:2.37
Anthony, William (Bill), 82:4.137, 85:3.182, 87:3.170, 88:3.119, 90:2.62–63*il*
    letter from, 85:3.136
Antonetti, Martin:
    broadside reviews by, 90:3.105–108
    essay by, 90:3.104–105
    reviews by, 87:4.203, 88:2.88–90, 88:3.122+, 89:1.12+, 33–34, 90:1.34–36
Antoninus, Brother. *See* Everson, William
Anvil Press (Carolyn Reading Ham-

mer), 79:1.10, 85:2.121, 85:3.158–159+, 86:1.29–31+*il*, 87:4.193–195+*il*, 89:3.119–120*il*, 90:1.21–22
Apollinaire, 89:2.87*il*
Appleman, Philip, 88:2.74–76+*il*
Appleton, Tony, 77:1.18
Aralia Press (Michael A. Peich), 76:2.30, 84:3.133, 89:2.85
Aratus, 75:3.27
Ardizzone, Edward, 89:1.4–5*il*
Arif Press (Wesley B. Tanner):
    books from, 81:4.121, 82:1.19, 83:2.53–54+*il*, 84:2.62, 85:1.51*il*, 86:1.31–32, 87:1.13–14+*il*, 87:3.128–129+*il*, 88:3.127–128+*il*
    press mark, 79:4.103*il*
    Fournier ornament banner, multicolor letterpress cover by, 83:3
Arion Press (Andrew Hoyem):
    books from, 76:2.28, 77:4.83, 79:2.51, 80:2.49–53*il*, 82:1.12–13*il*, 19–21, 22, 83:1.11–12*il*, 12–13+*il*, 84:2.62–63*il*, 84:4.144–146*il*, 85:4.223–224*il*, 86:2.79+*il*, 86:4.219+*il*, 88:4.181–184, 189*il*, 89:4.207–209+*il*
    press mark, 79:4.104*il*
    watermarks, 86:3.139–140+*il*
Arizona State University School of Art. *See* Pyracantha Press
Armitage, Merle, 79:1.26
Armstrong, Margaret, 80:4.126
Arnett, John Andrews, *pseud.* (John Hannett), 82:1.35
Arnholm, Ron, 90:1.19–20*il*, 90:2.71*il*
Arp, Hans [copy of], 84:3.126–128*il*
Arrabal, Fernando, 85:2.113–114+*il*
Arrighi, Ludovico Vincentino degli, 80:4.132–133*il*, 81:1.26+, 82:4.154, 89:2.88–89
Ars Liborum (Gotthard de Beauclair), 86:2.81*il*, 83, 99
Artaud, Antonin, 87:2.68
Artichoke Press (Jonathan Clark), 76:4.62–63
Artists Book Works (Pamela Barrie), 90:3.111–112*il*
Artzybasheff, Boris, 86:1.29
Ashbery, John, 84:4.144–146
Ashendene Press (C.H.J. St. John Hornby), 87:2.65–67*il*
Ashlar Press. *See* Heckscher, August
Ashling Press and Handmade Papers, 77:2.38, 78:2.35
    See also under papermakers
Atkins, Kathleen, 85:2.111
Atkins, Kathryn A., 89:2.88–90*il*, 90:1.49
Atkinson, Richard MacIntryre, 78:4.116–118
Atwood, Margaret, 84:3.97–98
Auden, W. H., 85:3.164–165*il*

Auerhahn Press (Dave Haselwood), 78:2.49–50
Avadenka, Lynne (Land Marks Press), 85:2.109*il*, 85:3.147, 90:3.114*il*
Avinor, Michael, 86:3.133–134
Avrin, Leila, 82:4.122, 86:1.21–27, 87:1.53–54
Axel-Nilsson, Christian, 85:1.45–46, 85:3.138

B

Bach, Johann Sebastian, 85:3.140
Bachaus, Theodore *pseud.* (Henry Morris), 79:1.22
Bacon, Roger, 75:4.40
Badius, Jodocus, 77:2.42
Bahr, Leonard F. (Adagio Press), 77:1.10, 84:1.5, 84:3.104
Baily, Jane, 77:1.11
Bain, Iain:
    books from, 81:2.49, 82:4.139–140*il*
    review by, 86:2.70+
Baj, Enrico, 85:4.214
Bakelantz, Louis, 88:2.74–75+*il*
Baker, Anthony (Gruffyground Press), 78:2.36, 78:3.74–75, 88*il*, 79:3.73
Baker, Arthur, 79:3.86–87
Bakker, Bert, 81:3.94–95
Balbus, Johannes, 86:4.232
Balkwill, John (Huckleberry Press), 90:3.133–134*il*
Ballou, Adin, 79:4.111
Balston, Thomas, 82:2.52
Balston, William, 82:2.52
Bank, Arnold, 79:3.72, 86:3.132
Bannister, Manly, 77:1.18–19
Banyan Press (Claude Fredericks and David Beeken), 77:3.59
Barbarian Press (Crispin and Jan Elsted):
    books from, 85:4.225–226*il*, 87:2.80, 87:3.127–128*il*
    broadsides from, 83:2.51–52*il*, 84:3.104+*il*
Barbour, Barton H., 85:2.108–109
Barcham Green & Co. *See* Green, John Barcham (Jack); Green, Simon Barcham
Barclay, Alexander, 85:1.62–63 (translator)
Bareiss, Molly and Walter, 86:4.188
Barker, Nicolas, 79:2.41, 83:1.4, 85:1.51, 86:3.170, 87:1.47–50 (author)
Barlow, William P., Jr. *(reviewer)*, 76:2.31–32, 82:2.50–52
    See also collectors and their collections in Index by Names
Barnett, C. Z., 85:4.225–226
Barnhardt, Dale, 84:3.98+

Barrett, Timothy, 78:1.13, 80:2.53–55*il*, 82:4.136–137, 90:2.56+
    articles by, 80:2.40–44*il*, 83:3.92–93
    book by, 84:2.52–53*il*
    letters from, 81:4.114–115, 84:1.3
    reviews by, 78:2.52, 79:2.57–59, 83:3.119–121
Barrie, Pamela (Artists Book Works), 90:3.111–112*il*
Barrow, W. J., 84:3.99–100
Bartkowiak, H. S., 89:3.110–111
Bartlett, Lee (Scarecrow Press), 84:4.174–175, 89:3.121–123
Baruch, Franziska, 86:1.24
Bash, Barbara, 78:1.30
Basilisk Press (Charlene Garry), 79:2.44, 79:3.97–98, 82:4.127
    press marks, 79:4.104+*il*, 90:3.145*il*
Baskerville, John, 76:2.31–32
Baskin, Leonard (Gehenna Press), 78:2.44*il*, 49, 54
Batey, Charles, 79:2.41
Battipaglia, Leonard, 82:1.7
Baudin, Fernand:
    books by, 85:1.46–48*il*, 90:1.8
    cover design by, 90:2.61+(*cover*)
    letter from, 79:2.42–43
    report by, 86:2.113–114
    review by, 89:4.201–202
Baumann, Gustave, 81:1.17+*il*
Bawden, Edward, 80:3.98–100*il*
Bayer, Herbert, 85:4.200–201*il*
Beach, Sylvia, 85:2.103
Beal, Jack, 81:3.89+*il*
Beale, G. A., 79:1.19–20, 79:3.73
Beard, Mark, 85:2.114–115+*il*
Beatty, Alfred Chester, 83:1.2
Beauchesne, Jean de, 81:1.29, 82:4.154
Beauclair, Gotthard de. *See* Trajanus Press
Beausoleil, Beau, 86:1.40–41
Beck, Bruce:
    reviews by, 82:4.149, 83:3.121–123, 90:3.130–131
    Turtle Press books, 85:3.162–163, 86:4.237
Becker, David, 79:4.127–128
    exhibition review by, 81:3.104–105*il*
    reviews by, 77:4.83, 83:1.30–31, 85:2.123–124
Beckett, Samuel, 77:3.66, 80:3.88*il*, 84:3.107
    broadside, 90:3.107–108+*il*
    illustrated editions (reviews of), 77:2.33–34+*il*, 85:1.51–54*il*, 86:2.73–74+*il*, 88:1.11–12+*il*, 88:3.111–112+*il*
Beeken, David (Banyan Press), 77:3.59
Beekman, E. M., 76:4.67–68
Behrendt, Steven, 81:4.132

Beil, Frederic C., 87:3.167*il*
Beilenson, Edna (Peter Pauper Press), 85:3.177
Belanger, Terry (Book Arts Press), 86:3.135 (now at University of Virginia)
Belch, David E. (*reviewer*), 84:1.17+
Bell, Julian, 88:2.82–83
Bell, Lilian A., 87:3.172–173
Bell, Vanessa, 75:1.4
Bellamy, B. E., 81:2.57–58*il*
Belloc, Hilaire, 84:1.34–35
Bennett, John Thomas (Gardyloo Press), 80:2.38–39, 83:1.11
Bennett, Paul, 86:3.158, 87:2.69+
Bensen, D. R., 83:2.55+
Benson, Richard, 82:2.61, 82:3.101–102
Bentinck-Smith, William, 85:3.187
Bentley, Beth, 78:3.75–76
Bentley, Wilder:
  letter from, 82:1.3
  memoir by, 75:4.33–35
  response to, 82:3.82
  reviews by, 76:4.65–66, 79:1.23–26
Benton, Linn Boyd, 81:4.141, 86:1.7+
Benton, Morris Fuller, 78:4.120, 81:4.141–144, 82:3.90, 85:1.35, 87:4.214–215, 90:2.70
Benvenuto, Jim (Full Moon Press), 87:3.119–120
Berger, Barb, 85:3.142–143+
Berger, Sidney E. (*reviewer*), 85:4.227, 87:4.192, 90:3.140–141
Berlin, Lucia, 84:3.96–97, 88:4.160–162
Berliner Handpresse (Wolfgang Jörg and Erich Schönig), 87:1.43–44+*il*
Berliner, Harold, 76:1.8, 78:2.42, 81:4.119, 84:2.49, 85:3.144+*il*, 160
Berlioz, Hector, 87:2.92
Bernard, Kenneth, 88:3.128–130
Bernhard, Lucian, 81:2.54
Bernstein, Bonnie (Goodmorrow Press), 82:3.100–101
Bernstein, Dennis (ear/say), 85:3.167–168+*il*, 89:2.96–99+*il*
Berry, Wendell, 80:2.48, 85:3.174+*il*
Bertelson, Christine (Christy):
  photograph of, 82:4.147*il*
  Rara Avis Press books, 79:3.74, 81:1.22+*il*, 83:1.10, 83:4.150
  reviews by, 81:4.129, 82:2.61–62, 86:2.119–120
Bettman, Otto L. (Bettman Archive), 89:2.73*il*
Bewick, Thomas (wood engraver), 76:2.34, 79:3.87, 81:2.49–50*il*, 82:4.139–140*il*, 85:4.204, 89:2.67–69+*il*
  museum, 85:2.81, 89:1.4*il*
Bidpai (fabulist), 75:2.15
Bidwell, John, 82:2.52, 82:4.154

articles by, 82:3.96, 116–117, 83:3.104–105+*il*
reviews by, 78:3.81–82, 82:4.150+, 83:1.29–30, 83:2.71–72, 84:3.129–131, 89:3.120–121
Bieler Press (Gerald Lange):
  books from, 76:2.29, 77:1.10, 77:3.59–60, 78:4.113, 81:1.16+*il*, 81:4.121–122, 82:1.3, 82:3.98*il*, 82:4.130*il*, 84:2.63–64, 85:1.57–59, 86:4.226–227*il*, 87:3.159, 88:1.5+
  broadsides from, 84:3.104*il*, 85:4.224–225
Big Bridge Press (Nancy Davis), 84:3.131–132, 90:3.116–117*il*
Bigelow & Holmes, 90:3.121+
  letter design (Leviathan), 80:2.49+*il*
  and Lucida type, 85:1.70, 86:3.150*il*, 87:3.162*il*, 88:1.41*il*
  as mentors, 85:3.149, 90:3.121+
  and Pellucida type, 86:4.238
Bigelow, Charles A., 79:1.12, 81:1.31, 84:1.7
  Corvine Press books, 80:1.3, 80:3.87–88+*il*, 85:4.235
  exhibition review by, 80:2.45
  letter to, 80:3.75
  MacArthur Prize Fellowship, 82:4.122
  named *On Type* Editor, 80:1.3
  On Type articles, 77:4.98–100, 79:1.27–30*il*, 80:1.3, 80:3.102–103*il*, 82:1.6–7+, 88:4.171–174*il*, 89:2.75–82*il*
  reviews by, 79:2.50–51, 80:4.131–132, 82:1.29–31, 83:3.124–125, 85:1.46–48, 88:4.170+, 188, 89:4.200–201
Bigelow, Jacob, 79:4.110–111
Bigly, Cantell A., 75:1.4
Bigus, Richard, 79:3.84–85
  article by, 82:2.53+
  relief engravings by, 89:2.62–63*il*
  essay by, 87:2.75
  FP cover design by screenless lithography, 89:2.60+(*cover*)
  letters from, 78:4.106, 81:3.108, 84:3.91–92
  response to, 81:3.108–109
  See also Labyrinth Editions
Bílek, František, 87:1.18, 26*il*
Binns, Betty, 77:4.94
Bird & Bull Press (Henry Morris):
  archives, 89:2.59
  bibliography, 82:1.27–29*il*
  books from, 77:4.88–89, 78:1.19–20, 78:4.112–113, 79:4.110–111, 80:2.53–55*il*, 81:3.86, 83:2.72+, 84:3.94–95, 85:1.56–57, 87:3.156+, 89:2.61*il*
  press mark, 79:4.104*il*
Biscuit City Press (Robert and Sylvia Gutchen), 78:4.113, 79:3.74, 80:4.120

press mark, 79:4.104*il*
Bissinger, Press of Mildred, 76:2.29, 78:3.78
Bixler, Michael and Winifred, 81:4.118
  FP issue design by, 76:1.16, 76:2.20 (note)
Black, M. H. (author, Cambridge University Press), 86:2.123
Black Mesa Press (Charles Alexander), 84:3.104
Black Pennell Press (Thomas Rae), 85:3.162–163*il*, 86:4.195–196*il*, 88:1.23+*il*, 89:2.67–69+*il*
Black Rock Press (Kenneth J. Carpenter), 80:1.15–16+*il*, 86:2.77–78*il*
  press mark, 79:4.104*il*
Black, Sarah, 87:1.14+*il*
The Black Stone Press (Peter Rutledge Koch and Shelley Hoyt-Koch), 76:3.40–41
  books from, 76:2.29, 77:1.11, 80:2.47, 83:1.22*il*
  cover design by Shelley Hoyt, 82:1
  press mark, 79:4.104*il*
Blackburn, Paul, 77:4.84+, 105*il*, 81:3.89+*il*, 86:1.56
Blackman, Alan (*reviewer*), 86:2.67, 70, 87:4.201+*il*
Blackwells Press (Nick Zachreson), 85:2.111
Blair, Sheila S. (*reviewer*), 89:3.147–150
Blaizot, Claude, 88:2.53
Blake, Norman F., 78:2.52, 80:3.74
Blake, William, 78:1.2–3, 79:2.60–61, 80:1.23, 80:2.70, 81:4.132–133, 82:2.49–50+*il*
Bland, David, 79:3.86+
Blažek, Otta, 87:1.22
Blinn, Carol J., 77:3.56
  FP cover design by, 80:2.39+(*cover*)
  letter from, 84:4.139
  photographs of, 82:4.147*il*, 85:3.176*il*
  profile of, 85:3.179–180
  See also Warwick Press
Bliss, Anthony S., 79:1.21–22, 79:2.43, 82:4.129+, 85:2.124–126
Bliss, Carey S. (*reviewer*), 76:3.52–53
  book by, 82:2.58*il*
Bliss, Douglas Percy, 80:3.98–100
Block, Irving, 85:4.226–227*il*
Block, Laurie, 83:4.149–150
Blocker, Mare (M Kimberly Press), 87:2.81
Blumenthal, Barbara B. (Catawba Press), 81:2.39, 82:1.5, 86:4.199–200*il*
Blumenthal, Joseph, 80:3.100, 85:1.7, 86:3.170, 88:3.106
  articles by, 80:1.4–9, 85:1.28–31*il*, 86:1.5
  books by, 77:4.95–96, 79:4.111, 86:3.157+*il*, 90:1.8, 90:2.73–75*il*

cover (with border by Simon de Colines), 87:3.137+(*cover*)
  letters from, 82:2.42, 86:4.235–236
  reviews by, 76:2.26–27, 77:3.65, 78:3.82–83
  Spiral Press books, 80:1.9, 81:4.118, 82:2.42, 83:2.56–58*il*
Bly, Robert, 80:4.123+*il*, 81:3.91–92*il*, 85:3.147
The Bodley Head. *See* Ryder, John
Bodoni, Giambattista, 76:1.15, 90:3.105
Boekie Woekie [Netherlands], 89:4.185+*il*
Boertzel, Barbara Moon, 86:3.146–147
Bogan, Kathy, 88:2.68+
Bohlken, Linda Ness, 78:4.115
Bohn, Mel, 81:4.132
Bolaño, Roberto, 77:1.11
Bolton, Claire, 90:2.75–76*il*
Bonet, Paul, 84:3.128, 88:2.53, 88:4.152
Bonham, Neal. *See* Sea Pen Press and Papermill (Suzanne Ferris and Neal Bonham)
Book Arts Press (Terry Belanger, Columbia University; later University of Virginia), 84:1.4, 86:3.135, 87:1.6–7
Book Works (London, England), 85:1.69–70
Boorstin, Daniel J. (Librarian of Congress) , 78:1.12–13, 84:2.86
Booth, Scott Laurence, 76:1.8
Boozer, William, 75:2.20
Borges, Jorge Luis, 77:1.7–9*il*, 81:3.105, 86:3.173–175+*il*
Born, Ernest, 84:3.105
Bosham, Herbert of, 82:2.67, 86:4.208
Boshier, Derek, 82:1.11
Bosman, Richard, 88:4.181, 189*il*
Bosqui, Edward (San Francisco printer), 85:1.64
Boswell, Winthrop Palmer, 75:2.15
Botnick, Ken:
  Bowery Press, 89:2.84–85
  See also Red Ozier Press (Steve Miller and Ken Botnick)
Boulton, Richard (Freehand Press), 76:4.71
Bournehall Press, 76:2.29
Bow & Arrow Press (Harvard University), 80:4.107
Bowen, Emanuel, 81:3.83+*il*
Bowery Press (Steve Miller and Ken Botnick), 89:2.84–85
Bowman, J. H., 87:2.108
Bracciolini, Poggio, 89:3.135*il*, 137, 139
Bradáč, Ludvíc, 87:1.22, 30*il*
Bradbury, Ray, 80:3.91
Brady, Denise (bradypress), 89:4.166–167+*il*
Brahms, Johannes, 75:4.40

Bramanti, Anna, 78:2.56
Bramanti, Bruno, 78:2.56
Brand, Chris, 89:4.197
Brandi, John (Tooth of Time Books), 83:1.10–11
Brandis, G. and Mazdy Brender à (Brandstead Press), 77:1.11
Brandis, Mazdy (Brandstead Press), 78:3.77
Brandt, Sebastian (1497), 85:1.62–63+*il*
Brannen, Noah S., 79:2.55–56
Bray, Walter, 81:2.62
Bread & Puppet Theater (Peter Schumann), 79:3.79–81*il*, 81:4.126–127*il*
Bremer Presse (Willy Wiegand and Ludwig Wolde), 79:4.111, 86:2.88–89, 92–93*il*, 103–107*il*, 86:3.149*il*, 86:4.235–236
Breslauer, Bernard H., 87:1.6–7, 88:1.34, 88:2.53–54, 88:4.167–168
Brett, Simon (Paulinus Press), 86:2.65–66
Brewer, Fredric (Echo Press), 88:2.74–76+*il*
Brewer, Roy, 78:4.124
Bridgers, Bill (Emanon Press), 83:3.102–103
Bridges, Robert, 81:4.134–135, 83:1.7–9*il*, 9, 86:3.160+, 89:3.151
Briem, Gunnlaugur SE, 87:4.201–202*il*
  FP cover design by, 85:3.138+(*cover*)
Bright, Betty, 89:2.60
Bright, William, 81:4.134
  articles by, 81:1.12–13+, 83:1.33–35*il*
  letters to, 83:2.44+, 83:3.87
  named Contributing Editor, 80:4.107
  reviews by, 80:3.88–90, 80:4.106, 122, 81:1.20, 81:3.91–92, 81:4.121, 83:2.58, 84:1.18–19, 84:2.70–71, 84:4.174–175, 85:3.165–166, 85:4.235, 87:3.127–128, 88:3.130–132, 89:2.99+
Brilliant, Alan (Unicorn Press), 76:2.30
Bringhurst, Robert, 84:4.139, 86:2.66–67
  book by, 87:3.127–128*il*
  broadside from, 83:2.51–52*il*
  named Contributing Editor, 86:2.66
  rejoinders to, 88:1.5+, 88:3.105–106
  reviews by, 84:2.63–64, 67, 85:1.57–59, 61–62, 85:2.105–107, 110–111, 85:3.164–165, 85:4.227–228, 86:1.32–33, 40–41, 86:2.68–69, 79+, 86:4.200–202+*il*, 87:3.159, 87:4.204–206+, 88:1.15–17, 88:3.112+, 88:4.186–188, 89:1.37
Brock, David, 90:2.66*il*
Brockman, James, 88:2.56, 65
  featured bookbinding, 89:1.8–11*il*
  letter from, 88:1.5
Bromer, Anne C. and David J., 78:1.20, 86:1.34–38*il*, 87:2.75, 88:2.54

letter from, 81:3.75
reply to, 81:3.109
Bromer (booksellers), 78:1.20–21, 82:3.98+, 86:1.34+*il*
Bronk, William, 80:1.16+*il*, 87:2.93–94+*il*
Brooding Heron Press (Sam and Sally Green), 88:2.52
Brook, Stephen (*reviewer*), 78:2.49
Broughton, James, 78:3.77
Brower, David, 77:2.35–36
Brown, Margaret R., 84:1.20
Brown, Nadya, 87:3.122+*il*
Browne, Thomas, 86:2.120–121
Browning, Elizabeth Barrett, 85:1.43
Browning, Robert Pack, 88:1.18, 88:2.72–74, 89:1.36–37
Brownlee/Ramsdale, Sandra, 89:2.96–99+*il*
Brownrigg, Linda L., 82:2.64–67+*il*, 70–73
Brownstone, David M., 84:1.19
Bruccoli, Matthew J., 87:4.216
Bruce, David, Jr., 81:1.24
Bruce, Deborah (D.B.) (*reviewer*), 90:3.100, 101+
Bruce, George, 78:1.29
Bruchac, Joe, 88:1.15–17+*il*
Brunell, Richard, 89:1.48–49
Brunner, Vratislav Hugo, 87:1.22
Brunsman, Laura, 87:2.79
Bryant, William Cullen, 87:4.188+*il*
Buchwald, Howard, 82:2.62–63
Buckley, Christopher, 81:4.121–122, 85:4.224–225
Buechler, John (*reviewer*), 86:4.195–196, 88:4.181–184, 90:2.88–90
  exhibition catalog by, 84:4.139
Bühler, Curt F., 79:1.18+*il*
Bullen, David, 85:1.14
Bullen, Henry Lewis, 86:3.161*il*
Bullock, Wynn, 76:4.62–63
Bultitude, Alan. *See* September Press
Bun-Ching Lam, 88:1.11–12+*il*
Bunseido Press. *See* Cannabis Press (Asao Shimura)
Burch, William, 82:3.93–95
Burdett, Eric, 77:1.19
Burgess, Anthony, 79:3.81–83+*il*, 80:1.2–3, 81:3.104*il*, 105
Burgess, Gelett, 85:1.64
Burke, Clifford, 77:4.78
  books by, 80:3.76–81, 88:2.55, 89:2.71+*il*
  exhibition review by, 75:2.9
  letter to, 81:1.2–3
  performance, 81:4.148
Burke, Jackson, 75:1.7, 76:1.14–15
  obituary (d. 1975), 75:3.31
Burne-Jones, Edward, 76:2.33, 86:3.156
Burnett, A. M., 87:4.181–183, 88:1.5

Burnett, Kenneth L., 75:4.42
Burns, Aaron (ITC), 88:1.40
Burns, Andrew, 85:2.108–109
Burnt Wood Press (Eileen Hogan, England), 77:3.58+*il*, 78:2.45–46, 79:2.47–48+*il*, 83:2.70–71*il*
Burroughs, William S., 82:2.62–63
Burstein, Mark (Lewis Carrol Society), 82:4.140–141*il*
Burton, Mike, 84:3.99–100
Burton, William, 79:4.115–116
Butcher, David, 83:4.156–157
Butler, Frances C., 84:1.4
  articles by, 78:3.70–73*il*, 80:4.108–112, 82:2.44–47+*il*, 85:1.23–25
  FP cover design by, 80:4.107+(*cover*)
  lectures by, 81:4.134, 82:4.146
  photograph of, 85:3.176*il*
  profile of, 85:3.180–181+*il*
  rejoinder to, 80:2.39
  report by, 86:1.18–19
  reviews by, 79:4.110–111, 80:1.18–19, 84:3.118–120, 85:2.114–116, 88:4.185–186, 89:3.127–128, 142–143
  See also Poltroon Press
The Buttonmaker Press (Donald Knoepfler), 88:1.18, 89:1.35–36*il*
Buxton, Frank, 82:2.42
Bynum, Diana, 90:2.56+

C

Cabbagehead Press (John Risseeuw), 87:3.120+*il*, 90:3.115–116*il*
Cabeza de Vaca, Álvar Núñez, 76:1.8, 89:2.99+*il*
Cadnum, Michael, 84:2.63–64
Caflisch, Max, 87:1.35
  anthology about, 89:1.18–19*il*
  book by, 82:2.48*il*
  FP cover design by, 82:2.73+(*cover*)
  On Type article, 83:4.138–142+*il*
Cains, Anthony, 78:1.14
Cains, Tony, 82:3.86
Calder, Alexander, 89:1.31*il*
Caliban Press, 87:1.10+*il*, 89:1.46–48+*il*
California Polytechnic State University (Shakespeare Press), 89:1.6
Calkins, Robert G., 85:4.197
Callen, Anthea, 80:4.126
Calliopea Press (Carol Denison and David Pascoe), 77:2.35
  broadsides from, 79:2.48, 85:3.147+*il*
Callner, Richard, 83:1.21–22
Camberwell Press, 84:4.182, 86:1.40
Camberwell School of Arts and Crafts, 86:3.147–148+*il*, 88:2.60–61+*il*
Cambridge University Press, 80:4.136, 82:2.43, 75, 86:2.123, 90:1.25
Campbell, Peter, 87:1.8–9

Campbell, Sandy, 76:3.48
Camus, Albert, 79:1.4+*il*
Canadau, Eugene G., 80:1.16+*il*, 82:3.112
Candau, Eugenie:
  article by, 76:1.1–5*il*
  bookbindings catalogue by, 78:2.33–34+(*insert*)
  review by, 80:2.56–57
Canham, Anthony, 86:4.200, 201*il*
Cannabis Press (Asao Shimura), 83:2.50–51, 86:3.146–147*il*, 88:2.52
Canning, Eileen, 81:3.107
Cantor, Margery:
  article by, 90:3.121–125
  FP cover design by, 89:1.34+(*cover*), 89:2.60
  reviews by, 89:1.5, 89:3.111
Capra Press (Noel Young), 75:2.13
Carey, John, 90:2.81–83*il*
Carey, Maureen, 82:2.53+
Carl, Malla Blumencranz, 82:4.122
Carlile, Henry, 87:3.121
Carlson, Lage Eric, 83:1.14–15*il*
Carlson, Susan, 90:3.109*il*
Carluccio, Marie, 85:1.73
  cover stencil by, 83:4.174+(*cover*)
  named Art Director, 82:1.2
Carnegie Institute of Technology (New Laboratory Press), 89:3.108
Carpenter, Kenneth J. (Black Rock Press), 79:4.104*il*, 80:1.15–16+*il*, 86:2.77–78*il*
Carpenter, Rod, 89:1.29
Carroll, Lewis, *pseud.* (Charles Lutwidge Dodgson), 78:2.42, 85:4.214, 88:2.62
  reviews of illustrated books by, 76:1.2*il*, 82:3.103–106+*il*, 82:4.140–141*il*, 84:1.38–41*il*
Carruth, Hayden, 77:2.37, 77:4.77+, 80*il*, 84, 81:3.89, 103*il*, 90:1.49*il*
Carter, Harry Graham, 79:2.41, 82:4.154, 83:1.4, 85:1.45–46, 89:3.134+
  obituary (1901–1982), 83:2.69–70*il*
Carter, Jimmy, 77:2.38
Carter, John, 75:3.31–32, 85:1.42–45, 88:2.88
Carter, Matthew, 85:1.36, 45–46, 88:1.24
  and Adobe Systems, 88:1.40*il*
  letter from, 87:1.7
  and the Linotype Co., 86:3.148, 88:1.25, 89:1+(*insert*)
  typefaces by, 79:1.27–30*il*, 80:2.45, 80:3.75, 81:1.20, 85:4.221, 86:3.148, 89:1+(*insert*), 89:1.28*il*
Carter, Sebastian:
  articles by, 88:2.96, 90:3.145
  book by, 87:4.204–206+
  FP cover design by, 81:4.115+(*cover*)
Carter, Sebastian and Will. *See* Rampant Lions Press (Will and Sebastian Carter)
Carter, Will, 86:3.170, 87:2.71*il*, 88:4.192
  letter from, 86:4.236–237
Carver, Raymond, 85:1.13
Cash, Barbara (Ives Street Press), 84:2.67–68*il*, 85:1.59–60, 86:4.198–199*il*, 87:1.54
Cash, George (Cellador Press), 85:3.140
Cassity, Turner, 80:1.14
Castañón, Adolfo, 88:3.130–131
Castell, Heinrich IV zu, 88:4.167–168
Castiglioni, Gino and Alessandro Corubolo (Officina Chimæra), 89:3.143–144
Castle Press (Grant Dahlstrom), 79:1.8, 81:1.34
catalogues, checklists, and bibliographies of fine presses (by name):
  Abattoir Editions checklist, 78:1.10
  Allen Press bibliography, 81:1.2, 82:1.17–19*il*
  Allen Press bibliography (review), 82:1.27–29*il*
  Auerhahn Press, 78:2.49–50
  Bird & Bull Press bibliography (review), 82:1.27–29*il*, 89:2.61*il*
  Cummington Press checklist, 78:1.9–10
  Golden Cockerel Press bibliography (review), 76:1.13
  Grabhorn press bibliography (review), 76:2.31, 82:3.83
  Kelmscott Press bibliographies (review), 85:2.127–128, 85:4.201–202
  Laguna Verde Imprenta (Ward Ritchie), 81:3.85+, 89:4.165–166*il*
  Nonesuch Press bibliography (review), 82:3.87–89
  Perishable Press checklist (review), 86:1.54–56
  Plain Wrapper Press checklist, 81:3.105
  Poltroon Press catalogue, 82:3.83
  Press in Tuscany Alley, The bibliography (review), 84:4.169–170+*il*
  Rampant Lions Press Miscellany (review), 90:2.81–82*il*
  Spiral Press, 83:2.56–58*il*
  Stinehour Press bibliography, 77:1.13, 89:3.152–154
  White Rabbit Press, (Graham Macintosh) 86:3.154–156
  Whittington Press (review), 83:4.156–157
Cataneo, Bernardino, 82:4.145+*il*
Catawba Press (Barbara B. Blumenthal), 81:2.39, 82:1.4, 5, 86:4.199–200*il*
Cate, Philip Dennis, 79:2.47–48
Cather, Willa, 88:4.159

The Complete Index to *Fine Print*

Catich, Edward Michael, 76:4.70, 77:3.55, 80:4.129
   Catfish Press, 83:4.153–154*il*
   obituary (1906–1979), 79:4.118*il*
Cavafy, C. P., 78:2.45–46, 81:3.104*il*, 86:3.147–148+*il*
Cavalcanti, Guido, 86:3.163–165
Cave, Roderick, 84:4.172–173
Caxton, William, 76:4.75, 77:2.42, 78:2.52–53, 78:3.95, 80:3.74*il*, 83:3.88–91
   indulgence fragment printed by, 87:2.68+
Celeyran, Mary Tapie de, 75:1.4
Cellador Press (George Cash), 85:3.140
Cendrars, Blaise, 87:3.117, 139–140, 141–150(*color foldout*)
Center for the Book, University of Iowa, 85:3.182–183, 86:2.73–74+*il*, 87:3.171
Century Company *Thumb-Nail Series*, 82:1.15–18+*il*
Čermínóval, Marie (Toyen pseud.), 87:1.29*il*
Chafetz, Sidney, 85:2.113–114+*il*, 89:1.48–49
Chaika, Betty Lou, 82:4.131+, 84:2.79
   featured bookbindings, 81:3.82–83+*il*, 86:1.47–52*il*
   reviews by, 86:4.217–218, 87:4.214
Challis, Tim, 90:3.101
Chalmers, John P., 85:2.121–123, 87:2.64–65
   exhibition review by, 83:4.171–172+
Chalon, Renier Hubert Ghislain, 87:4.203–204
Chamberlain, Sarah (Chamberlain Press), 84:1.34–35, 87:3+(*insert*)
   books from, 78:1.20–21, 78:4.113–114, 79:3.74*il*, 81:3.87, 82:2.58*il*, 86:1.28–29+*il*, 87:2.80, 88:3.109+*il*
   broadside from, 84:3.109+*il*
   FP cover design by, 84:3.90, 135+cover
Chambers, David, 87:4.203
   Cuckoo Hill Press book, 85:4.232–233
   review by, 81:3.88–89
Chandler, Bruce (Heron Press), 77:1.13
Chandler, Emily, 78:1.30
Chapman, Abigail D., 84:3.106–107
Chappell, Warren:
   address by, 85:2.86
   book about, 84:4.158+*il*
   books by, 76:3.50–51, 77:2.34–35, 41, 81:3.98
   illustrations by, 83:4.163*il*, 84:4.154*il*
   review by, 76:4.72–73
   typeface by, 90:2.70*il*
Charles XII of Sweden, 85:4.229–230*il*
Charrière, Gérard (bookbinder), 80:2.60–61+*il*, 83:1.14–15*il*, 83:4.170–172*il*

Chaucer, Geoffrey, 80:4.124–125, 128*il*, 83:3.108–109*il*, 85:4.202
Chayt, Meryl and Steven (Anachronic Editions), 84:3.118–120, 87:4.213+*il*
Cheever, John, 87:1.9–10*il*
Cheloniidae Press (Alan James Robinson)
   books from, 81:4.122–123*il*, 82:2.57, 82:4.124*il*, 131*il*, 83:4.149–150*il*, 84:2.64–66, 86:2.120–122*il*
Chen, Carol, 84:3.105
Chennells-Pinner, Prue, 86:2.123
Chenoweth, Mary (Press of Appletree Alley), 84:3.133, 84:4.141, 85:3.161–162, 87:4.188+*il*
Chesterton, G. K., 79:3.83
Chevington Press (D. R. Wakefield), 83:4.171+*il*, 86:3.177–178
Chevreul, Michel Eugène, 80:4.109
Chibbett, David, 79:1.23–26*il*
Child, Heather, 77:3.66–67, 87:4.202, 88:2.90
Chilford Hall Press, 86:2.70–71*il*
Chillida, Eduardo, 86:4.200–202
Chimaera Press (Michael and Helen Hutchins), 79:4.116, 81:2.48+*il*, 89:3.129+*il*, 90:3.130–131*il*
Chiostri, Carlo, 85:4.207*il*
Christensen, Pauline (Polly):
   goodbye to, 82:1.2
   reviews by, 78:1.21, 78:4.113, 114, 79:1.17, 79:2.61–62, 79:3.73, 74, 87, 79:4.115, 116, 80:1.16+, 80:2.47, 48, 80:3.88, 81:1.16, 19, 22, 81:2.69, 81:3.87, 92
Christensen, Thomas, reviews by, 87:2.67–68, 90:1.18+
Christie, Agatha, 89:3.147
Christopher, A. B., 82:4.148*il*, 151
Chu, Hung-lam, 90:3.138–140*il*
Cicero, 89:3.135*il*, 137*il*
Cinamon, Gerald, 88:3.105
Circle Press Publications (Ronald King), 79:4.124–125*il*, 85:3.168–172*il*
Citino, David, 90:2.89–90+*il*
Clampitt, Amy, 83:3.106*il*, 121+
Clare, John, 88:2.60*il*
Clarendon, Lord, 79:2.40, 64*il*
Clarino Press (Jeanette Olender-Papurt), 84:2.66–67*il*
Clark, Howard, 82:4.136, 83:3.93–95, 90:1.5
Clark, Jonathan (Artichoke Press):
   article by, 76:2.21–23
   FP cover design by, 90:4.149(*cover*)
   press mark, 79:4.103*il*
Clark, Kathryn, 81:4.126–127, 90:1.5
   articles by, 77:4.77–81*il*, 83:3.95
   lectures by, 81:4.133+, 82:4.136
   photograph of, 77:4.80*il*
   review by, 83:3.102–103

Clark, Kathryn and Howard. *See* Twinrocker Handmade Paper, Inc. (in the *Subject Index*)
Clark, Robert, 86:2.77–78*il*
Clark, Tom ('Quiller'), 79:2.52–54*il*
Clark, Walter H., Jr., 76:3.42
Clark, Walter Van Tilburg, 86:2.77–78*il*
Clark, Willard F., 88:3.106
Clarke, Bert, 82:4.146, 88:1.4
Clarke, Graham (Hayle Mill), 76:2.19*il*
Clarkson, Christopher, 85:2.107–108
Clay, Steven, 89:3.130–133
Clay, Susan (King Library Press), 82:4.147*il*
Clendinning, Ross, 85:2.80
Cleverdon, Douglas, 88:3.133–135*il*
   obituary (1903–1987), 88:2.96
The Close-Grip Press (Cary Wilkins), 88:3.109–111+*il*
Clover Hill Editions (Douglas Cleverdon), 86:3.156, 88:2.96
Cobden-Sanderson, Thomas James, 76:1.14, 76:4.72, 82:1.2, 83:2.53–54+*il*, 85:2.124–126, 85:3.136, 86:4.189, 90:2.60
   collection, 82:4.129+
   Doves Press, 78:3.82, 84:3.94–95, 87:2.66–67, 87:4.215–216
   featured bookbinding, 82:4.129+, 147*il*
   influence of, 86:2.88, 105
   lecture by, 83:4.162–163
Coberly, Elizabeth (Night Heron Press), 78:4.110–111+*il*, 125*il*
Cockerell, Douglas, 77:1.19, 82:3.86
Cockerell, Sydney Morris, 85:4.202
   obituary 1906–1987, 88:2.96
Coffee House Press (Allan Kornblum), 90:2.61*il*
Cohen, Arthur A., 82:4.141–145, 84:3.126–128, 85:4.200–201
Cohen, Elaine Lustig, 82:4.145
Cohrs, Timothy, 78:3.75–76
Cole, John Y. (Library of Congress), 78:1.13, 88:3.122
Coleman, Carroll (Prairie Press), 76:1.12
   obituary (1904–1989), 90:1.48–49*il*
Coleman, Thomas R., 85:1.28, 31
Coleridge, Samuel Taylor, 79:2.64*il*, 80:1.16+*il*
Colescott, Warrington, 77:4.85, 88:3.116–119+*il*, 128–130+*il*
Colette, Sidonie-Gabrielle, 83:4.154–156
Colines, Simon de, 87:3.137+*il*
Colish, A., 75:4.40
Collectors and their collections:
   Bank, Arnold, 86:3.132
   Beatty, Alfred [Arthur (sic)] Chester, 83:1.2
   Belder, Robert de, 87:4.212

Birdsall Collection, 75:3.30
Burke, Jackson (types of Arrighi and Blado), 75:1.7, 76:1.14–15
    obituary (d. 1975), 75:3.31
Burstein, Mark (Lewis Carrol Society), 82:4.140–141*il*
Casamassima, E., 83:1.19
Castell, Heinrich IV zu, 88:4.167–168
Cento Amici del Libro, I, 79:1.8
Cobden-Sanderson, Thomas James, 82:4.129+
Craemer, Jeff (collector of old presses), 86:3.132
de Bellis, Frank V., 85:4.212–215*il*, 86:1.5
de Vever, Henri, 89:3.147–150
Doheny, Carrie Estelle, collection of (auction catalogs), 87:4.180–181, 88:2.55–56, 89:1.12, 89:2.104, 89:4.163–164
Donnelly & Sons Co., R. R., 82:4.123, 83:2.44
Elliott, Harrison G., 78:3.91–92
Fell, John Bishop, 79:2.40+*il*, 82:4.154*il*
Franklin, Colin, 88:1.34+
Grabhorn collection, 76:1.14–15, 76:2.31, 82:3.83
Harding, George Laban, 76:4.75–76, 79:3.91
Heller, Elinor Raas, 89:2.56
Hewitt, Christopher, 89:3.110
Hofer, Phillip, 76:1.13, 85:3.187
Hoover, Herbert, 83:3.123–124
Kelly, Rob Roy, 83:2.46–47, 90:2.75–76
Kemble, Edward C., 76:4.76, 79:3.91
Lerner, Abe, 87:3.160–161
Lyons, T. J. (collector of advertising types), 83:2.49, 84:2.49, 89:1.19–20*il*
Maser, Frederick E., 85:2.121–123
Middleton, Bernard C., 84:2.48
Middleton, Robert Hunter, 87:2.61
Morgan, Douglas and Lloyd (wood type collectors), 83:2.47–49*il*
Norstedt collection, 85:1.45–46*il*, 85:3.138
Papantonio, Michael, 79:3.71
Phillips, Frederick Nelson, 88:1.45
Ray, Gordon, 83:3.91+
Rifkin, Robert Gore (expressionist art collector), 77:2.27–28+*il*
Rollins, Carl P., 84:4.177–178*il*
Rosenwald, Lessing, 80:2.70–71
Sackner, Ruth and Marvin, 88:4.176
Schlosser, Leonard B., 87:2.62
Sexton, Eric, 82:1.2
Strauss, Victor and Edith, 75:1.7
Van Vliet, Claire, 83:2.43+(cover)
von Kritter, Ulrich, 85:2.123–124*il*

Collings, Charles, 82:2.42
Collins, Jess, 88:2.81–82+*il*
Collins, John, 85:1.42–44
Colorado College, Press at (James Trissel), 80:2.48, 84:4.147–148, 87:1.6
Colt Press (Jane Grabhorn), 85:2.104*il*
Columbia University. *See* University of Virginia
Columbus, Christopher, 89:1.7, 90:2.88–90+*il*
Colverson, Tom, photograph of, 88:2.63*il*
Coman, Carolyn, 80:2.58–59*il*
The Compton Press Ltd., 77:1.11
Compulsive Printer (Elmore Mundell), 77:1.11
Cone, Claribel, 85:3.160–161
Conkwright, P. J., 78:1.30
Contre Coup Press (Timothy Hawley), 86:1.38–39*il*
Cooper, Oswald (Oz), 82:4.156
Coover, Robert, 81:3.93–94
Copper Canyon Press (Tree Swenson and Sam Hamill), 87:2.68
    books from, 78:4.114, 81:4.123, 83:2.77–79, 85:2.105–107
Le Corbusier (Charles Édouard Jeanneret), 76:3.52
Corderoy, John, 77:1.19
Corey, D. Steven, 75:2.10, 75:4.42, 76:1.15, 76:2.25
    articles by, 75:1.2–3, 75:4.33–35, 77:1.15–16, 80:2.38–39, 81:3.85+
    On Type article, 77:3.71+*il*
    reviews by (D.S.C.), 76:3.42, 76:4.62, 82:3.85, 83:4.149–150, 88:1.23, 89:4.209–210, 90:2.87–88, 90:3.133–134*il*
Cornford, Adam, 79:1.17
Correspondance des Arts (Poland, Janusz Pavel Tryzno), 88:4.157, 90:1.17+*il*
Cortese, James, 80:4.115–116+*il*
Corti Brothers, 76:4.66
Corubolo, Alessandro and Gino Castiglioni (Officina Chimæra), 89:3.143–144
Corvine Press (Charles Bigelow), 80:1.3, 80:3.87–88+*il*, 85:4.235
Cowell Press (University of California, Santa Cruz), 76:2.29, 78:1.11, 83:2.71–72
Cowley, Malcolm, 82:2.68, 82:3.101–102, 87:3.167+*il*
Cozine, John C., 76:3.48
Crabgrass Press (Philip L. Metzger), 81:4.123–126*il*, 82:4.156–157
Craig, Edward Gordon, 79:1.14–15, 81:4.117*il*, 86:2.89, 88:1.26–33*il*, 90:2.77–78+*il*

photograph of, 81:4.137*il*
Craighead, Meinrad, 77:1.14
Cranach-Presse (Harry Graf Kessler), 78:3.82, 81:4.117*il*, 86:2.88–89, 94–95*il*, 90:1.49, 90:2.77–78+*il*
    Shakespeare's *Hamlet* from, 88:1.26–33*il*
Crane, George, 78:2.43–44, 58*il*
Crane, Hart, 82:2.61, 82:3.101–102
Craven, David, 84:2.71
Craw, Freeman (Jerry), 80:3.82–83, 89:1.7
Crawford, John Wallace, 89:1.36–37+*il*
Crawford, Ralph and Bruce, 85:4.225–227
Creighton, Basil, 77:4.88
Crenshaw, Brad, 84:2.67
Crepuscular Press (Marta Anderson), 77:2.34, 80:4.123
Crerar, John, 86:2.123
Cresci, Giovan Francesco, 79:4.118, 81:1.28
Creuzevault, Colette and Henri, 88:2.54
Crisalli, Karen, 84:1.4
Croce, Benedetto, 78:4.114
Crocker, Alan, 89:3.120–121*il*
Crosby, Caresse, 85:2.112
Crosby, Harry, 85:2.112
Crown Point Press, 76:1.11
Cruikshank, George, 78:2.36
Crutchley, Brooke:
    article by, 75:3.31–32
    review by, 77:1.18
    writings by, 82:2.75, 82:4.152
Cuala Press (previously Dun Emer Press), 75:2.20
Cuckoo Hill Press (David Chambers), 85:4.232–233
Culley, Peter, 87:3.119*il*
Cumming, Dame Hildelith, 77:1.14
Cummington Press (Harry Duncan):
    about, 84:2.72, 86:3.180
    books from, 75:2.17, 76:1.12, 78:1.1–4+*il*, 87:4.185–187*il*
    checklist, 78:1.9–10
    collection, 78:1.11
    press mark, 79:4.104*il*
    See also Abattoir Editions (Harry Duncan)
Cunard, Nancy (Hours Press), 85:2.103
Currie, Kit:
    articles by, 84:4.164–167+*il*, 88:2.55–56, 89:4.163–164
    career of, 86:3.135
    response to, 78:4.106–107
    reviews by, 78:3.76, 82:2.58, 86:2.69–70
Curwen Press (Harold Curwen and Oliver Simon), 77:4.96, 80:3.99, 84:3.129*il*, 87:2.107
Cushing, J. S., 81:4.143
Cushman, Don, 82:3.108–109+*il*, 84:3.101

continuous tone offset lithograph printed for FP by, 84:3.103+(*insert*)
Cusick, Rick, 82:4.156, 83:4.163*il*
Cutliffe, Henry Charles, 83:4.170–171*il*

D

D'Ambrosio, Joseph (printer), 77:1.11, 89:4.210
D'Annunzio, Gabriele (complete works), *See* Mardersteig, Giovanni
D'Arbeloff, Natalie (NdA Press), 82:1.11, 82:4.148*il*, 151–152, 87:3.129*il*
D., H. *See* Doolittle, Hilda (H.D.)
DaBoll, Raymond F. (RFD), 77:3.55, 80:4.132–133, 84:4.158+*il*
obituary (1893–1982), 82:4.156
Dahlstrom, Grant (Castle Press), 79:1.8
obituary (1902–1980), 81:1.34
Daiber, Gretchen, 85:2.110–111*il*
Dailey, William and Victoria (Press of the Pegacycle Lady), 78:3.78, 80:1.23, 81:1.17+*il*
Damon, S. Foster, 75:2.14
Dana, Robert, 87:2.67–68, 87:4.185, 88:2.71–72+*il*
Dandelion Press. *See* Hidy, Lance
Dang Tran Con, 85:4.242
Daniel, Arnaut, 86:3.163–164
Daniel, Henry, 81:4.134–135
Daniel Press (Charles Henry Olive Daniel), 81:4.134–135, 89:3.150–152
Danne, Richard, 77:4.94
Dante Alighieri, 77:2.42+*il*, 81:1.1(*front and back cover wood engraving by Barry Moser*), 4–8*il*, 85:4.206, 220, 88:1.17–18+*il*
Darnton, Robert, 81:2.61
Darwin, Erasmus, 87:3.168+*il*, 88:2.70*il*, 74
Davenport, Guy, 87:2.97–98+*il*, 88:3.109–111+*il*
David, Ismar (Hebrew calligrapher and type designer), 86:1.21–27*il*
Davids, Betsy:
FP cover design by, 84:2.86+(*cover*)
photograph of, 82:4.147*il*
Rebis Press books, 78:4.114–115, 82:2.61–62+*il*, 82:3.119
report by, 85:3.153–155
reviews by, 85:3.167–168, 87:1.10+, 87:2.98–100, 87:3.120–121, 167, 88:1.38–39, 88:3.128–130+, 88:4.178+, 89:2.96–99, 89:4.173–174+
Davids, Kenneth, 78:4.114–115
Davies, Gwendoline and Margaret (Gregynog Press), 81:2.62
Davies, Jordan, 79:4.115
Davis, Dick, 87:4.185+*il*

Davis, Nancy (Big Bridge Press), 84:3.131–132, 90:3.116+*il*
Davis, Roger, 90:2.58–59
Davis, Tracy A. (Nomad Press), 85:2.113–114+*il*
photograph of, 84:2.78*il*
Dawes, Wallace (paper dealer), 83:3.97
Dawson, Muir, 85:1.53, 86:4.190, 235, 89:2.100
Day, Benjamin, 80:4.110–111
Day, Donald, *On Type* article, 81:1.31–32*il*
Day, Dorothy, 90:1.44
Day, Katherine (*reviewer*), 89:1.4–5, 6, 89:2.59–60
Dayton, Stuart, 78:2.38*il*
d'Azevedo, Warren L., 80:1.15–16+*il*
de Bartha, Georges, 90:1.33–34
de Belder, Robert, 87:4.212
de Bretteville, Sheila Levrant, 84:3.105
de Does, Bram, 84:1.9+*il*, 84:2.49, 89:4.162+*il*, 192*il*, 194*il*, 196–197
de Durfort, Claire, 77:4.88–89, 83:1.14–15*il*
de Espinosa, Antonio de, 81:1.12
de Fortsas, J. N.-A. pseud. (hoax), 87:4.203–204*il*
de Furnival, Richard, 88:2.74–75+*il*
De Gonet, Jean, 88:1.12, 88:2.54–55
de Groot, Z. H., 89:4.161
De Guérin, Maurice, 87:1.13–14+*il*
de Hamel, C.F.R., 87:1.51
de Lisle, Leconte, 78:4.109–110
de Pizan, Christine, 85:2.100
De Pol, John. *See* DePol, John
de Soto, Ernest, 77:4.78
De Vinne, Theodore Low, 78:1.29, 81:4.141, 82:1.15+, 84:4.170–171, 85:1.68, 89:1.23
book by, 84:4.170–171
Dean, H. Mallette, 82:3.83
obituary (d. 1975), 75:2.19
Dearth, Greg, 85:3.164–165*il*
Deaver, Georgia, 82:4.132–135*il*
FP cover design by, 88:3.119+(*cover*)
Degener, Amanda, 89:3.110
Degenhardt, Gertrude, 90:3.100*il*
Del Sol Press (David Streeter), 77:2.45
Dela Rosa, A. V., 77:1.14–15, 77:4.91
Delaunay, Sonia, 87:3.139–140, 141–150(color foldout)*il*
DeLittle, Robert Duncan, 90:2.75–76*il*
Demeter, Peter, 81:4.146–147
Demotte, Georges, 89:3.148–150
See also Islamic books and manuscripts, forgeries in Subjects Index
DeMouthe, Margaret, 85:4.194, 86:1.4
Deng Ming-Dao, 88:2.76–77+*il*
Denham, Robert (Iron Mountain Press), 77:1.14

Denison, Carol (Calliopea Press), 77:2.35, 79:2.48, 83:1.25*il*, 85:3.147+*il*
DePol, John:
wood engravings by, 83:2.43–44*il*, 84:1.41*il*, 84:2.49*il*, 84:4.146, 85:2.110*il*, 85:3.144*il*, 86:1.28*il*, 86:4.196–198*il*, 87:4.188–189+*il*, 88:1.18, 90:3.110–111*il*
Yellow Barn Press books, 87:4.188, 88:1.23*il*, 89:3.144+
Derain, Alice, 85:3.160–161
Deresiewicz, Bogdan, 77:2.32+
Derleth, August, 79:3.77–78, 90:1.48*il*
deRoos, Sjoerd H., 76:3.37, 89:4.190+*il*
Detterer, Ernest F., 88:4.152, 90:2.70*il*
Dickens, Charles, 76:1.10, 78:2.42, 85:4.225–227*il*
Dickey, James, 82:3.107–108*il*
Dickey, William, 86:2.68–69
Dickinson, Emily, 78:1.20–21, 86:3.150+*il*, 87:1.7+, 88:4.184–185
Diderot, Denis, 81:2.61
Didot, François Ambroise, 90:3.136
Dieu Donné Press & Paper, Inc. (Susan Gosin), 79:3.73, 83:3.98, 88:3.121+*il*
Dignon, James M. (Mason Hill Press), 79:2.51–52+*il*, 84:3.109+*il*
Dikstein, Judith (Officina Pluralo), 82:1.22–24
Dillard, Annie, 83:1.10
Dillon, Richard (*reviewer*), 85:3.160
Dittrich, Simon, 86:4.200+
Dixon, Paul B., 83:3.103, 85:2.113–114
Dobie, J. Frank, 82:1.22
Dobin, Deborah, 81:4.127+
Dobin, Hank (Goodmorrow Press), 82:3.100–101
Doebler, John, 86:2.75
Doggeral Press, 83:2.54
Doležal, Jaroslav, 87:1.22–23
D'Ooge, Craig, 85:1.64–65
Dooley, John, 85:2.121–123
Doolittle, Hilda (H.D.), 76:1.8, 78:3.77, 85:2.105–106
Dooryard Press (Barbara and Tom Rea), 84:3.95
dos Santos, Bartolomeu, 81:2.48, 63*il*
Dostale, Merce, 89:3.130–132
Dostoevsky, Fyodor, 90:1.42*il*
Doty, William Kavanagh, 79:4.116
Doves Press (Cobden-Sanderson and Emery Walker), 78:3.82, 84:3.94–95, 87:2.66–67, 87:4.215–216
Doyle, Arthur Conan, 83:2.55+, 89:3.147
Drake, Albert, 77:1.10
Dreadnaught Press (Elizabeth Abraham and Greg Gatenby), 78:4.104*il*, 107–108
Drenner, Don von R. (Zauberberg Press), 89:2.62+*il*

Dreyfus, John, 80:1.21, 88:1.4
  award to, 84:3.135
  exhibition review by, 82:4.125+
  obituary by, 88:3.104–105
  On Type articles, 85:4.219–222*il*, 87:2.69–73+*il*, 90:1.25–29*il*
  rejoinder to, 86:3.158
  reviews by, 81:4.139+, 82:4.146+, 152+, 84:3.94–95, 87:2.65–67, 89:3.119–120
  talks by, 83:1.4, 84:1.7, 85:2.86, 86:2.66, 88:1.41
  writings by, 77:3.68, 82:3.87–89+*il*, 90:2.73
Drogin, Marc, 81:4.136, 84:3.125
Drost, Henk, 84:1.10
Drucker, Johanna, 75:4.39
Drummond, Andrew, 80:4.120
Drury, John, 84:4.147–148
Dryden, John, 77:1.7, 87:1.8–9+*il*
Dubie, Norman, 76:3.49, 78:4.113
DuBois, Tad (Spheniscidae Press), 89:4.161
Duchamp, Marcel, 90:1.6–7
Dudin, M., 78:4.116–118
Dudley, C. (Opal Press), 80:4.122–123*il*
Duemer, Joseph, 89:1.41
Duensing, Paul Hayden, 78:1.29, 85:1.73, 86:2.65, 87:1.24, 88:1.25
  conference reports by, 83:1.4–5*il*, 4–5, 85:2.86–87
  letters from, 76:2.25, 76:3.47
  obituary by, 82:4.156–157
  On Type articles, 78:2.46–48*il*, 78:3.86–87+*il*, 80:2.67–68, 80:3.101–102*il*, 80:4.106, 134–135*il*, 85:1.20–22, 35–41*il*, 86:1.6–10*il*, 87:1.34–39*il*, 90:2.69–71*il*
  Private Press & Typefoundery of, 76:2.29–30, 77:1.13, 79:4.108+*il*
  reviews by, 82:4.154, 83:1.29–30, 83:2.66, 84:3.123–125, 84:4.174, 85:2.126–127, 85:4.204, 87:4.193–195+, 88:1.6, 9–10, 88:4.170, 89:1.18–19, 90:3.100–101
  types from, 87:1.15
Duff, E. Gordon, 86:1.38
Dun Emer Press (later Cuala Press Wales), 75:2.20
Duncan, Alastair, 90:1.33–34
Duncan, Harold M., 82:3.90
Duncan, Harry, 88:1.17
  books by, 84:2.71–72+, 88:1.45
  FP cover design by, 86:3.180+(*cover with etching by Keith Achepol*)
  influence of, 85:3.179
  interview with, 78:1.4–8*il*
  philosophy of, 78:1.4–6, 80:3.100, 81:4.135+, 84:2.71–72+, 85:1.14, 89:3.133
  photograph of, 78:1.8*il*
  press mark, 79:4.103*il*
  profiles of, 78:1.1–7+*il*, 81:4.132
  reviews by, 81:2.58–61, 86:3.157, 87:3.151–152, 88:3.127–128, 89:1.45–46, 89:4.171–173
  See also Abattoir Editions; Cummington Press
Duncan, Robert, 86:3.165+*il*
Dunlap, Joseph:
  review by, 78:3.84–85
  writing by, 77:3.68
Duras, Marguerite, 88:1.11–12+*il*
Dürer, Albrecht, 77:4.97–98, 85:1.62–63*il*
Durfort, Claire de, 77:4.88–89, 83:1.14–15*il*
Durgin, Michael, 89:3.110
Duston, Hannah, 88:4.181+*il*
Dutt, Toru, 79:2.48–49
Duval, Kulgin D., 81:2.38–39, 85:2.119+, 87:2.64–65
Dvořák, Anton, 88:4.178+*il*
Dwan, Kevin, 80:2.38, 84:3.93+
Dwiggins, William Addison, 76:1.13, 77:3.55, 78:1.30, 79:4.130–131, 80:3.92, 94, 81:3.106, 86:2.79, 119
  articles on, 75:2.18–19, 84:4.163+*il*, 87:2.82–86*il*, 87–89*il*
  and Dorothy Abbe (Püterschein-Hingham Press), 75:2.18–19, 80:1.18–19+*il*, 80:2.39, 87:2.62+*il*
  and Edward Michael Catich, 83:4.153–154
  FP cover honoring, 87:2.62+(*cover*)
  Hermann Püterschein (pseud.), 87:2.88
  illustrations of work by, 77:3.53*il*, 84:4.137(*cover*), 154*il*, 157*il*, 169*il*, 87:2.83–89*il*
  "M-formula," 89:1.26
  photograph of, 89:1(*insert*)
Dworkin, Angela P., 84:3.132–133

E

Eadfrith, Bishop, 82:2.73
Eagan, Tim, 86:1.39–40
Eakins Press Foundation (Leslie Katz and Harvey Simmonds), 77:3.60
  press marks, 79:4.105*il*, 80:1.9*il*
ear/say (Warren Lehrer and Dennis Bernstein), 85:3.167–168+*il*, 89:2.96–99+*il*
Easton, Phoebe Jane, 84:3.120–123
Eberhardt, Fritz, 83:1.14–15*il*
Eberhardt, Richard, 82:3.101
Echániz, Guillermo, 83:1.33–35*il*, 83:2.44+, 83:3.87
Echo Press (Fredric Brewer), 88:2.74–76+*il*
Eco, Umberto (movie), 87:2.102–103
Edelstein, J. M. (*reviewer*), 77:3.59, 79:3.72, 80:3.98, 81:1.17, 81:4.121–122, 82:3.103, 83:4.150, 85:2.112
Edition de Beauclair (Gotthard de Beauclair), 86:2.83
Edition Kaldewey (Gunnar Kaldewey), 88:1.11–12+*il*, 89:2.59
Edition Seefeld (Charles Whitehouse), 87:3.122*il*
Edition Tiessen (Wolfgang Tiessen), 86:4.200–203+*il*, 88:3.105–106
Editiones Dominicae (Franco Riva), 79:2.46, 82:3.116
  press marks, 79:4.105*il*, 80:2.44
Edizioni Ampersand (and Alessandro Zanella), 82:3.82, 88:3.143
Edizioni Rovio (Giorgio Upiglio), 85:4.212–215*il*
Edizioni Tallone (Tallone family), 80:1.13+, 21–22+*il*, 83:4.151*il*, 85:4.205–208, 215*il*, 238+
Edmonds, J. M., 81:2.46–47*il*
Edson, Russell, 79:1.17
Edwards, George Wharton, 82:1.17, 18
Edwards, Nancy Chandler, 78:1.20–21
Ehmcke, Fritz Helmut (Rupprecht Presse), 86:2.90, 104
Eichenberg, Antonie, 78:2.50–51
  FP cover design by, 90:1.9+(*cover*)
Eichenberg, Fritz, 78:2.50–51*il*, 79:3.74, 88:4.159*il*, 90:1.9+*il*, 43–45*il*
Eisenhower, Dwight D., 85:3.141*il*
Eisenstein, Elizabeth L., 79:2.46, 80:1.23–25+, 81:2.61, 84:4.139
Ekker, Remco Flip, 89:4.186+*il*
El Lissitsky. *See* Lissitzky, El
Elchers, Philip (Uitgeverij Philip Elchers), 89:4.185–186+*il*
Eldridge, Betty Palmer, 89:2.59
Elizabeth Press (James Weil), 80:1.16+*il*, 82:3.112
Elkind, M. Wieder, 82:4.122–123
Ellenport, Samuel B. (Harcourt Bindery), 82:1.5, 83:4.143
Elliott, Harrison G., 78:3.91–92
Elliott, James Welsh, 88:1.4
Elliott, William I., 79:2.55–56
Ellis, E. N., 85:4.225–226*il*, 89:1.35–36*il*
Ellis, Richard, 80:3.92+*il*
Elm Press, 87:1.14+*il*
Elmete Press (A. S. Maney), 79:3.88+*il*, 80:1.2
Elsted, Crispin:
  letter from, 89:2.56–57
  reviews by, 85:3.172–173, 86:2.120–122, 86:4.193–195, 219+, 87:4.215–216, 88:1.6–8, 88:2.68+, 82–83, 88:4.188, 89:2.71+, 89:4.166+, 90:1.16–17, 90:2.77–78+, 81–82, 91–92

Elsted, Crispin and Jan. *See* Barbarian Press (Crispin and Jan Elsted)
Eluard, Paul, 80:2.59*il*, 61
Ely, Timothy, 87:2.80–81, 88:4.176
Emanon Press (Debra Weier and Bill Bridgers), 82:3.106*il*, 83:3.102–103
Emerson, Ralph Waldo, 82:2.59
Emery, Jack, 84:3.97
Enschedé, Johannes, 77:2.42+
Enslin, Theodore, 88:1.15–16
Epes, Maria Poythress:
  FP issue design by, 76:4.78
  Poythress Press book, 77:3.59
  reviews by, 77:2.35, 78:3.74, 79:3.88+
Erespin Press (Carol Kent), 85:3.165–166
Erhardt, Hans Martin, 86:4.200, 201*il*
Ernst, David, 77:2.35
Ernst, Max, 82:4.127
Ernst-Ludwig-Presse, 86:2.90–91*il*
Eshleman, Clayton, 79:1.17–18
Esposito, Tony, 82:1.6+
Esser, Mark, 85:3.183
Essick, Robert N., 80:1.23
Esslemont, David, 88:1.45, 90:3.129–130
Estudio Gráfico (Raúl Veroni), 77:3.65
Etherington, Donald, 84:1.20+, 85:2.121, 87:3.169, 88:2.56+, 88+
  exhibition review by, 80:3.94–95+
  featured bookbindings, 83:1.14–15*il*, 83:2.59
Ettan Press (Milos Sovak), 76:4.63–64
Eucalyptus Press (Mills College), 78:4.114–115
Euripides, 86:4.200, 202+*il*
Evanescent Press (Lee Ruelle), 77:3.60
Evans, Edmund, 80:4.108
Evans, Emrys, 75:3.30
Evans, Ingrid, 89:1.38
Evans, Jean, 81:2.67
Evans, Margaret B., 81:4.118, 82:1.3, 85:1.29–30
Evelyn, John, 87:2.90–91
Everson, William (Brother Antoninus), 79:3.84–85, 88:3.115
  biography of, 89:3.121–123*il*
  controversial review of book authored by, 81:1.18–19*il*, 81:3.75, 108–109
  Lime Kiln Press books, 75:3.21–22, 76:2.26–27, 80:2.55–56, 82:2.53+*il*, 59–61+*il*, 85:1.7, 89:3.123
  rejoinder to, 78:3.80
  reviews by, 78:1.15, 80:2.51–53, 86:2.77–78
  woodcut of, 89:3.122*il*
  writings by, 76:2.31, 76:4.62, 80:2.55–56, 81:1.18–19*il*, 81:3.75, 108, 82:2.59–61, 84:4.174–175, 85:4.235, 89:3.121–123+, 90:3.127–128
Evetts, Deborah (bookbinder), 79:1.18+*il*, 83:2.59, 90:2.63*il*
Evetts, L. C., 80:4.126+
Evrard, Sün (bookbinder), 84:4.180, 90:1.37–39*il*
Ewert, William B., 87:3.121+*il*
Ex Ophidia press. *See* Rummonds, Richard-Gabriel
Eyssen, Jürgen, 82:3.86–87

F

Fabilli, Mary, 89:3.122
Fahey, Edna Peter, obituary (1897–1974), 75:1.7
Fair, Anthony, 84:3.128–129
Fairbank, Alfred, 78:1.30, 79:2.44–45, 80:1.26
Fandel, John, 78:3.77
Fanti, Sigismondo, 81:1.26, 89:2.78*il*
Farmer, Geoffrey, 86:2.123
Farnsworth, Donald S., 76:2.22, 90:2.58
Farrell, Charles, exhibition review, 80:3.92–94*il*
Farrell, David, 79:2.45–46, 81:4.133
  book from, 89:3.152–154
  On Type article, 78:4.121–123*il*
  reports by, 78:1.11–12, 81:2.66–67*il*
  review by, 83:4.166–167
Fass, John (Hammer Creek Press), 83:1.37
Fata Morgana Press (Bruno Roy), bookbindings for, 88:2.53, 88:4.175
Faulkner, William, 84:2.48–49
Faust, Dikko (Purgatory Pie Press), 78:3.75–76
Fawcett, Benjamin, 89:2.72–73
Fawcus, Arnold (Trianon Press), 82:2.50
Feather, John, 88:2.88–90
Fein, Samuel (Reflector Press), 78:2.37
Feliciano, Felice, 85:4.194+*il*, 89:1.8–9+*il*, 89:3.135*il*
  prize named after, 89:3.143–144, 90:2.59–60
Fell, John (Bishop), 79:2.40–41+*il*, 52, 82:4.154*il*, 83:1.7, 18
Ferlinghetti, Lawrence, 80:4.123–124, 84:3.107, 87:2.67–68, 88:3.128–130
Fern, Alan, 84:2.54
  reviews by, 80:4.120–121, 82:3.87–89
Ferris, Suzanne, 88:2.95
  letter from, 80:1.2
  See also Sea Pen Press and Papermill
Ferry, David, 81:4.129, 83:2.54–55
Feyrer, Gayle, 77:3.59–60
Fiedler, Conrad, 89:3.119+
Fine Arts Press, (Gerald Lange, University of Southern California), 89:1.7, 90:2.88–90*il*

Fine Print Broadside Round-Up (reviewers):
  1984 *Introduction* by Charles Seluzicki, 84:3.103
  1985 *Introduction* by Alastair Johnston, 85:3.139–140
  1990 *Introductions* by M. Antonetti, D. Goines, C. Robertson, C. Taylor, 90:3.104–117*il*
FINE PRINT cover designers:
  Abbe, Dorothy (with W. A. Dwiggins stencil ornaments), 87:2.62+*il*
  Achepol, Keith (cover print), 86:3.180+*il*
  Amert, Kay, 87:4.210+*il*
  Angelo, Valenti 83:1.35+*il*
  Baudin, Fernand, 90:2.61+*il*
  Bigus, Richard, 89:2.60+*il*
  Blinn, Carol J., 80:2.39+*il*
  Blumenthal, Joseph (with border by Simon de Colines), 87:3.137+*il*
  Briem, Gunnlaugur SE, 85:3.138+*il*
  Butler, Frances, 80:4.107+*il*
  Caflisch, Max (with Granjon ornaments), 82:2.73+*il*
  Cantor, Margery, 89:1.34+*il*, 89:2.60
  Carluccio, Marie (stencil), 83:4.174+*il*
  Carter, Sebastian, 81:4.115+*il*
  Chamberlain, Sarah, 84:3.135+*il*
  Clark, Jonathan, 90:4.149+*il*
  Davids, Betsy, 84:2.86+*il*
  Deaver, Georgia, 88:3.119+*il*
  Duncan, Harry (with Achepohl print), 86:3.180+*il*
  Eichenberg, Antonie, 90:1.9+*il*
  Gentry, Linnea (type ornament), 75:2.20+*il*
  Goluska, Glenn, 86:1.4+*il*
  Grycz, Czeslaw Jan (with Moser drawings), 81:1.3+*il*
  Gutsch, Herbert, 90:3.143+*il*
  Hidy, Lance, 84:1.43+*il*
  Holmes, Kris, 80:3.75+*il*
  Hoyt-Koch, Shelley, 82:1.3+*il*
  Huizenga, Janine, 89:4.175+*il*
  Jiskra, Jan, 87:1.24+*il*
  Lerner, Abe, 83:1.35+*il*
  Livingston, Mark, 80:1.3+*il*
  McLellan, Leigh, 86:4.238+*il*
  Mardersteig, Martino, 85:4.194+*il*
  Moser, Barry (with Jan Grycz design), 81:1.3+*il*
  Mott, Steve, 89:2.60+(*cover*)
  O'Connell, Bonnie Pratt, 88:4.176+*il*
  Powers, Will, 88:1.10+*il*
  Quadflieg, Roswitha, 86:2.109+*il*
  Randle, John (with Phipps linocut), 88:2.93+*il*
  Skaggs, Charles, 84:4.183+*il*
  Skelton, Christopher, 82:3.119+*il*

VOLUME 16, NUMBER 4, 2003
Complete Index to Fine Print 1975–1990
   Cover design: Jonathan Clark   90[2003]:4.149
   Designer: Will Powers   90[2003]:4.151+

Stewart, William, 82:4.157+*il*
Stone, Sumner (titles), 81:3.95+*il*
Swenson, Tree, 89:3.113+*il*
Tanner, Wesley B., 83:3.125+*il*
Unger, Gerard, 81:2.71+(*cover*), 71+*il*
Van Vliet, Claire, 83:2.43+*il*
Walkup, Kathleen, 85:2.128+*il*
Weimann, Christopher (marbling), 81:3.95+*il*, 83:4.174+*il*
Wilson, Adrian, 79:4.126+*il*
Zapf, Hermann, 85:1.70+*il*
See also FINE PRINT issue designers
FINE PRINT *Designing Literature* article writers:
Berlin, Lucia, 88:4.160–162
Gioia, Dana, 89:2.83–86
Hamady, Walter, 88:3.116–119
Nelson, Victoria, 88:2.92–93
Powers, Will, 87:4.196–200
Roatcap, Adela Spindler, 88:1.26–33
FINE PRINT Featured Bookbinders, 85:1.8
Brockman, James, 89:1.8–11*il*
Carlson, Lage, 83:1.14–15*il*
Chaika, Betty Lou, 81:3.82–83+*il*, 86:1.47–52*il*
Charrière, Gérard, 83:1.14–15*il*
Cobden-Sanderson, Thomas James, 82:4.129+*il*
Coman, Carolyn, 80:2.58–59*il*
Eberhardt, Fritz, 83:1.14–15*il*
Etherington, Don, 83:1.14–15*il*, 83:2.60–61*il*
Evetts, Deborah, 79:1.18+*il*
Evrard, Sün (bookbinder), 90:1.37–39*il*
fourteen different bookbindings on same book, 83:1.14–15*il*
Glaister, Donald, 80:3.84–85*il*
Hoyem, Andrew, 82:1.12–13*il*
James, Angela, 83:3.108–109*il*
Jones, Trevor, 85:2.119+*il*
Kampf, Jamie, 83:1.14–15*il*
Kyle, Hedi, 84:3.114–115+*il*
Lubett, Denise Y., 81:2.46–47*il*
Middleton, Bernard C., 79:3.86+*il*
Miura, Kirstin Tini, 84:1.15+*il*
Mowery, John Franklin, 85:1.26–27+*il*
Ramsey, Eleanore, 87:2.75–78+*il*
Schnabel, Bruce (and Harvey Redding), 81:1.10–11*il*, 81:2.39
Schopfer, Janice Mae, 87:2.75–78+*il*
Sheehan, J. C., 82:2.54+*il*
Smith, Philip, 79:4.124–126*il*
Smith, Sally Lou, 80:1.10–11*il*
Southworth, Nancy, 80:2.58–59*il*
Stackpole, Julie Beinecke, 80:4.118–119+*il*
Van Vliet, Claire, 89:3.114–118*il*
Waters, Peter, 79:2.38–39*il*

Wilcox, Michael, 83:1.14–15*il*, 83:4.168–169+*il*
Wilson, Susan Spring, 83:1.14–15*il*
Zwang, Christian, 86:2.116–117*il*
See also bookbinders (in the *Subject Index*)
FINE PRINT Guest Editors:
Fraser, James (Czech issue), 87:1.15, 24
Raecke, Renate (German issue), 86:2.65, 124
Strauss, Monica J. (Dutch issue), 894.175*il*, 89:4.214
FINE PRINT issue designers:
Agner, Dwight, 77:2.38
Bixler, Michael and Winifred, 76:1.16, 76:2.20
Epes, Maria Poythress, 76:4.78
Gentry, Linnea (various issues 1976–1981 and continuing 1982–on), 76:2.20, 81:4.115, 82:1+
Goldenberg, Carol, 78:4.111
Gordon, Ronald, 78:3.80
Harvard, Stephen, 77:3.58
Hoyem, Andrew, 75:1.8, 75:2.20, 75:3.32, 75:4.44
Merker, Kim, 78:1.13
Moser, Barry (with Sheila Waters banner), 79:2.65
Ritchie, George F., 78:2.46
Stauffacher, Jack Werner, 77:1.23
Tanner, Wesley B., 76:3.49
Walker, Scott (with Tim Girvin banner), 79:3.71
Wilson, Adrian, 79:4.126
See also FINE PRINT cover designers
On Type article writers, 85:1.8
Abrams, George, 86:2.103–107*il*
Bigelow, Charles A., 77:4.98–100, 79:1.27–30*il*, 80:3.102–103*il*, 81:1.32, 82:1.6–7+, 88:4.171–174*il*, 89:2.76–82*il*
Caflisch, Max, 83:4.138–142+*il*
Corey, D. Steven, 77:3.71+*il*
Day, Donald, 81:1.31–32*il*
Dreyfus, John, 85:4.219–222+*il*, 87:2.69–73+*il*, 90:1.25–29*il*
Duensing, Paul Hayden, 78:2.46–48*il*, 78:3.86–87+*il*, 80:2.67–68, 80:3.101–102*il*, 80:4.134–135*il*, 85:1.20–22, 35–41*il*, 86:1.6–10*il*, 87:1.34–39, 90:2.69–71*il*
Farrell, David, 78:4.121–123*il*
Gentry, Linnea, 77:2.42+*il*
Holmes, Kris, 80:1.26–30*il*, 85:3.148–152*il* (cover design), 87:3.162*il*
Johnson, Herbert H., 86:3.158–161*il*
Kirshenbaum, Sandra, 88:1.24–25+*il*
Level, Jeff, 89:1.23–30+(*insert*)
Mosley, James, 82:3.90–95*il*

Nelson, Stan, 86:4.228–229*il*
Ovink, G. W., 79:3.92–96
Shaw, Paul, 81:4.140–144*il*
Stanford, Donald E., 83:1.7–9*il*
Stone, Sumner, 79:4.120–123*il*, 88:3.123–126*il*
Tracy, Walter, 81:2.51–56*il*, 81:3.99–102*il*
Twomey, Juliet Spohn (influence of Roman inscriptions), 89:3.134–141*il*
van Krimpen, Huib, 89:4.189–197*il*
Fine, Ruth E., 78:2.53
article by, 80:2.70–71
exhibition by, 85:2.120–121
exhibition review by, 80:4.113
linoleum cut by, 89:2.71+*il*
review by, 88:2.76–77
Finlay, Nancy, 88:3.106
Finley, Susan and Curtis, 85:1.69
Finney, Charles G., 84:4.148–149+
Fish, Williston, 76:3.48
Fisher, Ed, Jr., 89:3.108
Fisher, Roy, 85:3.168+
Fitz Gerald, Vincent, press of 85:2.114–115+*il*
Fitzgerald, F. Scott, 76:3.49, 85:4.223–224
Five Seasons Press (Glenn Storhaug), 84:1.37–38*il*
Five Trees Press (Eileen Callahan, Cameron Folsom, Cheryl Miller, Jaimie Robles, and Kathleen Walkup), 84:2.79
books from, 76:4.66, 78:3.74, 78:4.114, 79:2.54, 79:4.115–116
Flamer, Richard, 78:1.11
Flanner, Janet, 83:4.154–156
Flatlands Press (Richard Zauft), 85:3.142–143+*il*, 87:3.120–121+*il*
Flaubert, Gustave, 75:1.3–4
Flavin, Richard, 80:2.53–55*il*, 85:1.60*il*
Jionji Press books, 86:3.146–147*il*, 87:2.100–101*il*
Fleece Press (Simon Lawrence), 88:2.65–66+*il*
Fleischmann, Joan Michael (type designer), 77:2.42+*il*, 89:4.196
Fletcher, Harry George, III:
book by, 90:1.34–36*il*
reviews by, 80:2.63–65, 84:4.170–171
response to, 85:1.68
Florin Press (Graham R. Williams), 81:2.49–50*il*, 85:4.233–234*il*, 86:3.139+*il*, 86:4.223–224+*il*
Fluke, Gordon (Grahame Cracker Press), 90:3.116–117*il*
Flynn, Patrick JB (Jackalope Press), 85:3.143+*il*
Follain, Jean, 78:2.44, 81:1.16
Fontaine, René, 90:3.132–133*il*

Ford, Charles Henri, 84:2.71
Ford, Hugh, 75:3.29
Ford, Margaret L., 86:2.80–84
Forest, John and Sarah, 87:3.129*il*
Forgue, Norman, 80:1.5–6
Forman, H. Buxton, 85:1.42–44
Forster, E. M., 76:3.48
Forster, Peter, 88:2.66*il*
Fortune Press (Charles Skilton), 79:2.48–49
Foss, Phillip, Jr., 82:4.130*il*
Foster, Peter (Vine Press), 90:1.28–29
Four Ducks Press mark, 79:4.105*il*
Four Winds Press (Henry Schniewind):
    books from, 76:2.30, 76:3.48, 78:3.77
    press mark, 79:4.105*il*
Fournier, Pierre Simon, 89:2.80, 90:3.136
Fowles, John, 77:4.88–89
Fox, Siv Cedering, 79:2.48
Franck, Irene M., 84:1.19
Franklin, Anne, 85:2.101
Franklin, Benjamin, 76:2.30, 77:1.13, 81:3.77
Franklin, Colin, 86:1.37
    articles by, 79:3.69–71+*il*, 81:3.88+, 82:4.151–152+*il*, 88:1.34+
    books by, 81:4.136+*il*, 84:3.94–95, 87:2.65–67, 75, 87:4.215–216, 89:3.150–152
    exhibition review by, 78:2.33–34*il*
    reviews by, 83:1.22, 83:2.58+
Franklin, James, 78:4.113
Franks, Kate, 76:3.45
Frasconi, Antonio, 84:4.170–171
Fraser, James H., 76:3.40, 81:3.87+*il*
    as FP Guest Editor, 87:1.15, 24
Fraser, James H. and Sybil, 85:2.80–81
Frazier, Katharine, 78:1.1, 85:3.177
Frederic W. Goudy Award, 86:1.5
Fredericks, Claude:
    Banyan Press, 77:3.59
    review by, 79:1.12–14
        rejoinders to, 79:2.42–43, 79:3.72
Freebairn, James, 85:3.162–163
Freedman, Joe Marc (Sarabande Press), 83:3.121+*il*
The Freehand Press (Jessica and David Mycroft), 76:4.64, 80:1.16+*il*, 82:3.100*il*
Freeman, Paul (calligrapher), obituary (1928–1980), 81:1.34
Freeman, Vera G. (paper dealer), 76:3.45–47
    report by, 83:4.159–161
French, Hannah Dustin, 87:2.63–64
French, William Fuller Kirkpatrick, 90:2.92–93
Friedlaender, Henri, 86:1.24, 87:1.53–54
Friedlander, Joel (Petrarch Press), 89:1.45–46+*il*
Friedlander, Lee, 77:3.60

Friedman, Joan M. (*reviewer*), 80:1.23
Fromek, Jan (Odeon), 87:1.20
Frontier, Roberto (Legatoria Piazzesi), 76:2.27–28, 76:3.41
Frost, Carol, 79:1.9–10
Frost, Gary, 82:4.137+, 87:3.171
    article by, 83:3.97–98
    exhibition reviews by, 85:2.83–85, 85:4.194
    reviews by, 79:4.128–129, 82:3.85–86, 83:2.50–51, 86:3.146–147
Frost, Robert, 78:2.40*il*, 83:2.57, 86:3.157+*il*
Frutiger, Adrian, 88:1.25
    signs and symbols by, 80:4.131–132
    typefaces by, 79:1.27, 80:2.45, 82:1.29–31*il*, 86:3.149, 88:3.124, 88:4.171–174*il*
    Univers typeface by, 82:1.30, 88:4.177+*il*
Fry, Christopher, 80:4.125+*il*
Fry, Edmund, 86:1.8, 87:4.203
Frye, Mary Ann (*reviewer*), 89:2.87–88
Fugger, Wolffgang, 89:2.90*il*
Full Moon Press (Jim Benvenuto), 87:3.119–120
Fust, Johann (15th-century printer), 86:4.212+, 89:1.12
Futernick, Robert, 75:2.12

G

Gachet, Henri, 79:4.117
Gadd, Jeremy, 76:2.29
Gage-Cole, H., 88:1.30*il*, 32
Gallagher, Tess, 79:1.10–11, 79:3.74, 85:3.141–142*il*
Ganda, Arnaldo, 90:2.59–60
Ganesan, Indira, 86:2.119–120*il*
Garamond, Claude, 83:4.139
García Terrés, Jaime, 88:3.130–131
Gardner, Martin, 82:4.140–141
Gardyloo Press (John Thomas Bennett), 80:2.38–39, 83:1.11
Garnett, Porter (New Laboratory Press, Carnegie Institute of Technology), 75:4.33–35, 81:2.52–53, 82:1.3, 82:3.82, 89:3.108
Garrett, Charlotte, 78:3.77–78
Garruba, Nancy J., 79:1.6
Garry, Charlene:
    Basilisk Press books, 79:2.44, 79:3.97–98, 82:4.127
    Basilisk Press marks, 79:4.104+*il*, 90:3.145*il*
    obituary (1932–1989), 90:3.145
Garvey, Eleanor M. (*reviewer*), 78:1.15–17, 79:4.112
Gass, William H., 86:1.33–34+*il*

Gatenby, Greg (Dreadnaught Press), 78:4.104*il*, 107–108
Gauguin, Paul, 89:1.6
Gavin, Carney E.S. (*reviewer*), 89:2.69–71
Gebhart, Horst, 89:1.16*il*
Gee, Eric (Gwasg Gregynog Press), 84:2.68–69
Gefn Press (Susan Johanknecht), 76:1.8–9, 78:1.17, 21
Gehenna Press (Leonard Baskin), 78:2.49, 54
    device of, 78:2.44*il*
Geilen, Jochen, 86:4.200, 203*il*
Gelfand, Morris A. (Stone House Press), 84:1.41*il*, 84:3.110*il*, 87:4.188+*il*, 88:2.52
    letter from, 86:3.179–180
Gentry, Helen, 76:4.57, 80:3.92, 83:4.173, 85:2.104
    obituary (1897–1988), 89:2.100
    quote from, 85:2.77(*cover*)
    reviews by, 78:2.42, 43–44
Gentry, Linnea:
    Amaranth Press books, 76:4.71, 78:2.41+*il*, 85:3.172–173*il*
    art by, 82:3.98+
    article edited by, 76:4.57–60
    articles by, 75:2.10, 75:3.21–22, 76:4.69–70, 77:2.42+*il*, 82:2.60, 82:3.114, 89:2.100
    exhibition review by, 75:3.28–29
    FP career of, 80:4.107, 85:1.6, 8
    FP cover design type ornament, 75:2.20+*il*
    FP issue designs (various 1976–1979, 1980, 1981, and final design continuing 1982–on), 76:2.20, 79:1.18
    On Type article, 77:2.42+*il*
    reviews by (L.G.), 76:3.42, 43–44, 45, 76:4.64, 77:1.10–12, 19–20, 77:2.37, 41, 77:3.58, 59–60, 65, 77:4.84, 86–87, 96, 78:2.38, 42, 43–44, 78:3.75, 78, 78:4.110–112, 79:1.9, 23, 79:2.59–60, 80:1.21–22, 80:2.65–66, 80:4.129, 82:3.113, 83:2.76–77, 84:4.171, 86:1.29–31, 87:1.42–43, 87:3.120+, 167, 168, 87:4.188–192, 89:2.62+
Genz, Marcella, 88:4.191
Gerard, David, 90:1.9
Gerhardt, Claus W., 89:3.111, 113
Gerry, Vance (Lord John Press), 80:2.47, 84:3.107
Gerry, Vance (Weather Bird Press), 80:2.48, 84:3.98+
Gerstenberg, Rainer, 88:3.143
Gesellschaft, Maximilian, 85:4.196–198
Gessner, Christian Friedrich, 85:2.79–80
Geyer Studio, 80:2.65
Ghotan, Bartholomeus, 88:2.56

Giampa, Gerald, 78:2.37
Gibb, Robert, 81:1.22
Gibbings, Robert (Golden Cockerel Press), 85:1.69, 88:3.134
Gilbert, Bennett, 82:4.150+
Giles, Laurence, 79:3.77–78
Gilgun, John, 82:3.98*il*
Gili, Phillida, 87:1.8–9*il*
Gill, Eric, 79:4.122, 83:1.17–18, 83:3.109, 86:4.197
    alphabet by, 88:3.133–135*il*
    art by, 82:3.92*il*, 110*il*, 88:1.23*il*, 31
    biography of, 89:4.201–203*il*
    catalogues of work by, 77:2.40–41, 84:3.129–131*il*, 88:3.133–135*il*
    cover design honoring, 82:3.119+*il*
    essay by, 79:1.2+*il*
    exhibitions, 82:3.82–83
    and Francis Meynell, 82:3.87–88
    Gill Sans types by, 77:2.40–41, 82:3.95, 119+*il*, 86:3.149+*il*
    and Harry Graf Kessler, 86:2.89
    lecture by, 82:3.96–97+
    Perpetua type by, 77:2.40–41, 79:1.2+*il*, 82:3.90–91+*il*, 93–95*il*, 84:3.105–106
    photograph of, 82:3.91*il*
    and Stanley Morison, 82:3.90+, 96, 89:1.5
    on typography, 90:2.87–88*il*
    lettering work donated, 77:1.13
Gillot, Charles, 80:4.108–109, 127*il*
Gilmour, Pat, 77:4.96
Ginger, E. M.:
    FP editor, 76:4.78, 85:1.73
    reviews by, 77:2.37, 78:3.77, 78:4.113–114, 79:1.17, 79:3.73, 84:3.96–97
Ginsberg, Allen, 79:1.17, 88:3.128–130
Ginzel, Roland, 77:4.84+
Gioia, Dana, 84:4.143–144
    writings by, 84:1.41, 88:1.21–23+*il*, 38–39*il*, 89:2.83–86*il*
Giorgio, Bob (cut text in wood), 81:3.87
Girvin, Tim, FP banner calligraphy by, 79:3.71+*il*
Giunti, printers of Florence, 81:1.25
The Glad Hand Press (Robert M. Jones), 85:3.158*il*
Gladstone, W. E., 85:1.56–57
Glaister, Donald, 80:3.84–85*il*, 88:3.137–141*il*
Glaister, Geoffrey Ashall, 81:1.23–24
Glick, Milton, 80:3.94
Gliwa, Stanislaw, 87:3.129
Gloss, Kenneth, letter from, 86:1.4
Godine, David R., 80:3.100, 87:2.68
    article by, 81:4.118–120+
    letter from, 75:4.35
    press marks, 79:4.102*il*

reply to, 82:2.42
    review by, 84:4.146
Goethe, Johann Wolfgang von, 85:4.230–232, 86:2.96–97*il*, 109+(*cover*), 86:4.200–201*il*, 87:2.92
Goines, David Lance, 80:4.111–112, 84:4.174, 88:4.184
    broadside reviews by, 90:3.115–117
    essay by, 90:3.114–115
Golahny, Berta, 81:3.93+
Gold, Marsha Eva, 83:3.106*il*, 121+*il*
Goldbarth, Albert, 87:3.159, 88:1.5+
Golden Cockerel Press (Christopher Sandford and Robert Gibbings), 76:1.6–7, 85:1.69, 88:2.57, 88:3.134
    bibliography, 76:1.13
    bookbinding of, 83:3.108–109*il*
Golden Cross Press mark (Valenti Angelo), 83:1.29+*il*
Goldenberg, Carol, FP issue design by, 78:4.111
Golding, Arthur, 76:2.28
Goldscheider, Irena, 87:1.5
Goldschmidt, Lucien, 83:3.91+
Goldstein, Daniel, 83:3.107*il*, 117–119
Goldstein, Laurence, 78:4.113
Goldwasser, Thomas A. (*reviewer*), 89:2.57
Goldyne, Joseph, 87:1.13–14+*il*, 87:3.128–129+*il*
Gollancz, Victor, 81:1.13
Goluska, Glenn (Canada):
    editor, *The Devil's Artisan*, 84:1.33
    FP cover design by, 86:1.4+(*cover*)
    response to, 87:1.7+
    reviews by, 84:2.70, 85:3.158, 86:3.150+, 87:1.7+
    See also imprimerie dromadaire; Nightshade Press
Gombrich, Edward A., 82:2.45, 47
The Good Book Press (Peter and Donna Thomas), 90:3.127–128*il*
Goodacre, Selwyn H., 82:3.104+, 84:1.38–41
Goodmorrow Press (Bonnie Bernstein and Hank Dobin), 82:3.100–101
Gordon, Arthur E., 86:1.44+
Gordon, Ronald (Oliphant Press), 80:3.91, 82:4.136
    FP issue design by, 78:3.80
    press mark, 79:4.105*il*
Gorey, Edward, 83:2.55+
Gorgas Oak Press, 84:2.75
Gorgonzola, Niccoló, 90:2.59–60
Gorrell, Gena K., 86:2.69–70
Gosin, Susan (Dieu Donné Press and Paper), 79:3.73, 83:3.98, 88:3.121+*il*
Goudy, Frederic W., 78:3.81, 79:4.131–132, 80:1.5, 81:2.45*il*
    and Dwiggins, 87:2.87+*il*

    proposed award to honor, 86:1.5
    type designs by, 76:4.67–68, 77:1.23*il*, 80:2.38, 81:1.24–25*il*, 82:2.60, 68, 82:3.99*il*
    wood engraved portrait of, 81:1.24–25*il*
Gourley, Paula, 87:3.170
Gowan, Al, 89:1.19–20
Grabhorn, Jane, 85:1.64–65, 85:2.104*il*
Grabhorn Press (Edwin and Robert Grabhorn), 79:1.1–2, 87:2.107, 89:2.100, 90:3.105
    bibliographies, 76:2.31
    collection, 76:1.14–15
    history of, 82:3.83, 85:1.64
    and Valenti Angelo, 83:1.26–28*il*, 37
Grabhorn, Robert, 75:3.26
Graczykowski, Andrej, 90:1.17
Grafe, Joyce, 86:4.216–217
Grafica Uno (Giorgio Upiglio), 85:4.212–215*il*
Graham, Rigby, 78:1.23–24
Grahame Cracker Press (Gordon Fluke), 90:3.116–117*il*
Grahn, Judy, 83:1.24+*il*, 83:4.148–149*il*
Gralla, Howard, 78:4.107–108, 85:1.48, 85:3.136
Granjon, Robert, 77:3.71, 79:1.27–30*il*, 82:2.48, 83:3.124–125*il*, 85:1.46, 86:2.67
    FP cover design by Caflisch after, 82:2.73+(*cover*)
    type designs by, 77:3.73*il*, 80:3.75, 82:4.154*il*
Grant, John Cameron, 84:3.123–125
Grant, Melinda, 81:2.38
Grasset, Eugène, 80:4.108–109, 127*il*
Grastorf, Dennis J. and Marilyn. *See* Angelica Press
Grastorf, Marilyn (*reviewer*), 76:1.12
Grauer, Dieter (Dieter Grauer Design), 87:4.187–188+*il*
Graves, John, 90:2.79–80
Graves, Michael, 85:4.223–224*il*
Graves, Robert (Seizen Press), 88:1.42–44
Graves, Tomás (New Seizen Press), 88:1.42–44
Gray, Don (Twowindows Press), 84:3.131–132, 85:2.112
Gray, Nicolete, 77:3.67–68, 87:3.154–156*il*
Graywolf Press (Scott Walker), 79:1.10–11*il*, 81:4.126, 85:1.11–12, 85:3.136–139, 89:2.86
    profile of, 81:4.116+
Graziano, Frank, 81:1.16+*il*
Green Gables press (Gene Holtan), 84:3.105
Green, John Barcham (Jack), 76:2.17, 86:3.136–143*il*
    obituary (1885–1982), 83:3.127

profile of, 75:3.31
Green, Remy (*reviewer*), 82:2.52
Green, Sam and Sally (Brooding Heron Press), 88:2.52
Green, Simon Barcham, 79:3.98, 84:2.47
    articles by, 76:2.17–20*il*, 81:2.40–43+*il*, 83:3.98–99, 84:1.11–13+*il*, 86:3.136–143*il*
    letters from, 80:4.133+, 87:4.183, 217
    response to, 81:4.114–115
    review by, 83:3.113–115*il*
Greenfield, Jane, 87:4.214*il*
Greenhill, Elizabeth, 87:2.64–65
Greenhood, David:
    articles by, 76:4.57–60, 77:1.4–6
    obituary (1896–1983), 83:4.173
Greenhouse Review Press (Gary Young, Elizabeth Sanchez, Gene Holton):
    books from, 84:2.67, 86:1.39–40, 88:4.185–186+*il*
    broadsides from, 84:3.106*il*, 87:3.122+*il*
Greenwood, Georgianna (calligrapher) (*reviewer*), 76:3.49, 88:3.120–122, 89:1.15–17
Greenwood Press (Jack Werner Stauffacher):
    books from, 76:3.46–47*il*, 79:1.12–14, 85:2.116–117*il*, 87:4.191–192*il*, 88:2.92–93, 90:3.132–133*il*
    Phaedrus, 79:1.5–6
    Phaedrus, letters about FP review of, 79:2.42–43, 79:3.72
    press mark, 79:4.105+*il*
    profiles of, 79:1.1–6*il*, 79:3.85
Greer, Jane, 87:4.185–187
Greet, Anne Hyde, 88:2.74–76
Greger, Debora, 85:2.110–111, 86:1.32–33*il*
Greger, Madel, 86:1.32–33*il*
Gregg, Linda, 81:4.116
Gregorovius, Ferdinand, 86:4.200
Gregory, Susan Myra, 85:3.160
Gregynog Press. *See* Gwasg Gregynog Press
Grenfell Press (Leslie Miller), 86:1.33–34+*il*, 86:3.165+*il*
Grenier, Robert, 85:3.144
Griffith, Chauncey Hawley, 83:4.153–154, 89:1.24+, 89:2.80
    photograph of, 89:1(*insert*)
Griffith, Richard R., 78:2.53
Griffith, Tom, 88:2.62
    photograph of, 88:2.64*il*
Griffo, Francesco, 80:1.26, 85:4.219–220, 87:1.47
Grillen-Presse (Richard von Sichowsky), 85:2.112–113*il*, 126–127, 86:2.86, 90
Groat, Jenny (*reviewer*), 80:4.132–133
Grooms, Chris, 88:4.152–153
Grooms, Thomas B., 83:1.2

Grosman, Tatyana, 77:4.79
Grossman, Laura, 87:2.81
Grosz, George, 85:2.80, 89:4.176, 179*il*, 90:2.66
Grover, Rachel, 75:3.30
Grover, Sherwood, 78:1.11, 82:3.83
    obituary (1912–1986), 87:2.107
Gruffyground Press (Anthony Baker), 78:2.36, 78:3.74–75, 88*il*, 79:3.73
Grumbach, Doris (*reviewer*), 83:4.154–156, 85:1.51–54, 85:3.160–161, 85:4.223–224, 87:1.9–10, 87:4.209–210, 88:3.111–112, 89:4.207–209
Grushkin, Philip, 80:4.126+, 84:4.163+*il*
Grycz, Czeslaw Jan:
    FP cover design by, 81:1.3+(*cover*)
    review by, 85:1.48+
Guernsey, Bruce, 84:2.67–68
Guigo the Carthusian, 77:3.59
Guiliano, Edward (*reviewer*), 82:3.103–106, 84:1.38–41
Guinee, Trudy S., 86:3.146–147
Guiney, Corinne (Wild Hare Press), 85:2.107*il*
Gullans, Charles (Symposium Press), 80:1.14
Gullick, Michael:
    articles by, 84:1.5, 86:4.204–208*il*
    letters from, 86:3.179–180, 87:2.107–108
    reviews by, 85:4.196, 86:1.34–38, 89:1.20–21, 89:3.110
    See also Red Gull Press
Gunn, Jeremy, 77:1.11
Gunn, Thom, 76:1.8, 76:3.48
Gunner, Jean, 80:3.95
Gürtler, André, 89:3.108
Gutchen, Sylvia and Robert:
    Biscuit City Press books, 78:4.113, 79:3.74, 80:4.120
    Biscuit City Press mark, 79:4.104*il*
Gutenberg, Johann:
    Andre Thevet imagined portrait of, 86:4.213*il*
    Bible typefaces (42-line Bible), 86:1.6*il*, 86:4.215+*il*
    Bible watermarks, 86:4.213, 233*il*
    Bibles, 78:4.102+, 82:3.150+, 83:3.87*il*, 86:4.212–215+*il*, 87:4.180–181, 88:2.56, 89:1.12+
    museum, 86:2.110
Gutenberg, Mrs. Johann, spoof about, 87:2.88*il*
Guthrie, A. B., Jr., 88:2.68+
Gutsch, Herbert (Handpresse Gutsch), 87:3.116, 89:1.38–39*il*
    FP cover design by, 90:3.143+(*cover*)
Guyot, Don, 81:3.76–78+, 84:3.120–123
Guyot, François, 85:1.46*il*

Gwasg Gregynog Press (University of Wales):
    books from, 76:1.7, 88:2.78+*il*
    and David Esselmont, 88:1.45
    and Eric Gee, 84:2.68–69
    history of, 76:4.75, 78:1.14, 81:2.61–62+*il*
    letters about review of, 88:4.152–154
    and Loyd Haberly, 79:4.129–130
    press mark, 81:2.65*il*

H

Haas, Irvin, 80:1.6
Haberly, Loyd, 79:4.129–130
Hack, Bertold, 85:2.126–127, 86:2.85–86+, 116–117*il*
Hadlač, Jiří, 87:1.24, 31*il*, 87:2.108
Hadrill, Robert (New Pyramid Press), 85:3.166–167+*il*, 89:3.127–128+*il*
Hague, René, 82:3.119
Haight, Anne Lyon, 85:2.104
Haiman, György, 84:4.178–180
Haines, John, 79:1.10–11
Hakv, Václav, 87:1.25*il*
Halbey, Hans A., 77:2.41, 83:4.146–147*il*, 86:2.110, 114
Halfer, Joseph, 81:3.86
Halfpenny Press, 78:3.77
Hall, Bert S., 83:3.123–124
Hall, Colin, 89:3.127–128+*il*
Hall, Dennis (Inky Parrot Press), 88:2.59–60+*il*
    photograph of, 88:2.63*il*
Hall, Fairfax (Stourton Press), 77:4.88
Hall, Martha Lacy, 82:3.107
Hallman, Frank, obituary (1943–1975), 76:2.23
Halperin, Mark, 76:1.8, 80:4.123, 81:4.129
Hamady, Walter, 82:4.136+
    Designing Literature article, 88:3.116–119*il*
    influence of, 78:3.75–76, 80:2.38–39, 80:4.123
    photograph of, 82:4.147*il*
    quote from, 90:3.143
Hamady, Walter and Mary. *See* Perishable Press Limited (Walter and Mary Hamady)
Hamburger, Michael, 84:1.37–38
Hamill, Sam, 87:2.68
    reviews by, 81:4.126, 87:4.185–187, 88:2.71–72, 81–82
    See also Copper Canyon Press
Hamilton, Christine, 80:2.60, 80:4.107
Hamilton, Colin, 85:2.119+
Hamilton, David, 86:3.176–177
Hammer, Carolyn Reading, 89:3.119, 90:1.21–22
    book design by, 79:3.75–77

See also Anvil Press
Hammer, Victor, 77:4.92, 78:1.2, 84:2.74, 85:3.158–159+*il*, 90:1.20–22*il*
   as artist and craftsman, 78:4.119
   philosophy of, 78:1.4, 89:3.119–120*il*
   uncial alphabets by, 78:4.121–123*il*, 87:4.193–195+*il*
Hampl, Patricia (Milkweed Editions), 88:4.178+*il*
Hampshire Typothetae (Harold P. McGrath and Barry Moser), 78:1.17, 82:2.57, 87:1.5–6
Handpresse Gutsch (Herbert Gutsch), 87:3.116, 89:1.38–39*il*
Handy, John, 80:1.29
Hanff, Peter E., 87:4.216
Hanka, Ladislav R. (Rarach Press), 84:4.171*il*
Hannett, John, 82:1.35
Hannon, Michael (Turkey Press), 87:3.167+*il*
Hansard, T. C., 88:4.155
Hansen, Matthew, 88:2.68+
Hanson, Jim, 80:1.14
Har-ma Hand Press (Harold F. Smith), 82:1.5, 85:1.32–34*il*
Harcourt Bindery (Samuel B. Ellenport)
   limited edition, 83:4.143
Hardenberg, Friedrich von (Novalis), 80:3.90–91+*il*
Harding, George Laban, 79:3.91
Harding, George Laban, obituary (1893–1976), 76:4.75–76
Harlan, Robert D., 83:2.57–58
   reviews by, 76:2.31–33, 81:3.96–97, 82:1.27–29
Harling, Robert, 77:2.40–41
Harman, Barbara, 90:2.56+
Harriott, John F. X., 85:4.192
Harris, Carroll T., 75:4.41
Harris, Elizabeth (Smithsonian Institution), 83:2.49, 83:3.86
   book by, 79:1.21–22
   reviews by, 81:3.96, 84:2.82–83
Harrison, Jeremy, 86:2.119–120*il*
Harrop, Dorothy A., 81:2.61–62+*il*, 87:4.215–216
Hart, James D., 79:2.49–50, 85:1.64–65
Harthan, John, 78:1.22–23, 83:1.30–31
Hartman, Charles O., 83:2.54–55
Hartz, Sem, 89:4.193, 194*il*, 196
Harvard, Stephen, 76:1.12, 78:1.11, 80:3.83, 81:1.20
   articles by, 77:3.49–52+*il*
   book by, 82:4.145+*il*
   FP issue design by, 77:3.58
   reviews by, 77:4.84–86, 78:3.83–84, 78:4.116, 79:3.88+, 81:1.26+
   a selection of calligraphic work by, 77:3.61–64*il*
   obituary (1948–1988), 88:4.192–193
Harvard University, Bow & Arrow Press, 80:4.107
Harvey, Michael, 76:4.72, 86:3.156–157*il*
Haselwood, Dave (Auerahn Press), 78:2.49–50
Hasucha, Christian, 85:3.166–167+*il*
Hauser, Robert, 78:2.53–54
Hausmann, Raoul, 82:4.142–143*il*
Haven, Gillian (Isis Press), 81:3.87
Hawk Press (Alan Loney), 80:4.120, 82:1.21
Hawkins, Bobbie Louise, 75:1.5
Hawks, Nelson C., 90:3.137
Hawley, Timothy (Contre Coup Press), 86:1.38–39
Hawthorne, Nathaniel, 88:4.181–183+*il*
Hayden, Mary Ann:
   original broadside for FP, 84:3.103+ (insert: continuous tone lithograph)
   See also Sombre Reptiles Press
Hayes, James, 82:4.126–127*il*, 84:1.5, 84:4.159*il*, 162*il*
Hayle Paper Mill (Barcham Green & Co.). *See the Subject Index*
H.D. *See* Doolittle, Hilda (H.D.)
Heaney, Seamus, 80:2.48
Hebborn, Wendy, 82:3.100–101
Heckel, Erich, 77:2.29*il*
Heckscher, August, 80:3.100
   Ashlar Press, 85:1.29–30
   exhibition reviews by, 80:2.45–46, 87:3.160–161
   photograph of, 85:1.28*il*
   press marks, 79:4.108+*il*, 80:1.9
   profile of, 85:1.28–31*il*
   quote from, 78:1.17
   review by, 89:3.124+
   Uphill Press, 85:1.30
   See also Printing Office at High Loft
Heiderhoff, Horst, 80:4.131–132, 84:1.25–31*il*
Hein, Max, 85:3.147+*il*
Heller, Elinor Raas, 76:2.31, 89:2.56
Heller, Joshua, 88:2.57–67+
Heller, Jules, 79:3.88
   review by, 78:4.109–110
Heller, Steven, 85:2.80–81, 87:2.82–86*il*, 90:1.43–45*il*
Hellinga, Lotte, 83:3.88–91
Hendel, Richard (*reviewer*), 78:2.41
Hendrickson, James, 80:4.132
Henke, Dellas, 80:3.88*il*, 86:2.73–74+*il*, 86:3.163–165+*il*
Hernández, David, 90:3.111–112*il*
Heron Press (Bruce Chandler), 77:1.13, 78:1.30
Herrick, Stephen Gale, 78:3.77
   letter from, 80:4.107
   reviews by, 76:1.14, 76:4.75, 79:1.14–15
Hess, Franz, 86:3.170
Hewitt, Christopher, 89:3.110
Hewitt, Graily, 77:1.21, 82:1.38
Hewson, David, 89:3.111
Heyeck, Robin (Heyeck Press), 81:1.17, 82:3.101, 84:3.95–96*il*, 86:2.68–69, 89:1.21–22
Heyen, William, 87:3.121+*il*
Hickin, Norman, 87:1.50–51*il*
Hicks, Richard, 79:2.43–44
Hidy, Lance, 80:2.58
   article by, 77:3.52–55*il*
   book designs by, 77:3.56–57, 60
   calligraphic work by, 80:4.125+*il*
   Dandelion Press book, 79:1.15–16
   FP cover design by, 84:1.43+(*cover*)
   lecture by, 81:2.66–67
   poster designs by, 84:2.54–55*il*, 85:2.81, 88:2.53
   reviews by, 77:2.35–36, 78:2.45–46, 82:2.61, 84:4.148–149
Hiersoux, Powers, Thomas (publishers), 82:4.131+*il*
Higgs, Kimball (*reviewer*), 90:3.127–128
High Loft. *See* The Printing Office at High Loft (August Heckscher)
Hilberry, Conrad, 81:3.89–90
Hilka, Thomas, 89:3.113
Hille, Jenny, 87:4.214
Hiller, Barbara, 79:4.117
Hillesheim, Alan (*reviewer*), 89:4.165–166, 90:2.79–80
Hills, Richard L., 90:3.140–141*il*
Hilton, David, 90:2.61*il*
Hindman, Sandra, 83:4.143–145+*il*
Hitchcock, Maureen Delaney, 78:4.120
Hobbs, Anne Stevenson, 89:1.31+*il*
Hobson, G. D., 87:1.51
Hodnett, Edward, 79:4.127–128, 81:2.49
Hodný, Ladislav, Sr., 87:1.23, 30*il*
Hoell, Louis, 86:4.236
Hofer, Philip, 76:1.13, 85:1.29
   obituary (1894–1984), 85:3.187
Hoffberg, Judith (*reviewer*), 76:2.33
Hoffer, William, 86:4.225
Hoffman, Jeffrey A., 87:1.10+*il*
Hoffman, Richard J., 88:1.8–10
Hoffmann, Lothar, 89:3.109*il*
Hofmannsthal, Hugo von, 79:2.55
Hofmannswaldau, Christian Hofmann von, 76:3.43–44
Hogan, Eileen:
   Burnt Wood Press, 77:3.58, 72*il*, 78:2.45–46, 79:2.47–48+*il*, 83:2.70–71*il*
   Camberwell School of Arts and Crafts (London), 86:3.147–148+*il*, 88:2.60–61+*il*
   photograph of, 88:2.64*il*

Holden, Karen (Red Dress Press), 85:3.173
Hölderlin, Johann Christian Friedrich, 79:4.112+*il*, 86:4.200
Holdsworth, F. Raymond (Ranelagh Editions), 77:2.37
Holiseventh Press (John Talleur and Linda Samson-Talleur), 85:2.111, 89:2.86, 90:1.15–16+*il*
Holland, Hollis, 84:4.159*il*
Hollander, John, 84:1.35–36
Holliday, Henry, 82:4.140–141*il*
Hollingsworth, Marsha, 82:1.5, 83:2.78
Holman, David (Wind River Press), 79:3.73, 84:3.110+*il*, 85:2.121
Holmes, Keith, 81:2.50+*il*
Holmes, Kris:
    FP cover design by, 80:3.75+(*cover*)
    and Isadora type, 80:3.73(cover), 85:3.148–152*il*
    and Lucida type, 85:1.70, 86:3.150*il*, 87:3.162*il*, 88:1.41*il*
    On Type articles, 80:1.26–30*il*, 85:3.148–152+*il*, 87:3.162*il*
    and Pellucida type, 86:4.238
    See also Bigelow & Holmes
Holmes, Stephen (Pynyon Press), 78:4.114
Holtan, Gene, 84:2.67
    Green Gables press, 84:3.105
    Quadq Press, 84:2.70*il*, 88:4.185–186+*il*
Hondius, Jacquemyne, 85:2.90*il*
Hoover, Herbert and Lou Henry, 83:3.123–124
Hopkins, Gerard Manley, 89:3.151
Hopkins, Richard L., 78:1.29, 90:3.136–138
Hornby, C.H.J. St. John (Ashendene Press), 87:2.65–67*il*
Hornschuch, Hieronymus, 85:2.79
Horton, Carolyn, 82:4.146, 88:2.94
Hosman, Ben (Regulierenpers), 88:3.143, 89:3.124+*il*
Houghton, Arthur, 89:3.147
Houle, James (Winter Harbor Press), 77:2.45
Hours Press (Nancy Cunard), 85:2.103
House, Glenn, 84:2.74, 77*il*
Hove, Arthur, 83:1.11
Howard, Ben, 79:4.115, 87:4.185–187*il*
Howell, John, 85:2.128–129
Howell, Warren, 85:2.128–129
Howes, Justin, 87:4.202
Hoy, Peter, 86:2.123
Hoyem, Andrew, 76:1.12, 85:1.65
    articles by, 82:1.12–13*il*, 87:2.107
    featured bookbinding by, 82:1.12–13*il*
    FP issue designs by, 75:1.8, 75:2.20, 75:3.32, 75:4.44
    lectures by, 81:2.67, 81:4.133
    reviews by, 76:4.74–75, 79:3.84–85
    See also Arion Press
Hoyt, Shelley, 88:4.152
Hoyt-Koch, Shelley:
    FP cover design by, 82:1.3+(*cover*)
    See also Black Stone Press
Hubert, Renée Riese (*reviewer*), 90:3.132–133
Huckleberry Press (Gregor Peterson and John Balkwill), 90:3.133–134*il*
Hudson, Mike (Wayzgoose Press, Australia), 82:3.83, 90:3.112+*il*
Hudson, Wil (Kingait Press), 78:3.74–75, 88*il*, 90–91 (Inuit art)
Hughes, Charles E., 81:4.144
Hughes, Sukey (papermaking):
    books by, 79:2.57–59*il*
    reviews by, 84:2.52–53, 85:1.60
Hugo, Harold, 87:1.6
Hugo, Richard, 84:3.95
Huizenga, Janine, FP cover design by, 89:4.175+(*cover*)
Hulse, Elizabeth, editor, *The Devil's Artisan* (Canada), 84:1.33
Humez, Alexander and Nicholas, 83:2.66, 88:1.6–8
Humphreys, Emyr, 81:2.50+*il*
Hunt, Rachel McMasters Miller, 80:3.95
Hunter, Dard, II, 76:2.24–25, 78:3.91–92, 78:4.119, 81:2.45*il*, 84:3.110
    Dard Hunter Paper Museum, 82:1.3+
    Mountain House Press, 83:4.151–153*il*
Hurd, Clement, 86:4.219+*il*
Hurd, Edith Thacher, 86:4.219+*il*
Hutchins, Michael:
    book by, 76:4.75
    reviews by, 79:4.129–130, 81:2.61–62+*il*
Hutchins, Michael and Helen (Chimaera Press), 79:4.116, 81:2.48+*il*, 89:3.129+*il*, 90:3.130–131*il*
Hutchison, F. M., 89:4.186
Hutt, Alan, 89:1.28–29
Huttner, Sidney F. (*reviewer*), 87:2.63–64, 90:1.33–34

I

I. M. Imprimit (Ian Mortimer), 80:4.122–123, 81:2.58, 88:2.96–97
Iacone, Salvatore J., 78:1.22
Ibbett, Vera, 76:1.10, 78:2.45
Ikegami, Ko[-]jiro[-], 86:4.217–218*il*
Iliazd (Zdanevitch, Ilia), 87:4.180
Illich, Ivan, 89:1.20–21
Image Gallery (Jack and Barbara McLarty), 79:2.55–56+*il*
Imprenta Glorias (Gloria Stuart), 89:4.209–210+*il*
imprimerie dromadaire (Glenn Goluska):
    books from, 84:3.95, 86:2.76–77+*il*
    broadsides from, 85:3.140–141*il*, 87:3.119*il*
Indiana Kid, The (James Lamar Weygand), 75:4.42
Ing, Janet, 84:2.79
    articles by, 80:3.74, 86:4.212–215+*il*
    book by, 89:1.12–13
    reviews by, 83:2.67, 84:4.139, 85:1.42–45, 85:2.110, 86:3.153–154
Inglis, Esther (17th-century writing mistress), 85:2.90–93*il*
    portrait of, 85:2.91*il*
Ingmire, Thomas (calligrapher), 78:1.12, 25*il*, 78:4.115, 82:4.132
Inkwell Press, 88:1.12+*il*
Inky Parrot Press (Dennis Hall), 88:2.59–60+*il*
Inman, Will, 88:1.15–17
Interval Press (Cheryl Miller), 83:4.148–149*il*
Iowa Center for the Book (University of Iowa), 85:3.182–183
Iowa, University of. *See* The Windhover Press (Kim K. Merker)
Ipert, Stéphan, 86:4.190, 235
Iron Mountain Press (Robert Denham), 77:1.14
Irving, Washington, 75:2.14
Ishi, Bob, 88:3.124
Isis Press (Gillian Haven), 81:3.87
Ismar, David, 80:2.65
Israel, Laura, 85:4.227
Ives Street Press (Barbara Cash), 84:2.67–68*il*, 85:1.59–60, 86:4.198–199*il*, 87:1.54
Ivins, W. M., Jr., 88:4.158*il*

J

Jackalope Press (Patrick JB Flynn), 85:3.143+*il*
Jackson, Bill, 79:4.105*il*
Jackson, Ian (*reviewer*), 84:3.131–132, 87:2.90–91, 87:4.212, 89:2.72–73, 89:3.109, 150–152, 90:1.36+
Jackson, Nancy Ruth, 86:2.69–70*il*
Jacobs, Allan, 86:3.133–134
Jaeckel, Willy, 77:2.44*il*
James, Angela, 83:2.59, 83:3.108–109*il*
Janeczek, Zbigniew, 90:1.17+*il*
Janouch, Gustav, 76:3.44
Janson, Anton, 84:1.25+
    See also Kis, Miklós Tótfalusi
Janta, Aleksander, 77:2.32
Janus Press (Claire Van Vliet), 81:4.134
    broadsides from, 85:3.141–142+*il*, 87:3.121+*il*
    profiles of, 80:4.115–117*il*, 85:3.177–178
    reviews of books from, 75:2.16, 76:1.8,

76:2.30, 76:3.48, 76:4.66–67, 77:2.37, 77:4.77, 84, 78:2.35, 78:3.74–75, 77, 78:4.109–110+*il*, 80:2.48
  reviews of books from, illustrated, 77:4.79–81*il*, 78:3.88*il*, 78:4.126*il*, 79:3.79–80*il*, 80:2.47*il*, 80:4.120–121+*il*, 128*il*, 81:4.126–127+*il*, 82:1.21+*il*, 83:3.103+*il*, 106+*il*, 84:4.148–149+*il*, 89:2.71+*il*, 90:1.10–11+*il*
  See also van Vliet, Claire
Janus Presse (Carl Ernst Poeschel and Walter Tiemann), 86:2.90
Jargon books, 89:3.130
Jeffers, Robinson, 76:2.26–27, 77:2.35–36, 82:2.59, 84:2.85, 85:1.7, 88:3.112–113+*il*, 90:3.127
Jeffers, Una and Robinson, 87:4.209–210*il*, 89:4.209–210+*il*
Jelínek, František, 87:1.24, 30*il*
Jensen, Gustav, 84:4.156*il*
Jensen, Laura, 81:4.129, 86:1.32–33
Jenson, Nicolas, 89:3.134–140*il*, 90:2.69–71*il*, 76–77
Jess (Jess Collins), 88:2.81–82+*il*
Jionji Press (Richard Flavin), 86:3.146–147*il*, 87:2.100–101*il*
Jirout, Alois, 87:1.22
Jiskra, Jan, FP cover design by, 87:1.24+(*cover*)
Jixing, Pan, 83:2.50
Johanknecht, Susan (Gefn Press), 76:1.8–9, 78:1.17, 21
Johns, Jasper, 77:3.66, 86:2.79, 119
Johnson, A. F., 83:1.24
Johnson, Bruce L., 84:2.50–51
Johnson, Bryan R. (*reviewer*), 85:4.236–237, 86:1.42–44, 89:2.61
Johnson, Eric A. (Okeanos Press), 89:2.99+*il*, 89:4.171–173+*il*, 90:3.109–111*il*
Johnson, Henry Lewis, 80:1.4–5
Johnson, Herbert H., 79:1.8, 86:4.237–238
  On Type article, 86:3.158–161+*il*
  rejoinder article to, 87:2.69–73+*il*
  reviews by, 80:4.132, 81:1.23–24, 84:1.19–20, 84:4.169–170
Johnson, Honor, 82:3.101
Johnson, M. Charlotte, 89:1.48–49
Johnson, Rod, 89:1.48–49
Johnson, Samuel, 89:1.41–42
Johnson, W. R., 78:3.77, 83:3.103+, 106*il*
Johnston, Alastair M.:
  articles by, 79:1.1–6*il*
  books by, 78:2.49–50, 83:3.124–125, 86:3.154–156
  broadside reviews by, 85:3.139–140, 147
  letter to, 79:2.41–42

letters from, 79:3.72–73, 86:2.109
reviews by, 80:3.96–98, 81:2.48, 83:1.17–19+, 84:3.125–126, 85:1.45–46, 85:3.156–158, 86:1.54–56, 87:4.203–204, 214–215, 88:2.90–91, 89:1.4, 89:2.67–69, 89:3.142–143
  See also Poltroon Press
Johnston, Edward, 76:4.72, 79:4.122, 82:1.19, 84:4.155*il*, 86:2.104–105, 86:3.149, 87:4.202*il*, 88:3.122
Johnston, Paul, 80:1.5
Johnston, Priscilla, 87:4.202
Jones, David, 82:3.84, 88:2.96
  obituary (1896–1974), 76:1.6–7
Jones, Herbert, 77:1.18
Jones, Owen, 82:2.44
Jones, Robert M. (The Glad Hand Press), 85:3.158*il*
Jones, Thomas (Gwasg Gregynog Press), 81:2.62
Jones, Trevor, 83:2.59+*il*, 85:2.119+*il*
Joplin, Scott, 84:3.95
Jörg, Wolfgang and Erich Schönig (Berliner Handpresse), 87:1.43–44+*il*
Josephy, Robert, 80:3.94+*il*, 94
Joyce, Carol, 83:2.60
Joyce, James, 76:2.29, 81:3.107, 83:2.59, 60–61*il*, 85:2.119+, 89:4.207–209+*il*
Juniperus Presse (F.H. Ernst Schneidler), 86:2.90, 111

K

Kafka, Franz, 80:4.118–119+*il*, 89:1.38–39*il*
Kafka, Robert, 87:4.209–210*il*
Kagitci, Mehmed Ali, 81:3.76+
Kahn, Sy, 85:2.112
Kairos Press (W. Thomas Taylor), 87:2.62, 88:1.17–18+*il*
Kalashnikov, Anatolii, 85:4.232–233*il*
Kaldewey, Gunnar (Edition Kaldewey), 88:1.11–12+*il*, 89:2.59
Kamensky, Vasily, 88:4.176
Kamo no Chomei, 77:3.59
Kamph, Jamie, 83:1.14–15*il*, 83:2.72+
Kandinsky, Wassily, 77:2.29*il*
Kane, George Robert, 85:2.107
Kant, Immanuel, 86:4.200+*il*, 219
Kaplan, Edward, 79:1.17
Kaplan, Jerome, 78:4.109+*il*, 80:4.118–119, 81:3.93+
Kaplinski, Jaan, 83:2.77–78
Kapr, Albert, 84:4.175–177
Karl, Michael (Ritchie), 76:3.48
Karmiole, Kenneth, 82:2.58, 84:1.17+
Karow, Peter, 79:1.30
Katakura, Nobumitsu, 86:3.146–147
Katz, Leslie G. (Eakins Press Foundation), 77:3.60, 79:4.105*il*, 80:1.9*il*

Kauffman, Richard, 77:2.35–36
Kaufman, Diane W., 80:4.133
Kaufman, Margaret, 89:2.71+*il*
Kaufmann, William, 86:3.177–178
Keene, Donald, 77:3.59
Keeping, Charles, 89:3.129+*il*
Keijser, Jan, 89:4.187–188
Kellar, Scott, 84:1.20, 87:3.170
Kelleher, Daniel (Wild Carrot Letterpress), 84:2.71
Keller, Ronald (Red Angel Press), 82:3.107–108*il*, 82:4.150
Kelly, Jerry:
  articles by, 84:4.164–167+*il*, 86:2.80–84+*il*
  broadside, 87:3.167*il*
  letter from, 90:1.49
Kelly, Rob Roy (wood type), 83:2.46–47, 90:2.75–76
Kelly, Robert, 82:4.131+*il*
Kelmscott Press (William Morris), 77:1.20, 77:2.35–36, 87:4.215–216, 90:2.70*il*
  bibliographies, 81:1.2, 85:2.127–128, 85:4.201–202
  See also Morris, William
Kemble, Edward C., 76:4.76, 79:3.91
Kendrew, James, 90:2.58–59*il*
Kennedy, Freda, 85:2.104
Kennedy, Lawton (San Francisco printer), 85:2.104
  obituary (1900–1980), 82:2.78–79
Kennedy, Richard, 77:4.89*il*, 83:4.156–157*il*, 85:2.103*il*, 89:2.69–71+*il*
Kennedy, X. J., 75:3.28
Kennerley, Mitchell, 87:4.216
Kent, Carol (Erespin Press), 85:3.165–166
Kent, Henry Watson, 86:3.170
Kent, Rockwell, 80:3.92, 82:1.34–35*il*
Ker, N. R., 83:2.65–66
Kerrigan, Philip (Tabard Private Press), 87:3.151–152+*il*
Kessler, Harry, Graf, 86:2.89–90, 88:1.26–33*il*, 90:2.78
Killion, Tom, 77:4.103, 81:3.75, 85:4.235
  illustration by, 81:1.18*il*, 90:3.127–128*il*
  Quail Press books, 79:1.17, 80:3.88–90*il*, 85:3.174, 89:3.113*il*
  reviews by, 85:2.108–109, 89:3.121–123
Kilvert, Francis, 84:2.68–69
Kimball, David (*reviewer*), 89:3.110
Kincaid, James R., 82:3.104–105, 84:1.38–41
Kindersley, David, 77:4.98–100, 79:3.72*il*, 84:1.8+, 86:2.70+*il*
King, Antoinette, 82:4.136
King, Jean Callan, 82:1.6+
The King Library Press (University of Kentucky), 75:3.27, 76:3.48, 77:4.86–87, 91, 78:1.11, 11–12,

79:3.75–77+*il*, 79:4.116, 82:1.21+*il*, 82:4.147*il*, 90:1.20–21
King, Ronald, 90:3.130*il*
  Circle Press Publications, 79:4.124–126*il*, 85:3.168–172*il*
King, Susan E., 90:2.61
  original letterpress broadside for FP, 87:3+(*insert*)
  reviews by, 83:2.54–55, 83:4.148–149, 85:3.166–167, 87:2.100–101
  See also Paradise Press
Kingait Press (Wil Hudson), 78:3.74–75+*il*, 90–91*il*
Kingston, Maxine Hong, 88:2.76–77+*il*
Kinnell, Galway, 81:3.89
Kipling, Rudyard, 90:3.108+*il*
Kirchner, Ernst Ludwig, 77:2.30*il*
Kirchner, Robert, 79:2.55
Kirkall, Elisha, 81:2.49
Kirkpatrick, Patricia, 82:4.149
Kirshenbaum, Sandra:
  articles by, 82:2.53+, 85:4.205–217*il*, 88:1.24–25+*il*, 88:4.192–193, 89:4.159–160
  decennary letter from, 85:1.3–10
  editorial news, 83:2.42, 89:4.159–160
  introductory letter by, 75:1.1
  reply to letter to FP, 85:4.194
  reports by (Book Arts Reporter), 81:4.132–135+, 86:1.5, 88:1.24–25+*il*
  reviews by, 75:4.37, 76:2.28, 76:4.63–64, 77:3.59, 60, 65, 77:4.82, 87, 78:1.20–21, 23–24, 78:3.77, 78, 78:4.111, 114, 79:1.14, 79:2.48–49, 79:3.74, 86, 79:4.116, 81:3.87, 86:2.67, 88:4.159+, 89:1.6, 89:2.59, 89:3.110–111, 90:1.8–9
Kis, Miklós, 86:1.7, 88:3.123*il*
  biography of, 84:4.178–180
  and "Janson" type, 84:1.25–31*il*, 84:4.178–180, 86:4.201–203*il*, 89:3.134–141, 90:2.69–71*il*
Kitaj, R. B., 86:3.165+*il*
Kitchen, Benjamin, 79:3.73
Kittredge, William, 80:3.92+*il*, 86:3.159, 88:2.68+*il*
Klabunde, Charles, 85:1.51–54*il*
Klinefelter, Walter, 87:4.203–204*il*
Klopp, Karyl (Pomegranate Press), 75:4.40
Klopstock, Friedrich, 85:2.126–127
Knapp, Joan, 81:3.76–78+, 83:1.2
Kner, Andrew, 84:4.178–180
Knoepfler, Donald (Buttonmaker Press), 88:1.18, 89:1.35–36*il*
Knopf, Blanche, 85:2.104
Knowlton, George, 82:1.23
Knuth, Donald, 81:1.31–32*il*, 82:3.82, 84:1.8+
  letter about, 84:3.93+

Koberger, Anton, 77:2.32, 77:4.96, 85:2.100*il*
Koch, Paul, 78:4.122
Koch, Peter Rutledge, 84:4.146, 85:3.158, 90:3.117+*il*
  Peter and the Wolf Editions, 88:3.112–113+*il*
  reviews by, 82:2.63, 83:4.151, 84:3.95, 89:1.5–6, 89:2.62
  See also Black Stone Press
Koch, Rudolf, 76:2.29–30, 76:4.75, 79:1.15–16, 79:4.122, 85:1.7
  alphabets by, 77:2.41
  the life of, 76:1.13, 76:4.69–70*il*, 81:4.133
  quotes from, 85:3.144*il*, 86:4.197*il*
  Workshop Rudolf Koch, 81:2.66–67*il*, 86:2.88, 98*il*
Kocman, J. H., 87:1.24
Koda, Paul S., 85:4.198, 199
Koeth, Alice, 82:2.62–63
Kokoschka, Oskar, 77:2.28, 43*il*
Kondoleon, Harry, 89:1.46–47+*il*
Konglomerati Press (Richard Mathews), 81:1.24–25, 82:3.101
Koren, Edward, 85:2.114
Koretsky, Elaine, 83:2.50–51, 87:3.156
Kornblum, Alan and Cinda (Toothpaste Press), 80:1.14, 81:3.93+*il*, 82:4.127, 84:1.4
Kosinski, Jerzy, 79:3.71
Koss, Jim, 87:2.81
Kotin, Daniel, 82:4.123
Kotin, David B., 90:2.91
Kraft, Norbert, 87:4.188–189*il*
Kramer, Kay Michael (The Printery), 76:1.9, 76:2.23, 77:3.65, 87:3.129–130+*il*
Krapf, Norbert, 84:1.41+*il*
Kredel, Fritz, 77:3.53*il*, 78:2.56, 81:2.67, 87:4.193–195+*il*
Krenzer, Jean, 90:2.91–92
Krich, John, 76:2.27–28
Kroeber, Theodora, 88:4.186–188*il*
Kroll, Ernest, 84:4.147–148
Kronfeld, Susan, 78:1.21
Krupat, Cynthia, 85:1.14, 85:3.138
Krupka, Lubomír, and Miroslava Krupková, 87:1.24, 30*il*
Kubota, Yasuichi, 78:3.85
Kuehn, Katherine, 88:1.15–16+*il*
Kühne, Hans, 89:2.56
Kuhner, David, 83:3.123–124
Kulche, Auguste, 77:1.1
Kumin, Maxine, 85:3.161–162
Kunsthaus Lempertz, 83:1.22–23, 85:2.112–113*il*
Kunz, Don, 85:2.115–116
Kupka, František, 87:1.18, 26*il*
Kurtz, John, 90:3.111–112*il*

Kutenai Press (Emily Mason Strayer), 88:2.68+*il*, 90:1.16–17*il*, 90:3.109*il*
Kuykendall, Karen Tucker, 82:3.101
Kuzma, Greg, 76:3.48
Kyle, Hedi, 84:3.114–115+*il*

L

Laboratory Press, New (Carnegie Institute of Technology), 89:3.108
Labrots, Syl, 80:4.109, 127*il*
Labyrinth Editions (Richard Bigus):
  books from, 78:1.15+*il*, 79:2.50–51+*il*, 81:1.18–19*il*, 81:3.75, 83:3.107*il*, 117–119, 84:3.91–92, 85:3.164–165*il*, 86:1.34+*il*, 89:2.62+*il*
  controversial review of, 78:4.106, 81:3.75, 108–109, 84:3.91–92
Lago, Greg, 87:3.119–120
Laguna Verde Imprenta (Ward Ritchie), 77:1.19–20, 77:2.37
  biographical bibliography, 89:4.165–166*il*
  checklist, 81:3.85+
  press mark, 79:4.105*il*
  See also Ritchie, Ward
Lakin, R. D., 78:2.37, 44
Lalande, Joseph Jérôme le Français de (papermaking reprint), 76:4.73–74
Lally, Michael, 76:1.9
Lam, Bun-Ching, 88:1.11–12
Land Marks Press (Lynne Avadenka), 85:2.109*il*, 85:3.147, 90:3.114*il*
Landacre, Paul, 84:3.109*il*
Landlocked Press, 88:1.15–17+*il*, 88:2.53
Lane, John, 87:4.216, 89:3.108
Lane, John A., 83:2.44+
Lang, Günter, 82:1.7
Lang, Lothar, 77:2.25+
Lange, Gerald:
  letter from, 88:1.5+
  USC Fine Arts Press books, 89:1.7, 90:2.88–90*il*
  See also Bieler Press
Langland, Joseph, 87:1.42–43+*il*
Lanskoy, André, 85:1.26+*il*
Lanyon, Ellen, 81:3.91–92*il*, 85:1.61*il*
Lao Tzu, 87:3.120
Larcher, Jean, 86:4.188
Lardent, Victor, 79:1.28, 80:1.29, 89:1.25
Larson, Arthur, 86:2.120–122
Larson, Jennifer S., 85:2.128–129
Latham, John, 82:1.11
Lathem, Edward Connery, 88:4.158–159
Lattimore, Richard, 90:2.66*il*
Laub, Randolph and Claudia (Tea Garden Press), 82:2.63*il*
Laughlin, James, 84:4.141–142, 86:3.165, 86:4.236, 87:2.67, 90:1.18+
Laughlin, Sarah, 89:1.36–37+*il*

Laursen, John (Press-22), 84:3.108+*il*, 87:2.80
Lavrentiev, Alexander, 90:1.31–33*il*
Lawrence, D. H., 84:2.64–65, 87:4.188–189+*il*, 89:2.69–71+*il*
Lawrence, Simon (Fleece Press), 88:2.65–66+*il*
 photograph of, 88:2.64*il*
Lawrence, Stanley, obituary (1900–1987), 88:2.96–97
Lawson, Alexander S. (*reviewer*), 76:4.67–68, 77:3.67–68, 78:3.81
Le Guin, Ursula Kroeber, 88:4.186–187
Le Witt, Sol, 86:3.173–175, 89:2.60
Leacock, Stephen, 87:1.8–9*il*
Lear, Edward, 78:3.77, 78:4.113–114
Lébédeff, Jean, 83:4.151*il*
LeCuire, Pierre, 85:1.26–27+*il*
Lederer, Wolfgang, 78:2.42, 85:3.144+*il*, 160*il*
Ledford, Sandy, 87:2.80
Lee, Dirk, 88:2.68+
Lee, Jim, 83:3.119–121
Lee, Marshall, 79:3.92+, 81:3.106–107
Leech, Thomas, 87:1.5, 6
Leeds, E. T., 89:2.69–71
Leese, Jerry, 88:2.52
Leeuwen, Jan Storm van. *See* van Leeuwen, Jan Storm
Lefevre, Theotiste, 86:1.1*il*, 4
Legatoria Piazzesi (Roberto Frontier), 76:2.27–28, 76:3.41
Leger, Fernand (broadside), 85:3.140–141+*il*
Legros, Lucien Alphonse, 84:3.123–125
Leguerrier, Pierre, 88:2.74–75+*il*
Lehman, Charles:
 obituary by, 79:1.7–8
 review by, 78:1.24+
Lehmann-Haupt, Hellmut:
 review by, 77:4.97–98
  response to, 78:1.30
Lehrer, Leonard, 86:2.72*il*, 75
Lehrer, Warren (ear/say), 85:3.167–168+*il*, 89:2.96–99+*il*
Leif, Irving P., 78:3.81–82
Lemonnier the Younger, 78:4.116–117
León-Portilla, Miguel, 88:3.130–132
Leonard, Ruth, 89:1.48–49
Leontief, Estelle, 76:1.8
Lerner, Abe, 80:3.100, 83:3.126
 articles by, 77:4.93–94, 78:4.102+, 83:1.26–29*il*, 84:4.150–153
 book by, 80:3.98
 collection exhibited, 87:3.160–161
 exhibition review by, 79:4.119
 FP cover design by, 83:1.35+(*cover*)
 letters from, 80:1.2–3, 81:3.108–109, 87:1.7+

 responses to reviews by, 81:3.75, 108, 85:1.68
 reviews by, 77:4.87–88, 78:2.52–53, 79:2.51–52, 79:3.79+, 80:2.55–56, 81:1.18–19, 84:3.97, 84:4.144–146, 86:3.144–146
Leslie, Robert "Doc," 76:1.11
Lessing, Karin, 82:4.149–150
Letbetter, Dennis, 90:3.132–133*il*
Levarie, Norma, 83:2.67
Level, Jeff, 89:1.23–30+(*insert*), 90:3.136–138
Levenson, Roger, 79:2.41–42, 79:3.72, 85:1.32–34
Levertov, Denise, 78:3.74, 81:4.123, 83:1.24+*il*, 83:2.78, 86:1.56
Levine, Philip, 77:1.11–12, 81:4.126
Lewis, A. W., 77:1.19
Lewis, Roy Harley, 86:3.167+
L'Heureux, John, 82:3.100–101
Li Po, 86:1.29–31+*il*
Li Shang-yin, 83:2.52*il*
Libanus Press (Michael Mitchell), 88:2.62+*il*
Libermann, Alexander, 86:1.31–32*il*
Libra Press (Ann A. Morris), 78:1.23, 81:1.19
Liddell, Sandra (Turkey Press), 81:1.22, 90:3.111+*il*
Lieberman, Ben, obituary (1914–1984), 85:2.129
Lime Kiln Press. *See* Everson, William (Brother Antoninus)
Lime Rock Press (T.V.N. Seymour), 81:4.127+
Limited Editions Club, 77:3.73, 81:1.20+*il*, 82:3.101–102, 83:1.28–29, 86:3.173–175+*il*
Lindegren, Erik, 78:4.118–119
Linden, James, 83:1.36–39, 88:2.55
Lindsley, Kathleen M., 86:4.195–196*il*
Linfante, Michele, 85:3.140
Lingen, Ruth, 88:1.15+
Lipton, Richard, 82:4.132–135*il*
Lissitzky, El, 82:4.143–144, 89:4.176, 178+*il*
Lister, R. P., 86:4.193–195+*il*
Livingston, Mark C.:
 articles by, 79:4.102–109*il*
 decorated initials by, 85:3.172–173*il*
 FP cover design by, 80:1.3+(*cover*)
 Mason Hill Press, 79:2.51–52+*il*, 84:3.109+*il*
 profile by, 84:2.57–60
 rejoinders to, 80:1.2–3, 87:2.108, 88:4.152–153
 replies from, 80:1.3, 88:4.153–154
 reviews by, 79:2.52–54, 79:3.81–83, 80:3.90–91, 80:4.122–123, 124–125, 81:1.24–25, 81:2.50+, 81:4.127+, 130,

 82:2.57, 62–63, 82:3.98, 107–108, 83:1.21–22, 83:2.54, 55+, 70–71, 84:1.37–38, 84:3.95–96, 84:4.141–144, 85:3.161–162, 85:4.228–230, 235, 86:1.40, 86:3.147–150, 87:3.119–120+, 167, 88:2.78+, 88:3.109–111, 89:1.41–42+, 89:3.144+
Lloyd, Les, 75:4.41
Lobisch, Mechthild, 85:4.193
Lock, Fred and Margaret (Locks' Press), 84:1.35–36, 85:4.228–230*il*
Lockhart, J. G., 75:4.37
Lockwood, Margo, 82:1.21+*il*
Lodge, David, 80:4.130
Loeb, Arthur, 82:1.19–21
Loeber, Edo G., 83:3.113–115*il*
 article by, 77:2.39–40
Logan Elm Press (Ohio State University), 82:2.61, 89:1.48–49, 90:2.89–90+*il*
Logan, Herschel C., 81:3.96*il*
Logan, John, 75:2.14
Lohman Breda, H. W., 89:4.200–201*il*
Lombard,, Peter the, 82:2.67
Loney, Alan (Hawk Press), 80:4.120, 82:1.21
Long, Haniel, 76:1.8, 89:2.99+*il*
Lorca, Federico García, 75:3.26–27
Lord John Press (Herb Yellin and Vance Gerry), 80:2.47, 84:3.107
Lorde, Audre, 83:1.25*il*
Losty, Jeremiah P., 84:1.18
Louie, Terry (*reviewer*), 90:3.138–140*il*
Lovejoy Press (Nathaniel Polster), 78:2.37
Low, Denise, 85:2.111
Lowe, Pardee, Jr., 80:4.123
Lowry, Glenn D., 89:3.147–150
Lowry, Martin, 84:4.170–171, 85:1.68, 90:2.76–77
 rejoinders to, 90:1.34–35
Lubbock, J. G., 78:1.18–19, 79:3.69–71+*il*, 81:3.88–89
Lubett, Denise:
 featured bookbinding, 81:2.46–47*il*
 review by, 78:4.116–118
Lucar, Elizabeth, 85:2.89
Lucas, Francisco, 81:1.28
Luck, Barbara:
 article by, 80:4.115–117*il*
 review by, 88:4.168–170
 See also Whirling Dervish Press
Lucky, Rochelle, 80:2.48
Lufkin, Raymond, 81:1.25*il*
Lutz, Hans-Rudolf, 88:4.170+*il*
Lutz, Winifred, 84:2.53
Luxembourg, Rosa, 88:4.177
Lydbury, Jane, 86:1.40*il*
Lyons, Joan, 86:1.18–19

Lyons, T. J. (collector of advertising types), 83:2.49, 84:2.49, 89:1.19–20*il*
Lyra, Nicholaus de, 82:2.54+*il*

M

M'Alpine, John, 86:4.195–196*il*
M Kimberly Press (Mare Blocker), 87:2.81
McAfee, Thomas, 82:3.101, 85:1.59–60
McBride, John, exhibition review by, 85:4.238+
McCance, William, 81:2.62+
McCarthy, Fiona, 89:4.201–202
McCarty, Willard (*reviewer*), 80:3.87–88, 82:1.22–24
McClure, Floyd Alonzo, 87:3.156+
McClure, Joanna, 77:1.10
McClure, Michael, 77:3.59, 79:4.115
McCormick, Nancy, 81:2.69+*il*, 87:3.129–130+*il*
McCrady, Ellen, exhibition review by, 80:3.94–95+
MacCulloch, Clare, 78:3.77
McCurdy, Michael:
    art by, 82:3.98*il*, 88:4.186–188+*il*
    letter from, 80:2.39
    press mark, 79:4.106+*il*
    See also Penmaen Press
MacDiarmid, Hugh, 80:1.10–11*il*
MacDonald, Susan, 76:4.66
McGough, Roger, 85:3.166–167
McGovern, John N., 90:1.5
McGowan, Dorian, 79:1.14
McGrath, Harold P., 87:1.5–6
    at Hampshire Typothetae, 78:1.17
    at Pennyroyal Press, 76:1.10
Macgregor, Miriam, 86:4.193–195+*il*
McGrew, Mac, 87:4.214–215
McGurk, Ruth:
    Peripatetic Press, 87:3.121+*il*
    report by, 90:3.142–143
McKendry, John J., 89:1.31
McKitterick, David, 79:4.130–134, 80:3.96–98, 82:3.87+, 83:1.17–19+
McLain, Raymond, 84:2.74
McLarty, Jack and Barbara (Image Gallery), 79:2.55–56+*il*
McLean, Antonia, 89:2.72–73
MacLean, Ruari (Shakespeare Head Press), 76:1.7, 85:1.42, 87:3.151–152, 89:2.72–73
    books by, 76:3.51–52, 82:1.31+, 90:1.8
McLellan, Leigh:
    articles by, 81:4.116+, 82:1.4–5+
    broadside reviews by, 85:3.140, 141–142, 174
    broadsides from, 84:3.108+*il*, 87:3.167+*il*
    FP cover design by, 86:4.238+(*cover*)
    named Contributing Editor, 81:1.3
    philosophy of, 81:1.20–21
    photograph of, 85:3.176*il*
    profile of, 85:3.178–179
    reviews by, 80:1.14, 80:2.47+, 80:4.123, 81:1.21–22, 81:3.87, 93, 95, 82:1.21, 82:2.58, 82:3.98+, 101, 107, 112, 82:4.130, 149–150, 83:1.10–11, 83:3.121, 84:1.41, 84:2.71–72+, 84:3.95, 97–98, 85:2.109, 111, 86:1.28–29, 38–39, 89:1.48–49
    See also Meadow Press
McMurtrie, Douglas C., 80:1.5
McNeil, Barton W. (Wild Hare Press), 78:1.17
McPherson, Michael (*reviewer*), 82:1.31+, 82:4.141–145, 83:1.12–13+, 85:2.127, 85:4.200–201, 86:2.76–77, 89:2.87–88
McPherson, Sandra, 81:1.20–21
Macaulay, David, 89:1.48–49
Mace, Carroll Edward, 79:3.75–77
Machiavelli, Niccolo, 85:4.210*il*
Machida, Seishi, 86:3.146
Mackey, Aidan, 79:3.83
Mackie, George (*reviewer*), 80:3.98–100
Mackintosh, Graham (White Rabbit Press), 86:3.154–156
Mackley, George, 85:4.233, 234
Macy, George, 80:1.7, 82:3.89, 83:1.28
Magee, David B., obituary (1905–1977), 77:4.102–103
Magee, Dorothy and David, 76:2.31
Maia, Pedro Moacir (Dinamene) Brazil, 77:3.74
Maillol, Aristide, 86:2.89, 88:1.31
Malanga, Gerard, 75:4.40
Malik Verlag, 85:2.80–81*il*
Malin, Charles, 77:3.57, 80:1.21, 29, 81:4.139, 82:1.24+, 82:3.93–94, 85:4.206, 88:3.134
    and Giovanni Mardersteig, 85:4.219–220
    and Stanley Morison, 86:3.160+, 87:2.70–71
Mallarmé, Stéphane, 83:1.21, 88:4.176
Mallison, Jane C., 77:2.38–39
Maloney, Margaret Crawford, 90:2.58–59
Mamet, David, 85:2.114–115
Mandelbaum, Allen, 81:1.4–6
Mandelstam, Osip, 79:4.112–114
Mánes, Josef, 87:1.16
Maney, A. S. (Elmete Press), 80:1.2
Manhire, Bill, 80:4.120
Manroot (Paul Mariah and Richard Tagett), 77:4.87, 78:3.77
Mansfield, Blanche McManus, 82:1.17–18
Mansfield, Edgar, 78:3.79–80, 82:1.21
Mantegna, Andrea, 89:3.136*il*, 139

Manutius, Aldus Pius. *See* Aldus Manutius (Aldine Press)
Marantz, Kenneth, 84:1.34–35, 89:1.31+
Marcks, Gerhard, 83:1.22–23*il*, 85:2.112–113*il*
Marcus, Joyce, 80:4.106
Marcus, Stanley, 82:1.22
Marcus-Aurelius Antonius, 82:4.129+, 147*il*
Mardersteig, Giovanni, 77:1.9, 81:4.139+*il*, 147*il*, 85:4.208–212*il*, 86:3.168
    books on, 79:1.26, 84:3.133
    and the Dante types, 85:4.219–222+*il*
    obituary (1892–1977), 78:2.55–57*il*
    prize honoring, 88:3.143, 90:2.59–60
    See also Officina Bodoni
Mardersteig, Martino, 78:4.119, 80:1.16+*il*, 81:4.146, 85:4.208–212*il*, 88:3.143, 90:2.59
    FP cover design by, 85:4.194+(*cover*)
    photograph of, 85:4.217*il*
    See also Stamperia Valdonega
Mariah, Paul (Manroot), 77:4.87, 78:3.77
Mariani, Paul, 78:4.111–112+*il*
Marinetti, Filippo Tomasso, 82:4.142*il*, 89:4.176, 179*il*
Mark, Enid (color lithos), 87:1.14+*il*
Marks, Saul and Lilian (Plantin Press), 75:2.11, 79:4.107*il*, 81:3.96–97
    obituary of Saul (1905–1974), 75:1.8
Married Mettle Press (Benjamin and Deborah Altman), 88:2.55, 90:2.63*il*
Marrow, James H., 84:1.23–24+
Martin, Connie, 87:2.94–95+*il*
Martin, Fred, 76:1.11, 77:4.83, 105*il*, 80:4.110
    exhibition review by, 76:4.68–69
Martin, John, 87:2.68
Martín Pescador Press (Juan Pascoe) (Mexico):
    books from, 77:1.11, 14, 78:1.21, 78:4.114, 80:4.122, 81:4.134, 88:3.130–132*il*
    press mark, 81:1.12*il*
    profile of, 81:1.12–13+
Martin, Pierre-Lucien, 88:2.53
Martin, Walter, 86:3.176–177
Marx, Groucho, 89:2.57
Marx, Karl, 88:4.177
Maryatt, Kitty (Two-Hands Press), 80:2.39
Maschio, Geraldine, 80:1.14
Maser, Frederick E., 85:2.121–123
Maslyn, David, 88:4.159
Mason, Biddy, 90:2.61
Mason, Emily. *See* Strayer, Emily Mason
Mason Hill Press (James M. Dignon), 79:2.51–52+*il*, 84:3.109+*il*
Mason, J. H., 78:3.82–83

Mason, John (Twelve by Eight Press), 78:2.54, 79:4.109*il*
Massé, Ron, 77:3.66
Massin, Robert, 89:2.87–88
Mather, Cotton, 88:4.181–182+
Matheson, William, 85:2.120–121
Mathews, Richard (Konglomerati Press), 81:1.24–25, 82:3.101
    report by, 78:4.115
    reviews by, 79:1.20
Matisse, Henri, 78:3.73*il*, 87:4.187–188+*il*
Matrix Press (Kathleen Walkup and Connie Thorpe), 83:1.23–25*il*
Matthews, Jack, 78:1.22
Matthews, William, 78:3.79–80, 83:4.162–163+*il*
Mattson, Francis O. (Frank) (N. Y. Public Library), 81:3.105, 82:4.136, 85:4.194
    reviews by, 82:2.59–61, 85:2.120–121, 89:3.129+
May, Eric, 89:1.48–49
Mayakovsky, Vladimir, 86:2.76–77+*il*, 89:4.178+*il*
Mayes, Frances, 84:3.95–96
Maynard, Robert, 81:2.61*il*, 62+*il*
Mead, John, 85:1.68
Meadow Press (Leigh McLellan):
    books from, 76:3.48, 77:2.37, 78:1.21, 81:1.20–21+*il*, 82:4.149, 84:2.69*il*, 85:4.227, 86:1.32–33*il*, 88:2.76–77+*il*
    broadsides from, 84:3.108+*il*, 87:3.167+*il*
Meatyard, Christopher, 79:3.75–77
Meier, Hans Eduard (type designer), 79:4.120–123*il*, 85:3.149
Melinsky, Claire (woodcuts by), 90:2.81–83*il*
Melville, Herman, 77:2.38–39, 78:3.78, 80:2.49–53*il*, 82:4.150+*il*, 87:1.6
    edition bindings, 88:2.55, 90:2.63*il*
Mengerhausen, Cornelia v., 76:4.63
Menhart, Oldřich, 87:1.15, 34–39*il*
Mercator, Gerardus, 81:1.28*il*
Meriden-Stinehour Press, Inc. (Roderick Stinehour), 76:1.12, 86:1.5, 88:4.192–193, 90:1.6, 8
Merker, Kim K., 81:4.148
    article by, 78:1.4–6
    and Dana Gioia, 89:2.84
    FP issue design by, 78:1.13
    letter from, 86:4.236
    photograph of, 82:4.147*il*
    profile of, 81:4.116+
    review by, 83:2.53–54
    See also The Windhover Press
Merrill, James, 77:3.59, 83:4.150, 85:4.227–228
Merwin, W. S., 83:3.121–123
Metcalf, Paul, 79:4.115, 84:3.104
Metzger, Philip L.:
    Crabgrass Press books, 82:4.156–157
    type specimen sheets by, 81:4.123–126*il*
    obituary (1915–1981), 82:4.156–157
Metzker, Ray K., 82:1.21+*il*
Meunier, Charles, 76:1.5–6+*il*
Meyerson, Simon, 82:4.151
Meynell, Francis, 80:4.129, 82:3.96, 83:1.17, 90:2.66*il*
    Eric Gill drawing of, 82:3.92*il*
    history of Nonesuch Press and, 82:3.87–89, 92*il*
    obituary (1891–1975), 75:4.41
    quote from, 79:3.84
Michaels, Leonard, 80:4.130–131
Michaux, Henri, 85:4.236–237
Micheaels, Cathleen (Mt. Ararat Press), 86:2.119–120*il*
Middlebrook, Dianne, 83:1.23–25
Middleton, Bernard C., 77:4.92, 80:3.95, 82:1.35, 82:3.86
    bookbinding collection of, 84:2.48
    featured bookbinding, 79:3.86+*il*
    review by, 78:4.116–118
Middleton, Christopher, 76:4.68
Middleton, Robert Hunter, 81:2.49–50*il*, 87:2.61, 90:2.70*il*
    life and career of, 85:4.204+
    review by, 79:3.87
Midnight Paper Sales Press (Gaylord Schanilec), 82:4.130*il*, 88:2.72–74+*il*, 90:2.61*il*, 90:3.129–130*il*
Miélot, Jean, 86:3.154
Miguet, Colette and Jean-Paul, 88:4.175
Mikolowski, Ken and Ann, 80:1.14
Mikula, Jiřrí, 87:1.15, 24, 32–33*il*
Miles, John, 89:1.5
Milkweed Editions (Patricia Hampl, Antonin Dvořák) 88:4.178+*il*
Miller, C. William, 77:1.13
Miller, Cheryl, 83:1.25*il*, 85:1.50*il*
    Five Trees Press books, 76:4.66, 78:3.74, 78:4.114, 79:2.54, 79:4.115–116
    Interval Press books, 79:2.54, 83:4.148–149*il*
    Iowa Center for the Book publications, 85:3.182–183
    review by, 90:1.15–16
Miller, Leslie (Grenfell Press), 86:1.33–34+*il*, 86:3.165+*il*
Miller, Liam, 75:2.20
Miller, Richard (Peppermint Press), 86:2.69–70
Miller, Steve, 80:4.123–124*il*, 89:1.7, 90:2.58
    Bowery Press, 89:2.84–85
    See also Red Ozier Press (Steve Miller and Ken Botnick)
Millerton, John, 82:2.61
Millington, Roy, 83:1.4
Mills College (Eucalyptus Press), 78:4.114–115
Mills, William, 77:3.60+
Milton, John, 87:3.167*il*
Minář, Emil, 87:1.15, 21–24+*il*, 24, 87:2.108
Mirabai, 81:3.91–92
Mitchell, Breon:
    article by, 77:2.25–28*il*
    reviews by, 79:2.55, 81:4.122–123, 82:3.86–87, 83:1.22–23, 83:4.166–167, 85:1.62–63, 85:2.112–113, 87:1.43–44, 87:4.187–188
Mitchell, Charles, 82:4.140–141
Mitchell, Frederick, 77:3.56–57
Mitchell, Michael (Libanus Press), 88:2.62+*il*
    photograph of, 88:2.64*il*
Mitchell, S. Weir, 76:4.66
Mitchell, Stephen, 88:3.127–128+*il*, 89:4.171–173
Mitsuharu, poem by, 84:3.104
Mitsui, James Masao, 87:3.159, 88:1.5+
Miura, Kirstin Tini, 84:1.15+*il*
Moholy-Nagy, Laszlo, 82:4.144
Momaday, N. Scott (*reviewer*), 76:4.63–64, 80:1.15–16, 81:1.17, 82:3.100, 84:2.66–67, 68–69
Montale, Eugenio, 84:4.141–142
Montero, José Antonio, 77:1.11
Moore, Henry, watermark, 76:2.18*il*
Moore, Suzanne, 88:3.137–141*il*
Moran, James [of California] (*reviewer*), 81:3.87
Moran, James [of England], 79:3.88+*il*, 86:3.170
    obituary (1917–1978), 78:4.124
Moran, Penny, 90:2.79–80*il*
Morgan, Edwin, 82:1.22–24
Morgan, Frederick, 85:4.227–228
Morgan, Gwenda, 86:4.193+*il*
Morgan, Janet, 80:4.123, 81:1.22
Morice, Dave, 81:3.93+*il*
Morison, Stanley, 81:3.100–101, 86:4.237, 88:1.9, 88:4.159, 89:1.24–26+(*insert*)
    Appleton, Tony (book on Stanley Morison), 77:1.18
    books by, 82:4.154*il*, 83:1.17–19+
    and Daniel Berkeley Updike, 79:3.72–73, 79:4.130–134, 80:3.96–98, 83:1.18, 86:3.169
    drawing of, 89:1(*insert*)
    and *The Fleuron*, 80:1.4, 80:4.129
    and Eric Gill, 82:3.90+, 96, 88:3.134
    and Frederic Warde, 86:3.159+, 87:2.69–73+*il*
    handlist of writings by, 77:1.18
    and the Monotype Corporation, 89:4.195

typographic quotes from, 79:2.43, 79:3.92+, 81:2.51–2, 54–55, 60
Morley, Malcolm, 86:1.33, 34
Morris & Co. (William Morris), 75:2.20
Morris, Anne A. (Libra Press), 78:1.23–24, 81:1.19, 81:2.39
Morris, Henry:
   article by, 75:3.31
   letters from, 76:2.20, 78:3.80, 84:2.47
   responses to, 78:4.106, 79:1.6, 79:3.73
   review by, 79:1.19–20
   writings by, 82:1.27–29*il*, 82:2.52, 84:1.12, 89:2.61*il*
   See also Bird & Bull Press
Morris, John, 83:1.4
Morris, William, 75:2.20, 86:3.156, 89:4.163–164
   and American book design, 78:3.84–85
   biographies of, 77:3.54, 68, 79:1.20, 85:4.192
   collection catalogue, 81:1.2
   influence of, 82:2.46, 86:2.88, 103, 87:1.21, 90:2.70
   and John Ruskin, 90:1.9
   See also Kelmscott Press
Morrow, Elizabeth Post, 76:2.25
Morse, Alice C., 82:1.17
Mortimer, Ian (I. M. Imprimit), 80:4.122–123, 81:2.58, 88:2.96–97
Mortimer, Ruth, 87:1.14+*il*
   response to, 81:3.74–75
   reviews by, 81:1.25, 85:1.55–56, 88:4.184–185
Moser, Barry:
   art by, 77:4.82*il*, 78:2.49, 78:4.104*il*, 111–112+*il*, 125*il*, 79:4.104*il*, 80:2.49+*il*, 81:1.4–8*il*, 36*il*, 86:4.199–200*il*, 88:2.74–75+*il*
   articles by, 78:3.65–69*il*, 81:1.4–8*il*
   catalogue, 82:2.43
   cover art by, 81:1.1*il*
   FP issue design by, 79:2.65
   reviews by, 78:2.42, 50–51
   See also Hampshire Typothetae; Pennyroyal Press
Moser, George, 81:1.21–22
Mosley, James (St. Bride Printing Library), 86:2.67+, 88:1.41
   On Type article, 82:3.90–95*il*
Mote, Frederick W., 90:3.138–140*il*
Motherwell, Robert, 89:4.207–209+*il*
Mott, Frank Luther, 75:2.13, 86:1.28
Mott, Steve, FP cover design by, 89:2.60+(*cover: screenless litho*)
Mountain House Press (Dard Hunter), 83:4.151–153*il*
Mowery, John Franklin, 83:4.171–172, 85:1.26–27+*il*
Moxon, Joseph, 89:2.68

Moy, Don M. (D.M.M.):
   articles by, 79:4.118, 82:4.126–127*il*, 132–135*il*
   named Contributing Editor, 85:1.73
   reviews by, 81:3.97–98, 82:1.29, 83:4.153–154, 84:3.125, 84:4.175–177, 86:1.44+, 86:3.156–157, 86:4.216–217, 223–224, 87:4.201–202, 88:2.90
Mt. Ararat Press (Cathleen Micheaels), 86:2.119–120*il*
Mucci, Paul, 76:3.41
Muir, John, 88:4.186–188+*il*
Mulcaster, Richard, 81:1.29
Munari, Bruno, 88:4.168–170*il*
Mundell, Elmore (Compulsive Printer), 77:1.11
Munn, Jesse, 83:3.99–101+
Munn, Judith A. (*reviewer*), 80:2.53–55
Munsell, Joel, 82:2.52
Munter, Robert, 89:1.17–18
Murray, Elizabeth K. M., 79:1.19
Murray, James A. H., 79:1.19
Musika, František, 87:1.20–21, 29*il*
Mycroft, David, 76:4.64
Mycroft, Jessica (Freehand Press), 76:4.64, 71, 80:1.16+*il*, 82:3.100*il*
Myridade Press (Ben Lieberman), 85:2.129

N

Nachman, Rabbi, 90:3.114*il*
Nadja Press (Carol Sturm and Douglas Wolf), 84:1.35–36
   books from, 80:2.47–48, 81:3.89, 103*il*, 82:4.136, 84:3.134, 85:4.227–228
Nadler, Elie, 89:3.142–143*il*, 90:1.5*il*
Nägele, Hildegard, 88:4.159
Nakanishi, Akira, 83:2.58
Narita, Kiyofusa, 78:2.52
Nash, John Henry, 79:1.1–2, 79:4.133, 83:2.57–58
Nash, Ray, 80:1.8, 80:3.75
Naumann, Walter, 86:3.150+
NdA Press (Natalie d'Arbeloff), 82:1.11, 82:4.148*il*, 151–152, 87:3.129*il*
Neavill, Gordon B., 84:2.74–77*il*
Needham, Paul, 83:3.87
   publications by, 77:3.68, 86:4.213–215+, 87:2.68+
   reviews by, 80:1.23–25+, 83:3.88–91, 88:4.167–168
Nelson, Robert W., photograph of, 86:3.161*il*
Nelson, Stan, 82:2.42, 84:1.10, 88:1.24, 88:2.92–93, 90:2.58
   address by, 85:2.86
   On Type article, 86:4.228–229*il*
Nelson, Victoria:

books by, 78:4.114–115, 87:4.191–192*il*
   Designing Literature article, 88:2.92–93
   review by, 90:1.17
Neruda, Pablo, *Ode to Typography*, 78:1.15+, 25*il*, 83:3.102–103, 106*il*, 85:2.105–107, 89:1.37+*il*
   letters about design of book by, 78:3.80, 78:4.106
   and Tallone, Alberto, 85:4.206, 238
Nesbitt, Alexander:
   article by, 87:2.87–89*il*
   review by, 84:2.62–63
Neugebauer, Friedrich, 76:3.49
Neugebauer, Richard, 84:4.171
Neuman, Robert S., 85:1.62–63*il*
Neustadt, Barbara, 87:1.42–43+*il*
Nevins, Iris, 88:1.4
New Directions Press (publisher), 81:4.116+, 85:4.236–237*il*
New Laboratory Press (Carnegie Institute of Technology), 89:3.108
The New Overbrook Press (Charles Altschul), 85:1.51–54*il*
New Pyramid Press (Robert Hadrill), 85:3.166–167+*il*, 89:3.127–128+*il*
New Seizen Press (Tomás Graves), 88:1.42–44
Newdigate, Bernard H., 86:2.106, 87:3.151–152+*il*
Newman, John Henry, 77:3.58+*il*, 72*il*
Nexus Press, 87:2.98–100+*il*
Nicholas, Robin, 89:1.29+(*insert*)
Nichols, Ashton:
   article by, 79:2.33–39*il*
   review by, 78:1.22–23
Nicholson, James B., 82:1.35
Nicholson, William, 76:3.47*il*, 79:1.14–15*il*, 83:4.157
Nickel, Peter, 88:1.17–18+*il*
Niebauer, Abby, 81:1.17
Nielson, Deann, 77:4.87
Night Heron Press (Elizabeth Coberly), 78:4.110–111+*il*, 125*il*
Nightowl Press. *See* Press of the Nightowl (Dwight Agner)
Nightshade Press (Glenn Goluska), 84:3.97–98, 86:4.225*il*, 90:2.91
Nixon, Howard M., 79:4.128–129
Noguchi, Isamu, 84:2.71*il*
Nolde, Emil, 77:2.30*il*
Nomad Press (Tracy A. Davis), 85:2.113–114+*il*
Nomadic and Almond Tree Presses, 87:4.192
Nonesuch Press (Francis Meynell), 90:2.66*il*
   history, 82:3.87–89, 92*il*
Nonpareil, Marquesa, *pseud.* (Susan S. Wilson), 79:1.22

Noordzïj, Gerrit, 81:3.94–95*il*
Norris, Frank, 87:4.196–200*il*
Norris, Leslie, 85:2.110–111
North Point Press (Jack Shoemaker and William Turnbull), 81:4.116+, 145
Novalis (Friedrich von Hardenberg), 80:3.90–91+*il*
Nudelman, Edward D., 84:2.49
Nuthead, Dinah, 85:2.101
Nyholm, Janet, 78:4.109–110+*il*, 126*il*

O

Oak Knoll Books, 83:2.72+, 84:3.134
Oates, Joyce Carol, 75:4.40
O'Brien, Fitz-James, 75:3.27
Obrtel, Vit, 87:1.21
Occasional Works (Ann Rosener), 85:3.160–161, 88:2.82–83
Ocharte, Pedro, 83:1.33–35, 83:2.82
O'Connell, Bonnie, 81:4.148
    FP cover design by, 88:4.176+(cover)
    Penumbra Press, 76:1.11, 76:3.49, 79:4.106*il*
O'Connor, Jeannie, 90:2.80–81
O'Connor, John, 90:2.80–81*il*
Odell-Foster, Dee, 82:1.11
Offenbach Workshop (Rudolf Koch), 81:2.66–67*il*, 86:2.88
Officina Bodoni (Giovanni Mardersteig):
    books from, 77:3.57–58+*il*, 72*il*, 79:1.8, 79:2.45–46, 81:4.128*il*, 88:3.143, 89:1.8–9+*il*
    complete works of Gabriele D'Annunzio (1927–1936) 49 vols., 78:2.55
    history of, 78:2.55–57*il*, 81:4.139+*il*, 82:1.3, 86:3.168
    press marks, 79:4.105, 80:2.44*il*
    typeface, 86:3.149*il*
Officina Chimæra (Alessandro Corubolo and Gino Castiglioni), 89:3.143–144
Officina Pluralo (James Taylor and Judith Dikstein), 82:1.22–24
Officina Serpentis (Eduard Wilhelm Tieffenbach), 86:2.90
Ogden, Linda K., 87:2.75
    reviews by, 82:1.35, 87:1.50–51
Ogg, Oscar, 84:4.154*il*, 163+*il*
Ohio State University, Logan Elm Press, 82:2.61, 89:1.48–49, 90:2.89–90+*il*
Okeanos Press (Eric A. Johnson), 89:2.99+*il*, 89:4.171–173+*il*, 90:3.109–111*il*
Oldtown Press (Susan M. Allen), 88:4.184–185
Olender-Papurt, Jeanette (Clarino Press), 84:2.66–67*il*

Oliphant Press (Ronald Gordon), 80:3.91, 82:4.136
    press mark, 79:4.105*il*
Oliva, Viktor, 87:1.18
Olivera, Miguel Alfredo, 77:3.65
Olivieri, Ruggero, 85:4.222*il*
Olšák, Jaroslav, 87:1.30*il*
Olson, Charles, 89:3.130
Olson, Rik (Wooden Rabbit Press), 87:3.168+*il*, 87:4.200, 90:3.108+*il*
Olson, Toby, 88:3.128–130
Omega Workshop, 89:3.127
O'Neill, Eugene, 90:2.91–92
Opal Press (C. Dudley), 80:4.122–123*il*
Oppen, George, 88:1.16
Oppenheimer, Joel, 85:1.61–62*il*, 88:3.128–130
Oppenheimer, Michael, 77:2.45, 77:4.87
Oracle Press (Rancho Linda Vista), 75:3.27
Orlen, Steven, 75:4.40
Ortiz, Simon, 90:3.111
Ortner-Zimmerman, T., 78:2.44
Osley, A. S.:
    book by, 81:1.26+
    exhibition review by, 81:1.14–15
Ossman, David, 90:3.111+*il*
Oster, Harry, 78:1.21
Otero, Paul, 86:1.28, 29*il*
Otto Rohse Presse, 86:2.85–86, 90, 96–97*il*, 108–109*il*
Ovid, 86:2.66, 86:3.150+*il*, 87:1.7+
Ovink, G. W., On Type (reprint and postscript), 79:3.92–96
Owen, John, 81:3.83+*il*
Owen, Wilfred, 84:3.98+
Owens, L. T., 78:3.82–83
Oxford University Press, 75:3.25–26, 86:2.66
    Bible, Lectern, 79:2.41, 82:1.2, 87:2.65
    history of, 79:2.40–41+*il*, 81:4.134–135, 82:4.154, 83:2.69–70*il*
Oyez Press (Thomas Whitridge), 76:4.62

P

Pacific Editions, 87:3.128–129+*il*
Padgette, Paul (reviewer), 76:1.9
Padrick, Deborah, 77:2.35
Painter, George D., 78:2.52–53
Palatino, the scribe, 81:1.26+
Paley, Morton D., 79:2.60–61
Palladino, Robert, 85:3.148
Pan, Jixing, 83:2.50
Pankow, David:
    article by, 80:3.82–83+
    report by, 84:1.7–10
    reviews by, 88:3.133–134, 90:2.73–75
Pankowski, Marian, 87:1.43–44+*il*
Papantonio, Michael, 79:3.71

Paradine Developments Limited, David, 77:4.87–88
Paradise Press (Susan E. King):
    books from, 86:3.175–176+*il*, 87:2.98–100+*il*, 89:4.173–174+*il*, 90:2.61
    broadside from, 84:3.105
Parallel Editions (Richard-Gabriel Rummonds), 84:2.75, 89:2.86
Pardoe, F. E., 76:2.31–32
Parisod, F. A., 89:3.111–112
Parker, Agnes Miller, 81:2.62+*il*
Parker, John, 88:2.78+
Parker, Mike, 80:3.75
Parkes, Harry, 85:1.56–57
Parkes, M. B., 83:2.65–66*il*
Parkinson, John, 80:4.120
Parrot, Edward Gray (bookbinder), 82:4.130–131
Parry, Nicholas and Mary (Tern Press), 88:2.58–59+*il*
    photograph of, 88:2.63*il*
Partick Press (Thomas Rae), 86:3.176–177
Pascal, Blaise, 89:2.81
Pascoe, David (Calliopea Press), 77:2.35, 79:2.48, 85:3.147+*il*
Pascoe, Juan (Martín Pescador Press, Mexico), 77:1.11, 78:1.21, 78:4.114, 80:4.122, 88:3.130–132*il*
    on oral literature, 81:1.13+, 81:4.134
    profile of, 81:1.12–13+
Pass, John (*See* Barbarian Press), 83:2.52
Paterson, Crawford, 85:3.162–163*il*
Paulinus Press (Simon Brett), 86:2.65–66
Pavie, Marie, 85:2.93–96*il*
Payne, Tim, 79:1.6
Paz, Octavio, 80:4.122, 90:3.105+*il*
Peacock, Thomas Love, 77:1.11
Peckham, John, 84:4.177–178
Pederson, Johannes, 85:3.156–158
Peich, Michael A., 79:2.61
    Aralia Press books, 76:2.30, 84:3.133, 89:2.85
    article by, 90:1.48–49
    reviews by, 80:2.47, 81:1.20–21
Peignot, Charles, 78:1.12
Penmaen Press (Michael McCurdy):
    bibliography (review), 79:2.61
    books from, 76:2.30, 78:4.111, 79:3.74, 80:4.123*il*, 81:3.93–94, 88:4.186–188+*il*
    broadside from, 84:3.107*il*
    press mark, 79:4.106+*il*
Pennyroyal Press (Barry Moser, Harold McGrath), 76:1.10, 87:3.134
    "Alice," binding for, 83:4.168–169+*il*
    books from, 76:4.67–68, 78:4.104*il*, 111–112+*il*, 125*il*, 81:1.21–22, 82:3.103–106+*il*, 83:4.168–169+*il*,

84:1.38–41*il*, 86:2.70+*il*, 87:1.5–6, 88:2.52, 74–75+*il*
  broadside from, 87:3.168+*il*
  press marks, 79:4.106*il*
Penstemon Press (Kathleen Gray Schallock), 80:1.14, 84:3.109+*il*
Pentagram Press (Michael Tarachow), 82:4.149–150, 84:3.110
Penumbra Press (Bonnie Pratt O'Connell), 76:1.11, 76:3.49
  press mark, 79:4.106*il*
Peppermint Press (Richard Miller), 86:2.69–70
Perepelitza, Daniel W., 76:4.71
Perfect, Christopher, 85:4.202–204
Peripatetic Press (Ruth McGurk), 87:3.121+*il*, 90:3.142–143
The Perishable Press Limited (Walter and Mary Hamady):
  about colophons of, 81:3.90
  books from, 77:4.84–86+*il*, 102, 105*il*, 79:3.77–79*il*, 81:3.89–91+*il*, 83:3.116–119*il*, 119–121, 85:1.61–62*il*, 88:3.116–119+*il*, 128–130+*il*, 144
  checklist, 86:1.54–56
  press mark, 79:4.106*il*
Perkins, Maxwell (editor), 82:2.53
Perrault, Charles, 83:4.151*il*
Perreiah, Grace, 78:3.78
Perry, Ronald, 84:1.41, 89:2.85*il*
Persuy, Annie, 84:4.180
Peter Pauper Press (Edna Beilenson), 85:3.177
Peter and the Wolf Editions (Peter Rutledge Koch and Wolf von dem Bussche), 88:3.112–113+*il*
Peters, Jean, 84:1.19
Peters, John:
  Vine Press, 90:1.28–29
  obituary (1917–1989), 90:1.25–29*il*
Peters, Norman, 87:4.183
Peterson, E. R., 84:4.147–148
Peterson, Gregor (Huckleberry Press), 90:3.133–134*il*
Peterson, William S., 81:4.132–133, 84:4.147, 85:4.201–202
Petherbridge, Guy T., 85:2.107–108, 87:1.7, 87:4.181
Petrakis, Harry Mark, 77:4.84+
Petrarch Press (Joel Friedlander), 89:1.45–46+*il*
Petrequin, Scott O. (Mohawk Paper Mills), 84:3.100
Petrillo, Jim and Betsy Davids (Rebis Press), 78:4.114–115, 82:2.61–62+*il*, 82:3.119
Pettas, William A., 81:1.25, 81:3.74–75
Pfäffli, Bruno, 88:4.174
Philips, Tom, 88:4.176
Phillips, Frederick Nelson, 88:1.45

Phillips, Matt, 82:4.131+*il*
Phinney, J. W., 81:4.143
Phipps, Howard, 88:2.93+(cover)
Picano, Felice, 88:3.110–111*il*
Pickering Press (John Anderson), 84:4.146, 85:2.110, 85:3.144*il*, 86:4.196–198*il*
  profiles of, 76:3.40, 81:3.87+*il*, 103*il*
Pickering, William, 85:2.110
Pierce, Lillian W., 84:3.132–133
Pierpont, Frank Hinman, 79:1.28, 82:3.90+
Pigno, Antonia Quintana, 89:2.62+*il*
Plain Wrapper Press (Richard-Gabriel Rummonds), 77:1.12, 79:1.8, 87:3.135
  Zanella, Allesandro, 79:3.81–83+*il*, 81:3.105, 82:3.82
  Zanzotto, Andrea, 81:3.104*il*
  books from, 77:1.7–9*il*, 79:2.46, 79:3.81–83+*il*, 80:1.2–3, 81:4.135, 82:3.82, 84:1.4, 84:2.75
  press marks, 79:4.107+*il*, 80:2.44
  retrospective exhibition, 81:3.104–105*il*
  closing of, 82:3.82
Plantin, Christopher, 75:2.11, 81:3.96–97, 85:1.45–46, 86:1.7–8, 88:4.192
Plantin Press (Saul and Lillian Marks), 75:1.8, 77:2.32–33
  press mark, 79:4.107*il*
  press motto of, 89:1.18*il*
  profile of, 81:3.96–97
  retrospective exhibition, 75:2.11
Plath, Sylvia, 86:4.199–200*il*
Plato, 76:3.46–47*il*, 79:1.5–6, 12–14, 88:2.62
Pleiades Press (Steven and Meryl Chayt), 87:1.42–43+*il*
Plomer, H. R., 89:1.17
Plumet, Georges (punchcutter), 86:3.160, 171*il*, 86:4.237, 87:2.69–73+
Plummer, John, 84:1.23
Poage, Michael, 76:2.29, 80:2.47
Pobanz, Nancy, 85:3.136, 87:2.79, 87:3.172–173
Pocock, Marian, 88:2.63–64*il*
Poe, Edgar Allan, 77:3.65, 81:4.122–123*il*, 82:3.98+, 86:2.120–122*il*, 88:4.155*il*, 89:3.129+*il*, 90:1.42*il*
Poeschel, Carl Ernst (Janus Presse), 86:2.90
Poitou, Guillem de, 77:4.84+, 105*il*
Pollard, Graham, 85:1.42–45
Polster, Nathaniel (Lovejoy Press), 78:2.37
Poltroon Novelty Company, 84:3.134
Poltroon Press (Frances C. Butler and Alastair M. Johnston):
  an author's apprenticeship at, 88:4.160–162

  books from, 77:1.11, 78:2.50, 78:4.114, 79:2.52–54*il*, 80:4.111, 83:3.124–125*il*, 84:3.96–97, 88:2.81–82+*il*
  broadsides from, 85:3.144+*il*, 87:3.168+*il*, 90:3.107–108+*il*
  catalogue, 82:3.83
  press mark spoof, 79:2.52*il*
  press marks, 79:4.107*il*
Poltroon, pseud. (Frances C. Butler and Alastair M. Johnston), 85:3.181–182, 89:3.142–143
  book reviews by, 82:1.24+, 87:1.47–50
  exhibition reviews by, 79:3.84, 89:4.177–178+
Polyglot Press, 78:3.78, 81:2.39
Pomegranate Press (Karyl Klopp), 75:4.40
Pomodoro, Arnaldo (sculptor), 77:1.7+*il*
Pond, Mimi, 82:2.61–62+*il*
Ponge, Francis, 85:2.116
Pons, Louis, 88:2.54–55
Poole, Monica, 85:4.234*il*
Pope, Robert, 77:2.37
Post, Herbert (Herbert Post Presse), 86:2.90+
Postman, Frederica (reviewer), 76:3.43
Potter, Beatrix, 82:3.83+
Poulin, A., Jr., 79:1.10–11
Pound, Ezra, 76:3.40, 78:2.37, 81:3.89, 84:4.141–142, 86:2.79, 86:3.163–165+*il*, 86:4.228, 236
Powell, Lawrence Clark, 88:3.106
  review by, 84:2.85
Powell, Roger, 77:2.38, 82:1.2
Powers, Will, 85:1.73, 87:1.45
  and Amaranth Press, 76:4.71
  articles by, 83:3.110–112, 87:4.196–200*il*
  FP cover design by, 88:1.10+(cover)
  letter from, 86:4.236
  named Production Manager, 80:4.107
  publisher (Hiersoux, Powers, Thomas), 82:4.131+*il*
  reviews by, 79:1.19, 80:4.130–131, 81:3.93–94, 82:3.100–101, 85:4.201–203, 87:4.213, 89:1.19–20, 89:3.152–154
Poythress Press (Maria Poythress Epes), 77:3.59
Pozzatti, Rudy, 88:2.74–76+*il*
Prairie Press (Carroll Coleman), 90:1.48–49*il*
Preisler, Jan, 87:1.18–19, 25*il*
Preissig, Voitěch (Orlov), 87:1.16–18*il*, 25*il*, 35, 38–39 (footnote)
Prentice, Margaret, 82:4.138, 89:1.48–49
Presot, Marie, 85:2.89–90+*il*
Press of Appletree Alley (Barnard Taylor and Mary Chenoweth), 84:3.133, 84:4.141, 85:3.161–162, 87:4.188–189+*il*

Press of Arden Park (Bud Westreich), 77:1.14

Press at Colorado College (James Trissel), books from, 80:2.48, 84:4.147–148, 87:1.6, 88:1.38*il*

Press of the Good Mountain at Rochester Institute of Technology, 78:4.120

Press of the Nightowl (Dwight Agner), 77:3.60+, 78:1.30, 78:3.77–78, 82:3.107, 83:4.153–154*il*
    history of, 76:3.37–40
    press mark, 79:4.107*il*

Press of the Palace of Governors, New Mexico (Pamela S. Smith), 85:2.108–109, 88:3.106, 89:1.36–37+*il*, 90:2.56+

The Press of the Pegacycle Lady (William and Victoria Da*i*ley), 78:3.78, 80:1.23, 81:1.17+*il*

The Press in Tuscany Alley (Adrian Wilson and Joyce Lancaster Wilson):
    bibliography (review), 84:4.168–170+*il*
    books from, 77:4.96+, 78:3.76, 88*il*, 78:4.106–107, 79:3.85, 80:1.12, 84:4.168–170*il*, 85:4.235
    press marks, 79:4.107*il*, 80:3.85*il*

Press-22 (John Laursen), 84:3.108+*il*, 87:2.80

Press-22 (John Laursen), 84:3.108+*il*

Prestianni, John,
    review by, 80:4.125+

Price, Reynolds, 78:4.108–109

Price, Robin, 90:2.91–92

Prince, Edward, 87:2.66–67

The Printery (Kay Michael Kramer), 76:1.9, 76:2.23, 77:3.65, 87:3.129–130+*il*

The Printing Office at High Loft (August Heckscher), 78:1.17
    books from, 79:4.111, 81:2.69+*il*, 85:1.62–63*il*, 87:3.129–130+*il*, 174
    checklist (1978–1983), 85:1.31
    press marks, 79:4.108+*il*, 80:1.9
    profile of, 85:1.28–31*il*

Private Press & Typefoundery (Paul Hayden Duensing), 76:2.29–30, 77:1.13, 79:4.108*il*

Probst, Gerhard F., 77:4.86–87*il*

Prochnow, William, 76:2.26

Proctor, Robert, 87:1.47

Purcell, Henry, 90:1.10+*il*

Purdy, James, 80:2.47–48

Purgatory Pie Press (Dikko Faust), 78:3.75–76

Püterschein, Hermann (pseud.). *See* Dwiggins, William Addison

Püterschein-Hingham Press (Dorothy Abbe and William A. Dwiggins), 75:2.18–19, 80:1.18–19+*il*, 80:2.39

Pynson Printers (Elmer Adler), 78:2.37, 80:1.6–7, 80:4.113+

Pynyon Press (Stephen Holmes), 78:4.114

Pyracantha Press (John Risseeuw), 84:3.108, 86:2.75+*il*, 87:3.120+*il*

Q

Qais Ibn al-Mulawwah, 86:3.144–146+*il*

Quadflieg, Roswitha, 78:1.15–17, 86:2.116+*il*
    FP cover design by, 86:2.109+(cover)
    photographs of, 78:1.26*il*, 86:2.82*il*
    press marks, 79:4.108*il*
    See also Raamin-Presse (Germany)

Quadq Press (Gene Holtan), 84:2.70*il*, 88:4.185–186+*il*

Quail Press (Tom Killion), 79:1.17, 80:3.88–90*il*, 85:3.174, 89:3.113*il*

Quandt, Elizabeth, 85:2.116–117*il*

Quindacqua Ltd., 77:3.56–57

Quinn, John, 81:4.148, 89:1.35–36*il*

R

Raabe, Paul, 86:2.84–85+*il*, 111–112

Raamin-Presse (Roswitha Quadflieg):
    press marks, 79:4.108*il*
    reviews of books from, 76:3.43–44, 77:2.33–34, 78:1.15–17, 85:4.230–231
    reviews of books from, illustrated, 77:2.43*il*, 78:1.26*il*, 79:4.112+*il*, 80:3.90–91+*il*, 82:1.24+*il*, 83:4.166–167+*il*, 86:2.84–85+*il*, 117*il*, 89:3.128+*il*

Racine, Jean, 87:4.193–195+*il*

Radice, Betty, 77:3.57

Rädisch, P. H. (punchcutter), 80:1.28, 81:2.52*il*, 81:3.100

Rae, Thomas (Black Pennell Press), 85:3.162–163*il*, 86:4.195–196*il*, 88:1.23+*il*, 89:2.67–69+*il*

Rae, Thomas (Partick Press), 86:3.176–177

Raecke, Renate, as Guest Editor (Germany), 86:2.65, 124

Ragab, Hassan, 79:4.117, 83:2.50–51

Ramer, James D., 84:2.74

Rampant Lions Press (Will and Sebastian Carter), 82:3.117
    books from, 76:3.47, 77:4.87, 78:1.18–19, 79:2.51, 79:3.83, 80:2.46, 81:3.88–89, 84:3.97*il*, 86:3.156, 88:3.111–112+*il*, 90:2.81–83*il*
    checklist (Miscellany), 90:2.81–82*il*
    offset book, 89:3.150–152
    press marks, 79:4.108+*il*, 82:4.152*il*, 90:2.82*il*
    retrospective exhibition, 82:4.125+*il*

Rams Head Press (P. J. Spitzmueller), 78:3.78

Ramsey, Eleanore, 87:2.75–78+*il*

Rancho Linda Vista (Oracle Press), 75:3.27

Rand, Paul, 88:4.159+

Randle, John:
    FP cover design (with Phipps linocut), 88:2.93+(cover)
    photograph of, 88:2.63*il*

Randle, John and Rosalind. *See* Whittington Press

Ranelagh Editions (F. Raymond Holdsworth), 77:2.37

Ransom, Will, 86:3.158+, 87:2.71

Rara Avis Press (Christine Bertelson), 79:3.74, 81:1.22+*il*, 83:1.10, 83:4.150

Rarach Press (Ladislav R. Hanka), 84:4.171*il*

Ratch, Jerry. *See* Sombre Reptiles Press

Rattray, David, 85:2.114–115

Rauschenberg, Robert, 76:1.11*il*

Ray, Gordon N., 76:3.51, 83:3.91+

Ray, Man, 80:2.59*il*, 61

Rea, Barbara and Tom (Dooryard Press), 84:3.95

Reading, Gay (Windell Press), 90:1.21–22

Reagh, Patrick, 84:3.107

Reason, Sarah, 88:2.60*il*

Rebis Press (Betsy Davids and Jim Petrillo), 78:4.114–115, 82:2.61–62+*il*, 82:3.119

Red Angel Press (Ronald Keller), 82:3.107–108*il*, 82:4.150

Red Dress Press (Karen Holden), 85:3.173

Red Gull Press (Michael Gullick), books from, 84:1.16, 85:2.107–108*il*, 86:3.144–146+*il*

Red Ozier Press (Steve Miller and Ken Botnick), 87:3.134, 89:1.7
    books from, 78:3.75–76, 78:4.110, 79:1.17, 80:4.123–124*il*, 82:2.62–63, 83:1.21–22+*il*, 84:2.48–49, 70–71*il*, 87:2.93–98*il*
    broadside from, 90:3.105+*il*
    press mark, 79:4.108+*il*

Redding, Harvey, and Bruce Schnabel, 81:1.10–11*il*

Redgrave, William, 76:3.44–45

Reed, Orrel P., Jr., 77:2.27–28

Reeds, Karen (reviewer), 81:2.61, 82:3.101, 83:2.65–66

Rees, Ioan Bowen, 88:2.78+*il*

Reese, Harry (Turkey Press), 81:1.22, 81:3.92, 87:3.167+*il*, 90:3.111+*il*

Reese, Jane H., 89:3.111

Reeves, James, 78:3.74–75, 88*il*

Reflector Press (Samuel Fein), 78:2.37

Regulierenpers (Ben Hosman), 88:3.143, 89:3.124+*il*

Reichl, Ernst, obituary (1900–1980), 81:3.106–107
Reid, Alastair, 88:1.38–39*il*
Reid, Frederick, 88:1.42–44
Reid, Nancy, 82:2.52
Reilly, Elizabeth Carroll, 76:3.52–53
Reiner, Imre, 77:3.60
Reitzes, Richard, 85:2.114–115
Renner, Paul, 79:4.122, 87:3.155*il*
Rennie, Silvia, 86:2.66
Renouard, A. A., 80:2.63
Renton, William, 82:1.37*il*
Reuss, Heinrich, 88:4.167–168
Revere, Paul, 76:3.53
Rexroth, Kenneth, 83:3.106*il*, 117–119
Rey Rosa, Rodrigo, 84:2.70–71
Reynes, John, 87:2.104–105
Reynolds, Lloyd J. (calligraphy teacher), 77:1.20, 85:3.148–149
 review by, 76:3.50–51
 students remember, 85:3.148+149, 88:3.126
 obituary (1902–1978), 79:1.7–8
Rhode, Hiero, 80:3.101–102
Rhodes, Curtis, 77:4.79+
Rice, Anthony, 90:2.89–90+*il*
Rice, Roy, 82:1.19
Rice, Stanley, 82:1.6+
Richmond, Mary L., article by, 78:1.1–4
Ricks, Christopher, 80:4.130–131, 88:3.111–112+*il*
Riding, Laura (Seizen Press), 81:4.130, 88:1.42–44
Ridler, Vivian, 83:2.69–70
Riessinger, Sixtus, 82:4.150+
Rilke, Rainer Maria, 76:3.42, 78:1.2, 4, 79:1.11, 84:2.62–63
 illustrated editions (reviews of), 89:1.45–46+*il*, 89:1.171–173+*il*
Rimbaud, Arthur, 81:4.121, 85:2.114–115
Rimmer, Jim, 85:2.86–87
Rippey, Carla, 77:1.11
Risseeuw, John:
 Cabbagehead Press, 87:3.120+*il*, 90:3.115–116*il*
 Pyracantha Press, 84:3.108, 86:2.75+*il*, 87:3.120+*il*
Ritchie, George F., 77:4.104, 85:1.6
 books from, 77:1.19–20, 79:4.112–114, 83:4.154–156
 FP issue design by, 78:2.46
 as publisher, 81:3.85+
 review by, 77:1.10
Ritchie, Jean, 84:3.108
Ritchie, Ward:
 article by, 81:1.34
 biographical bibliography, 89:4.165–166*il*
 broadside from, 84:3.109*il*
 lectures by, 87:1.6, 88:1.45–46

 profile of, 81:3.85+
 review by, 83:2.56–57
 See also Laguna Verde Imprenta
Ritsos, Yannis, 84:3.106*il*
Rittenhausen, Wilhelm, 90:2.61
Riva, Franco (Editiones Dominicae), 79:2.46, 79:4.105*il*, 80:2.44, 82:3.116
Rivas, José Luis, 88:3.130–131
Riverside Press, 81:1.23
Riviere, Robert, 78:2.36
Rizzo, Tania, 83:3.123–124
Roark, Joseph Bruce, 78:4.114
Roatcap, Adela Spindler, 88:1.26–33*il*, 90:1.31–33
Roberts, David, 81:3.92
Roberts, Matt T., 84:1.21, 88:2.88+
Roberts, Michael, 87:4.183
Robertson, Carolyn and James, 84:2.57–60+*il*, 86:2.66
 broadside reviews by Carolyn, 90:3.111–114
 photograph of James, 84:2.56*il*
 See also Yolla Bolly Press
Robinson, Alan James:
 letter from, 83:1.2
 See also Cheloniidae Press
Robinson, Ivor, 77:1.19
Robinson, John M. (Jack), 82:4.137, 84:1.3–4
Robles, Emmanuel, 77:3.65
Robles, Jaime, 78:4.114, 83:1.24+*il*
Roby, Daine, 83:2.54
Rochester Institute of Technology, 86:3.170–171*il*
Rocket Press (Jonathan Stephenson), 88:2.61–62+*il*
Rodchenko, Alexander, 90:1.31–33
Roditi, Edward, 78:3.78
Rodney, Janet, 79:3.77–78
Roether, Susan, 83:1.22*il*
Rogers, Bruce, 76:2.30, 77:4.102, 79:2.41, 80:1.8–9, 80:3.97, 81:1.2, 23, 82:1.2, 86:3.163, 86:4.237, 90:2.70*il*
 biography of (1870–1957), 90:2.73–75*il*
 design principles of, 84:4.150–153*il*
 exhibitions, 83:3.126–127
 and Frederic Warde, 86:3.159+, 87:2.69–73+
 photograph of, 86:3.161*il*
 title pages by, 79:2.63*il*, 84:4.150–151+*il*
Roggia, Sally, 84:1.21–23, 84:2.86
Rohse, Otto (Otto Rohse Presse), 79:1.23, 85:2.126–127, 86:2.85–86+*il*, 116
 photograph of, 86:2.108*il*
Rollins, Carl Purington, 80:3.82–83+, 100, 84:4.177–178*il*, 85:1.30, 87:2.87+*il*
Rome-Hyacinth, Michele, 87:3.171
Romtvedt, David, 85:1.57–59, 90:1.16–17*il*

Ronart Press (Ronald A. Ruble), 77:3.65
Ronsard, Pierre de, 84:4.152*il*, 87:4.187–188+*il*
Rood, Arnold (reviewer), 81:4.136+
Rookledge, Gordon, 85:4.202–204
Root, William Pitt, 79:1.11
Roquet, Jacob, 78:4.108–109
Rorer, Abigail, 81:2.39*il*, 81:3.75
Rosa, Rey, 84:2.71
Roscoe, William, 78:1.20–21
Rosenberg, Betty, 84:1.17+
Rosenberger, August, 80:1.29, 80:4.134, 85:1.36*il*
Rosener, Ann (Occasional Works), 85:3.160–161, 88:2.82–83
Rosenthal, Bernard M., 88:4.191
 letter from, 81:3.74–75
Rosenthal, Jane, 83:4.148–149
Rosenwald, Lessing J., 83:4.143–145+
 obituary (1891–1979), 80:2.70–71
Ross, Bob, 78:2.38
Rota, Anthony, obituary by 77:4.102–103
 review by, 77:1.7–9
Rota, Bertram, 78:1.18–19
Roth, Henry, 79:4.116
Rothenberg, Jerome, 88:3.128–130+*il*
Rothenberg, Michael, 90:3.117+*il*
Rothenstein, John, 78:4.119
Rous, Jan, 87:1.15, 19–21+*il*, 24
Roy, Bruno (Fata Morgana Press), 88:4.175
Royal Printing Office, Stockholm, 85:1.45–46
Roylance, Dale (Princeton University Library), 86:4.188
 exhibition review by, 80:2.60–61+*il*
Rubieri, Jacopo (15th-century woodcuts), 90:3.103
Ruble, Ronald A. (Ronart Press), 77:3.65
Rubovits, Frank, 79:3.77–78
Rubovits, Norma, 81:3.86, 107
Rück, Peter, 88:1.5
Ruder, Emil, 84:3.125–126
Rudge, William Edwin, 80:1.8, 80:4.132
Ruelle, Lee (Evanescent Press), 77:3.60
Rueter, Marilyn, 78:4.119–120, 82:4.123
Rueter, William:
 art by, 86:2.72*il*, 76
 broadside from, 84:3.104
 editor, *The Devil's Artisan* (Canada), 84:1.33
 reviews by, 82:2.48, 83:1.11–12, 84:2.62, 67–68, 86:1.31–32, 87:1.8–9, 43, 88:4.163–164
 See also Aliquando Press
Ruggie, Cathie, 77:1.10, 77:3.59
Ruiz, Nancy Roark, 78:4.114
Rumi, Jalaluddin Mohammad, 85:2.115
Rummonds, Richard-Gabriel, 89:1.7

articles by, 80:1.13+, 82:3.116,
    87:3.134–137
  at the University of Alabama, 77:1.12,
    84:2.74–76
  Dana Gioia and, 89:2.86*il*
  Ex Ophidia books, 87:1.9–10*il*,
    87:3.134, 88:1.21–23+*il*, 89:2.86*il*
  Parallel Editions, 84:2.75, 89:2.86
  photographs of, 82:4.147*il*, 84:2.77*il*
  rejoinder to, 87:4.181–183
  reply from, 88:1.5
  reviews by, 86:3.173–175, 87:2.91–93
  See also Plain Wrapper Press
Runge, Philipp Otto, 83:1.22–23*il*,
  83:4.166–167+*il*
Rupprecht Presse (Fritz Helmut Ehmcke), 86:2.90
Rusch, Adolph, 89:3.138*il*, 140
Rushmore, Arthur, 80:3.94
Ruskin, John, 77:1.20, 77:2.42, 82:2.44,
  90:1.9
Russell, Patrick J., Jr., 82:1.2
Russell, Thomas W., III, 86:3.134–135
Ruzicka, Rudolf, 88:4.158–159*il*
Ryan, Michael T., 89:1.17–18
Ryder, John, 75:4.41, 76:2.34, 76:4.74–75*il*,
  77:1.20–21, 77:2.42, 80:2.65–66, 88:2.57
  Gwasg Gregynog Press, 88:2.78+*il*
Ryder, Mona, 85:4.228–229

S

Sacerio-Gari, Enrique, 78:1.15
Sackett, DeForrest, 82:4.156
Sackner, Ruth and Marvin, 88:4.176
Sahagún, Bernardino de, 88:3.130–132*il*
Sahlstrand, Margaret, 81:4.129, 87:2.80
St. Birgitta of Sweden, 84:2.66–67
St. Jerome, letters by (1466–67, leaf
  book), 82:4.150+*il*
Salamander Press, 84:3.97–98*il*
Saleh, Dennis, 81:1.16
Salter, George, 77:3.53*il*, 81:3.106,
  84:4.154*il*, 163+*il*
  alphabet by, 84:4.137(cover)
Samson-Talleur, Linda (Holiseventh
  Press), 85:2.111, 89:2.86, 90:1.15–16+*il*
Sanchez, Elizabeth, 88:4.185–186
Sandberg, Willem, 89:1.7, 89:4.183–184+*il*
Sanders, Barry, 89:1.20–21
Sandford, Christopher (Golden Cockerel Press), 76:1.6–7, 13, 82:3.96,
  83:3.108–109*il*, 88:2.57, 88:3.134
Sanfield, Steve, 83:1.10–11
Sangorski and Sutcliffe bookbinders,
  82:2.70–227, 82:4.122–1237
Santa Susana Press (California State
  University, Northridge), 85:4.226–227
Sappho, 85:1.51*il*
Sarabande Press (Joe Marc Freedman),
  83:3.107*il*, 121+
Saudel, Jean, 78:3.73*il*
Sauser, Frederic. *See* Cendrars, Blaise
Saxe, Stephen O., 83:2.45–49+*il*,
  88:4.163–164, 90:3.100–101
  address by, 85:2.86
Scalapino, Leslie, 78:4.114, 80:4.110, 127*il*
Scarecrow Press (Lee Bartlett),
  84:4.174–175, 89:3.121–123
Schanilec, Clayton and Robert,
  88:2.72–74+*il*
Schanilec, Gaylord (Midnight Paper
  Sales Press), 82:4.130*il*, 88:2.72–74+*il*,
  90:2.61*il*, 90:3.129–130*il*
Schappler, John, 80:3.100, 89:1.28
Schedel, Hartman, 77:2.32+
Scheffler, Christian, 86:2.110–111
Schenck, Robert, 89:4.166+*il*
Scherrer, Carlos, 84:3.128
Schiller, Friedrich von, 86:4.200
Schimmel, Annemarie, 86:1.11–17*il*
Schimmel, Stuart B.:
  exhibition review by, 83:3.126–127*il*
  review by, 83:2.72+
Schlosser, Leonard B., 76:4.73–74,
  85:1.56–57, 87:2.62
Schlosser, Mary Coxe, 79:1.22–23, 83:1.14
Schmandt-Besserat, Denise,
  78:3.78–79*il*, 78:4.120 (origins of writing)
Schmied, François-Louis, 77:1.17*il*,
  19–20, 87:1.6
Schmoller, Hans, 81:4.139, 84:3.110+*il*,
  85:1.56–57, 88:3.105*il*
  letter from, 78:1.30
  Mardersteig obituary by, 78:2.55–57*il*
  obituary of (1916–1985), 87:2.107
Schnabel, Bruce, 81:2.39
  and Harvey Redding, 81:1.10–11*il*
Schneidler, F.H. Ernst (Juniperus
  Presse), 86:2.90, 111
Schniewind, Henry (Four Winds Press),
  76:2.30, 76:3.48, 78:3.77
Schöffer, Peter (Gutenberg's assistant),
  86:4.212+
Scholder, Fritz, 84:3.108
Scholderer, Victor, 86:3.149*il*
Scholes, R. W., 85:1.57–58
Scholten, D., 89:4.190+*il*
Schönig, Erich (Berliner Handpresse),
  87:1.43–44+*il*
Schönsperger, Johann, 83:2.71–72
Schopfer, Janice Mae, 79:4.117, 84:4.149+,
  169
  article by Eleanore Ramsey and,
    87:2.75–78+*il*
Schram, Frances, letter from, 85:3.138
Schreiber, Jan, 86:2.76
Schreyer, Alice D., 88:3.122+, 89:2.57+
  review by, 84:2.54
Schroeder, Jack (Songs Before Zero
  Press), 89:1.37+*il*
Schull, Diantha, 85:4.194
Schulz, Bruno, 81:1.22, 90:1.17
Schulz-Anker, Erich, 79:4.121
Schulze, Richard C., 90:3.133–134*il*
SchumacherGebler, Eckehart, 89:2.60,
  89:3.113 (foundry types)
Schumann, Peter, 79:3.79–81*il*,
  81:4.126–127*il*, 85:3.141–142+*il*,
  87:3.121+*il*
Schuricht, N., 78:4.122
Schuyler, James, 76:4.66–67
Schwaberow, Micah, 85:3.147+
Schwenke, Paul, 86:4.213
Schwerner, Armand, 77:4.85+, 105*il*,
  80:3.98
Schwimmer, Sandra, 87:3.120
Scripps College Press, 77:1.23, 80:2.38
Sea Pen Press and Papermill (Suzanne
  Ferris and Neal Bonham), 88:2.95
  books from, 78:3.75–76, 79:3.74,
    80:4.123, 83:2.54–55, 85:2.110–111*il*,
    87:2.79–80
  broadsides from, 81:4.129, 84:3.110,
    87:3.121+*il*
  press marks, 79:4.108*il*
Seamark Press (Kay Amert and Howard
  Zimmon), 78:2.42–43
Seastone, Leonard (reviewer),
  80:4.123–124, 84:4.147–148
  See also Tideline Press
Seattle, Chief of the Suquamish Tribe,
  86:4.198–199*il*
Segovia, Francisco, 78:4.114
Seiffer, Alison, 89:1.46–47+*il*
Seizen Press (Robert Graves and Laura
  Riding), 88:1.42–44
Sellars, David, 82:1.11
Sellers, Nathan, 83:3.104+
Seluzicki, Charles:
  broadside reviews by, 83:1.23–25*il*,
    85:3.143–144, 147
  Broadside Round-up 1984,
    84:3.103–114*il*
  exhibition review by, 87:2.79–81
  publisher, 78:3.78, 79:1.14, 80:2.48,
    81:1.20–21+*il*, 83:4.150, 87:3.167+*il*
  reviews by, 82:3.101–102, 83:2.51–53,
    83:3.103+, 117–119, 84:2.64–66,
    84:3.92–93, 98+, 84:4.141,
    85:1.54–55, 85:3.168–172, 86:3.165+,
    87:3.128–129, 89:3.128
Semonides, 85:4.228–229
September Press (Christopher Skelton
  and Alan Bultitude), 84:3.129–131,
  85:1.68, 87:1.8–9*il*, 90:2.77–78+*il*
Serge, Victor, 80:4.122
Serpa, Robert (Imago Handmade Pa-

permill), 77:4.92, 81:2.38, 82:3.114, 88:3.117–119+*il*
Seuphor, Michael, 82:4.148*il*, 151
Seven Acres Press, 79:4.129–130
Sexauer, Roxanne, 83:3.121–123*il*, 88:2.71–72+*il*
Seymour, T.V.N. (Lime Rock Press), 81:4.127+
Shaar, Edwin W., 89:1.27+*il*, 89:2.99
  photograph of, 89:1(insert)
Shaffer, Ellen, 78:4.106–107
Shahn, Ben, 88:3.137–141*il*
Shakespear, George (reviewer), 77:1.13, 77:2.34, 41
Shakespeare Head Press (Ruari MacLean), 76:1.7, 77:1.13, 77:2.34, 41, 85:1.42, 87:3.151–152, 89:2.72–73, 90:1.8
Shakespeare Press (California Polytechnic State University), 89:1.6
Shakespeare, William, 79:3.81–82
  bookbindings for editions of, 76:1.4+*il*, 79:4.124–126*il*, 89:3.114–118*il*
  Edward Gordon Craig, stage figures for, 81:4.138, 88:1.26–33*il*, 90:2.77–78+*il*
  fine press editions of, 76:1.9, 76:2.28, 86:1.40
  fine press illustrated editions of, 80:1.21–22+*il*, 82:3.100*il*, 86:2.75+*il*, 87:3.130+*il*, 88:1.26–33*il*, 90:1.42*il*
Shallock, Kathleen (Penstemon Press), 80:1.14, 84:3.109+*il*
Shaver, Neil (Yellow Barn Press):
  books, 86:1.28–29*il*, 88:1.23*il*, 89:3.144+
  broadside, 90:3.110–111*il*
Shaw, Bernard, 78:4.112–113
Shaw, Paul, 88:3.120–122*il*
  On Type article, 81:4.140–144*il*
Shecter, Ben-Zion, 81:1.16*il*
Sheehan, J. C. (bookbinder), 82:2.54+*il*
Shelley, Mary, 86:2.70+*il*
Shelton, Richard, 83:2.77–79
Sheridan, Michael (reviewer), 83:3.124–125, 85:1.70, 88:3.106
Sherman, Stuart C. (reviewer), 80:2.49–51
Shewring, Walter, 89:3.144+
Shimura, Asao, 77:4.100–101, 78:3.85, 80:2.68
  Cannabis Press books, 83:2.50–51, 86:3.146–147*il*, 88:2.52
Shire, Peter, 82:2.63*il*
Shmavonian, Sarkis, (reviewer) 79:4.112–114
Shoemaker, Jack, 78:4.108–109
  North Point Press, 81:4.116+, 145
Siberell, Lloyd Emerson, 80:1.6
Sibum, Norm, 86:4.225*il*

Sichowsky, von. *See* von Sichowsky, Richard
Sidgwick, Frank, 76:1.7
Siegenthaler, Fred, 77:2.38
Siegl, Helen, 80:2.47*il*, 84:2.69*il*
Silva, Arturo, 87:2.100–101*il*
Silver Buckle Press (University of Wisconsin), 88:2.53, 88:4.152
Šima, Josef, 87:1.20, 27*il*
Simic, Charles, 78:3.78, 84:2.69
Simmonds, Harvey (Eakins Press Foundation), 77:3.60, 79:4.105*il*, 80:1.9*il*
Simmons, Margaret, article by, 78:1.14
Simon, Herbert, 80:4.129
Simon, Oliver (Curwen Press), 77:4.96, 80:1.4
Simons, Anna (Bremer Presse), 86:2.88, 103–107*il*, 86:4.235–236
Simpson, Henry I., 79:2.49–50
Singer, Isaac Bashevis, 83:1.21–22+*il*
Singularity Press, 89:3.142–143*il*, 90:1.5*il*
Sipper, Ralph B. (reviewer), 78:2.49–50
Sirmai, J. A., 85:4.193
Sisson, Clinton, 79:1.21–22
Sitter, Jim, 86:3.134–135, 89:3.130–131
Sitwell, Dame Edith, 85:2.115
Sitwell, Pauline, 80:4.122–123
Sizensky, Liz (L.S.), 85:1.73, 86:1.39–40, 89:1.46–48
Skaggs, Charles E.:
  on American calligraphy (1945–1965), 84:4.155–163*il*
  cover design by, 84:4.183+(cover)
Skelton, Christopher, 85:1.68, 87:1.8–9*il*, 90:2.87
  FP cover design by, 82:3.119+(cover)
  See also September Press
Skilton, Charles (Fortune Press), 79:2.48–49
Skiöld, Birgit, 84:1.11–13+, 90:1.8–9
Sklar, Morty, 78:2.44
Skycraft, Peggy, 81:3.107
Slivka, Rose, 90:3.143
Smith, Cyril Stanley, 83:3.123
Smith, Harold F. (Har-ma Hand Press), 85:1.32–34*il*
Smith, Jessie Wilcox, 84:2.49
Smith, John R., 88:2.61*il*
Smith, Karl U., 78:1.27
Smith, Margaret M., 87:2.68+
Smith, Pamela S. (Press of the Palace of Governors), 85:2.108–109, 88:3.106, 89:1.36–37+*il*, 90:2.56+
Smith, Philip (bookbinder):
  articles by, 77:1.1–4, 78:3.79–80, 82:3.86
  articles on, 76:1.1–5*il*, 88:1.34+
  books by, 76:1.13–14, 83:2.58+*il*
  exhibition reviews by, 82:1.11+, 85:3.184–185

  featured bookbinding of, 79:4.124–126*il*
  letter about, 85:4.193–194
  letters from, 76:1.6, 87:2.108
  news of, 76:3.40, 78:1.13, 83:2.59
Smith, Richard Shirley (wood engraver), 78:3.74–75, 88*il*, 85:4.233*il*, 88:2.62
Smith, Sally Lou, 80:1.10–11*il*, 90:2.66*il*
Smith, William Jay, 76:2.30, 79:4.115
Smitherman, Geneva, 80:4.130
Smyth, Elaine, 87:3.152–154
Smyth, Paul, 77:4.82
Snodgrass, W. D., 79:1.14, 80:2.47–48
Snyder, Gary, 81:3.87
Sobota, Jan (bookbinder, Poland), 87:2.108
Solo, Dan X., 75:1.6
Sombre Reptiles Press (Jerry Ratch and Mary Ann Hayden), 80:4.124–125+*il*, 82:3.108–109+*il*, 85:3.147*il*, 86:1.40–41
Sommaruga, Renzo, 79:2.46
Songs Before Zero Press (Jack Schroeder), 89:1.37+*il*
Sönmez, Nedim and Yvonne, 86:4.190
Sonnichsen, Joanne (J.S.):
  articles by, 87:3.169–171, 88:2.53–55, 96, 89:1.8
  letter from, 85:4.193–194
  named Bookbinding Editor, 87:2.62
  response to, 88:1.5
  review by, 84:4.180
Sonta, Frederick, 81:2.39
Sorman, Steven, 88:4.178+*il*
Součková, Věra, 87:1.15
Sourget, Patrick and Elisabeth, 90:1.36+
Southall, Richard, 88:1.24, 88:2.84+
Southwick, Marcia, 89:2.62+*il*
Southworth, Nancy, 80:2.58–59*il*
Sovak, Milos (Ettan Press), 76:4.63–64
Sovik, Nils, 78:1.24+*il*
Sparrow Press, 82:3.112
Spawn, William, 85:2.121–122, 87:2.63–64
Spemann, Rudo, 83:4.146–147*il*
Spencer, G. A. (reviewer), 78:1.22
Spencer, Herbert, 89:1.26–27, 89:2.87–88*il*
Sperisen, Albert,
  exhibition review, 75:3.22–25*il*
  obituary by, 76:1.6–7
  reviews by, 75:3.29, 77:2.40–41, 77:3.60, 65, 77:4.88
Sperry, Ann, 88:1.11–12+*il*, 89:3.113
Spheniscidae Press (Tad DuBois), 89:4.161
Spicer, Jack, 84:3.104, 86:3.155
Spieker, Ewald, 89:4.186+*il*
Spiekermann, Erik, 88:4.164*il*
Spiral Press (Joseph Blumenthal), 80:1.9, 81:4.118, 82:2.42, 83:2.56–58*il*

Spitzmueller, P. J. (Rams Head Press), 78:3.78
Stackpole, Julie Beinecke, 80:4.118–119+*il*
Stafford, William, 78:4.110–111+*il*, 79:3.77–78, 80:2.47, 81:4.129, 82:3.113, 83:2.77–79
Staley, Carolyn, 86:4.188
Stamperia del Santuccio (Victor Hammer), 78:4.122–123
Stamperia Tallone (Bianca, Ernesto, and Aldo Tallone), 80:1.13+, 21–22+*il*, 83:4.151
Stamperia Valdonega (Martino Mardersteig), 77:1.10, 77:2.37, 85:4.208–212, 217*il*
Stan, Tony, 81:4.144
Stanbrook Abbey Press, 77:1.14
Standard, Paul, 82:4.156, 84:4.163+*il*, 86:3.169–170, 87:1.38
  book by, 80:4.132–133*il*, 82:3.116–117
  review by, 80:2.65
Stanford, Donald E., 81:4.134–135
  On Type article, 83:1.7–9*il*
Stanislavsky, Constantin, 88:1.28
Stanton, Blair Hughes, 81:2.62+*il*, 88:1.45
Starr, Edwin, 77:3.67
Starrett, Vincent, 76:1.9
Stauffacher, Jack Werner, 84:1.10, 84:4.178, 89:3.108
  on Alberto Tallone, 80:1.20, 83:4.151*il*
  Center for Typographic Language, 80:2.38
  FP issue design by, 77:1.23
  hand-set type specimens by, 84:1.31*il*, 88:1.40, 88:3.123–126*il*
  Phaedrus, letters about FP review of, 79:2.42–43, 79:3.72
  photograph of, 79:1.9*il*
  profiles of, 79:1.1–6*il*, 79:3.85*il*
  review by, 76:3.51–52
  teaching by, 78:1.11, 79:1.4–5, 80:2.38
  typography of, 88:2.92–93
  See also Greenwood Press
Stéen, Denis, 86:4.200–203
Stegner, Wallace, 85:3.144+, 90:1.18+
Stein, Gertrude, 81:3.106, 85:2.103, 85:3.160, 86:4.219+*il*
Steinbeck, Carol, 77:4.87
Steinbeck, John, 77:4.87
Steinberg, Lois, 78:4.114
Steinberg, Steven, 76:2.22–23
Steiner, Robert, 81:3.93+
Steiner-Prag, Hugo, 90:1.6
Steltzer, Fritz Max, 82:3.90
Stepanova, Varvara, 90:1.31–33*il*
Stephenson, Jonathan (Rocket Press), 88:2.61–62+*il*
  photograph of, 88:2.64*il*
Stermer, Dugald:
  review by, 82:4.130–131

response to, 83:1.2
Stern, Gideon, 87:2.107
Stevens, Meic, 84:2.68–69
Stevens, Wallace, 78:1.1+, 86:2.79+*il*
Stevenson, Robert Louis, 78:3.76, 78:4.106–107, 81:1.20, 87:3.129–130+*il*, 90:2.92–93
Stewart, Bruce, 85:4.235
Stewart, Pamela, 76:2.30
Stewart, William, 82:4.132–135*il*
  FP cover design by, 82:4.157+(cover)
Stiff, Ruth L. A., 89:3.109
Stifter, Adalbert, 86:4.200
Still Point Press (Gould and Charlotte Whaley), 86:4.237, 87:2.90–91
Stilwell, Robert W. (reviewer), 76:1.13
Stinehour, Christopher (reviewer), 78:1.21
Stinehour Press, The (Roderick Stinehour), 80:1.8–9, 14, 81:4.118, 88:4.192–193
  bibliographical lists, 77:1.13, 89:3.152–154
  press marks, 79:4.108*il*
Stinehour, Roderick, 89:3.152–154
  award to, 86:1.5
Stinehour, Stephen, 82:3.102
Stockdale, Percival, 89:1.41
Stomps, V. O., 86:2.99
Stone, Harry, 85:4.226–227
Stone House Press (Morris A. Gelfand), 84:1.41*il*, 84:3.110*il*, 87:4.188+*il*, 88:2.52
Stone, Joan, 78:3.75–76, 81:4.129, 84:4.147
Stone, Reynolds, 78:3.83–84, 82:4.157
Stone, Sumner, 88:1.39–40
  ATyI logo by, 84:1.7*il*
  FP cover titles by, 81:3.95+cover
  On Type articles, 79:4.120–123*il*, 88:3.123–126*il*
  reviews by, 78:4.118–119, 79:1.15–16, 79:2.55–56, 87:3.121+, 168
  types by, 88:1.40–41*il*, 88:2.53, 88:3.123–126*il*
Storhaug, Glenn (Five Seasons Press), 84:1.37–38*il*
Stourton Press (Fairfax Hall), 77:4.88
Stover, Dean, 87:4.192
Strachan, William, 82:2.53+
Strauss, Monica J.:
  articles by, 87:3.139–140+*il*, 89:4.176–186*il*
  exhibition review by, 88:4.176
  FP Guest Editor (for Netherlands), 89:4.175, 214
  reviews by, 81:3.89–91, 82:4.131+, 85:4.230–232, 86:3.175–176, 88:1.11–12
Strauss, Victor and Edith, 75:1.7
Strayer, Emily Mason (Kutenai Press), 88:2.68+*il*, 90:1.16–17*il*, 90:3.109*il*

Streeter, David (Del Sol Press), 77:2.45
Strick, Louis, article by, 81:1.34
Strick, Maria, 85:2.96–98*il*
  portrait of, 85:2.91*il*
Strindberg, August, 89:3.128
Strouse, Norman and Charlotte, 82:4.129+
Strutt, Arthur John, 87:2.91–93+*il*
Stuart, Gloria (Imprenta Glorias), 89:4.209–210+*il*
Sturm, Carol. See Nadja Press
Štyrský, Jindřich, 87:1.20
  and Toyen, 87:1.29*il*
Subin, Nina, 90:3.105+*il*
Sumac Press (Emerson G. Wulling), 76:1.12, 81:2.39, 83:2.57–58
Sumner, Melody, 85:1.73
  article by, 84:2.79–81+*il*
Sundberg, Alan Frederick, 86:4.200+
Sutcliffe, Judy, 85:1.33*il*
Sutcliffe, Peter, 79:2.41
Sutherland, James E., exhibition reviews by, 79:2.45, 80:4.113+
Sutnar, Ladislav, 87:1.20, 28*il*
Svoboda, Jindřich, 87:1.22–23, 31*il*
Swain, Gwenyth (reviewer), 88:3.105–106, 88:4.159, 164, 89:2.57+, 73, 90:1.9
Swamp Press, 79:1.17
Swann, Cal, 84:3.125–126
Swearingen, Roger G. (reviewer), 90:2.92–93
Swenson, Tree, 87:2.68
  FP cover design by, 89:3.113+(cover)
  See also Copper Canyon Press
Swift, Jonathan, 77:2.34–35
Swinburne, Algernon Charles, 77:4.88, 82:1.21+*il*
Symons, Julian, 89:3.144+
Symposium Press (Charles Gullans), 80:1.14
Szabo, Steve, 77:3.56–57
Szántó, Tibor, 88:1.43
Szirmai, J. A., 85:4.193
Szukalski, Stanislaw (type designer), 89:4.166*il*

T

Tabard Private Press (Philip Kerrigan), 87:3.151–152+*il*
Tagett, Richard (Manroot), 77:4.87, 78:3.77
Tagliente, Giovanni, 81:1.26+, 90:1.49
Talamantez, Ines, 76:4.63–64
Taller Martín Pescador See Martín Pescador Press
Talleur, John (Holiseventh Press), 85:2.111, 89:2.86, 90:1.15–16+*il*

Tallone, Alberto, 79:1.3, 80:1.13+,
    21–22+*il*
  Alberto Tallone Editore book,
    83:4.151*il*
  life of, 85:4.205–208
  photograph of, 80:1.20*il*
  types by, 85:4.206*il*
Tallone, Bianca, 80:1.13+, 85:4.207–208,
  216*il*
Tallone family (Stamperia Tallone),
    80:1.13+, 21–22+*il*, 85:4.207–208+*il*
  exhibition, 85:4.238+
  photograph of, 85:4.216*il*
Tanchis, Aldo, 88:4.168–170*il*
Tanis, James, 85:2.121–123
Tanner, Wesley B., 82:4.146, 85:1.73
  article by, 79:2.40–41+*il*
  book design by, 78:4.108–109+*il*, 126*il*,
    81:4.121, 87:4.196–200+*il*
  FP cover design by, 83:3.125+(cover)
  FP issue design by, 76:3.49
  photograph of, 82:4.147*il*
  reviews by, 77:3.57–58, 78:2.38+,
    78:3.74–75, 87:1.43
  See also Arif Press
Tanselle, G. Thomas, 87:3.116
Tarachow, Michael (Pentagram Press),
    82:4.149–150, 84:3.110
Targ, William:
  Targ Editions, 79:4.116, 80:3.91,
    81:4.130, 83:2.55+, 84:4.170–171
    response from, 85:1.68
Tarn, Nathaniel, 79:3.77–78
Tate, Allen, 78:1.2, 81:2.45*il*
Tate, Nahum, 90:1.10+*il*
Tauber, Robert, 82:4.146, 89:1.48–49
Taurus Books, 82:2.43
Taylor & Taylor printing (San Francisco), 88:1.4
Taylor, Barnard (Press of Appletree Alley), 84:3.133, 84:4.141, 85:3.161–162,
    87:4.188+*il*
Taylor, Christine, 90:3.109
Taylor, E. H. [Pat] (Out of Sorts Pres and
    Letter Foundery [sic]), 78:3.91, 83:1.5
Taylor, James (Officina Pluralo),
    82:1.22–24
Taylor, Mary Ann, original broadside
    from, 84:3.103+(insert: continuous
    tone lithograph)
Taylor, Michael (reviewer), 85:2.116
Taylor, Robert N. (compiler, Eric Gill
    collection), 84:3.129–131
Taylor, W. Thomas, 88:3.106
  articles by, 82:1.2, 83:1.14–15*il*,
    83:4.162–163*il*, 85:1.15–19
  book by, 82:1.27–29*il*
  books from, 76:4.68, 77:4.88–89,
    78:4.112–113, 84:2.71–72+, 84:4.139,
    168–170*il*, 85:2.120–121,
    87:3.152–154, 90:2.73–75*il*, 79–80*il*
  exhibition reviews by, 79:3.84–85,
    83:2.59+*il*, 83:4.171–172+
  fourteen bookbindings on same
    book commissioned by, 83:1.14–15*il*
  Kairos Press books, 87:2.62,
    88:1.17–18+*il*
  lecture by, 81:4.135
  letter from, 78:2.35
  reviews by, 78:1.19–20, 79:2.61, 83:2.75,
    83:4.172, 86:3.167+
Tea Garden Press (Randolph and Claudia Laub), 82:2.63*il*
Tebbel, John, 84:2.50–51
Teige, Karel, 87:1.19–21, 27–28*il*
Teiser, Ruth, 82:2.78–79
Tenniel, John, 87:2.106*il*, 88:2.62
Tern Press (Nicholas and Mary Parry),
    88:2.58–59+*il*
Testa, Fulvio, 88:1.21–23+*il*, 89:2.86
Teter, Holbrook (Zephyrus Image
    Press), 88:4.160, 90:3.111
Tetterode, Nicolas, 89:4.190
Themerson, Stefan, 89:2.87
Theobald, John, 78:3.77
Theodore Press (Michael Alpert),
    87:3.130+*il*, 89:3.114, 90:1.10–11+*il*
Thiele, Edmund, 80:4.106
Thom, Karo, 81:3.79–81+*il*
Thomas, Aliza, 83:2.50–51
Thomas, Calvin F. S., 88:4.155*il*
Thomas, Dylan, 78:1.15–17, 26*il*,
    79:2.33–39*il*
  handwriting of, 79:2.36*il*
Thomas, Edward, 77:4.89–90
Thomas, Isaiah, 80:4.136
Thomas, Lewis, 87:3.128–129+*il*
Thomas, Peter and Donna (The Good
    Book Press), 90:3.127–128*il*
Thomas, Stephen (reviewer), 78:1.18–19
Thompson, E. A., 80:4.107
Thompson, E. P., 79:1.20
Thompson, Jack C., 84:2.47, 86:4.188
Thompson, Marilyn, 76:3.48
Thompson, Michael R., article by, 75:2.11
Thompson, Susan Otis, 78:3.84–85,
    80:3.82
  reviews by, 80:4.126, 83:4.151–153,
    85:2.127–128
Thomson, Barry, 87:4.192
Thomson, Peter, 85:2.114–116
Thoreau, David, 78:3.78, 79:4.111,
    82:1.37*il*, 88:4.181–183+
Thorkelsdóttir, Rúna, 89:4.185+*il*
Thorpe, Constance (Connie),
    83:1.23–25*il*
  article by, 79:3.97–98
  reviews by, 81:2.57–58, 83:4.156–157
Thorpe, John, 86:3.154–156
Thurber, James, 79:3.93
Tidal Press (Charles E. Wadsworth),
    79:2.54, 80:4.125+*il*, 85:1.55–56
  press mark, 79:4.109*il*
Tidcombe, Marianne, 80:3.95, 82:3.86,
    85:2.124–126, 90:2.60
Tideline Press (Leonard Seastone):
  books from, 78:2.43–44+*il*, 82:3.113
  broadside, with Jack Fitterer, 84:3.110
  press mark, 79:4.109*il*
Tieffenbach, Eduard Wilhelm (Officina
    Serpentis), 86:2.90
Tiemann, Walter (Janus Presse), 86:2.90
Tiessen, Wolfgang (Edition Tiessen),
    86:4.200–203+*il*, 88:3.105–106
Tilson, Joe, 79:3.81–83+*il*, 81:3.104*il*,
    85:4.215*il*
Timperly, Charles H., 79:1.20–21
Todd, Glenn, 83:1.12–13+*il*
Todd, William B., 86:4.215
Tolkien, John Ronald Reuel, 76:1.4–5,
    88:1.34
Toller, Ernst, 90:2.66*il*
Tomkinson, G. S., 75:2.20, 75:3.26
Tomlinson, Charles, 80:4.122
Tompkins, Demaris Ide, 86:1.38–39
Tompkins, Hawley T. (pseud.),
    90:1.19–22
Tooth of Time Books (John Brandi),
    83:1.10–11
Toothpaste Press (Allan and Cinda
    Kornblum), 80:1.14, 81:3.93+*il*,
    82:4.127, 84:1.4
  press mark, 79:4.109*il*
Torre, Vincent, 88:1.12+*il*
Torresani, Andrea, 80:2.63
Tottoroto, Rosemary (illustrator),
    83:2.72+, 87:2.90–91
Toussaint, André, 88:2.74–75+*il*
Toyen, pseud. (Marie Čermínóvá),
    87:1.29*il*
Tracy, Walter, 87:4.204–206+,
    89:1.26–28+
  letter to, 82:1.3
    letter from, 82:3.82
  articles by, 81:2.51–56*il*, 81:3.99–102*il*
  photograph of, 89:1(insert)
Trajanus Press (Gotthard de Beauclair),
    86:2.80–84*il*, 99
Trakl, Georg, 82:1.24+*il*
Traxel, David, 82:1.34–35*il*
Treadwell, Michael, 83:1.4
Tremain, R. J., 77:1.11
Trianon Press (Arnold Fawcus), 82:2.50
Trissel, James:
  article by, 87:3.118–119
  Press at Colorado College books,
    80:2.48, 84:4.147–148, 87:1.6,
    88:1.38*il*
Trithemius, Johannes, 79:2.61–62

Troyer, Johannes, 76:1.15*il*, 76:2.25
Tryzno, Janusz Pavel (Correspondance des Arts), 88:4.157, 90:1.17
Ts'ai Lun, 78:2.52, 87:3.156, 172
Tschichold, Jan, 77:3.54, 77:4.94, 87:3.155*il*, 89:2.75, 79*il*
    biography of, 76:3.51–52
    influence of, 79:1.3–4, 27+
    obituary (1902–1974), 75:1.7
Tsien Tsuen-Hsuin, 86:1.42–44, 87:3.156+
Tufte, Edward R., 85:1.48+*il*, 85:3.136
Turkey Press (Harry Reese and Sandra Liddell), 81:1.22, 81:3.92, 87:3.167+*il*, 90:3.111+*il*
Turkey Press (Michael Hannon), 87:3.167+*il*
Turnbull, William (North Point Press), 81:4.116+, 145
Turner, Decherd, 86:1.37, 86:3.156, 87:1.6, 87:2.75
    exhibition review by, 82:2.70
    letter to, 82:4.122–123
    reviews by, 82:1.22, 85:4.201–202, 90:1.10–11+
Turner, Silvie, 84:1.11–13+, 90:1.8–9
Turtle Press (Bruce Beck), 85:3.162–163, 86:4.237
Tusser, Thomas, 83:2.70–71
Tvrdý, Antonín, 87:1.22
Twain, Mark, 88:1.18
Twelve by Eight Press (John Mason), 78:2.54
    press mark, 79:4.109*il*
Twinrocker Handmade Paper, Inc. *See* Clark, Howard; Clark, Kathryn; the Subject Index
Two-Hands Press (Kitty Marryat), 80:2.39
Twombly, Carol:
    photograph of, 90:3.125*il*
    profile of, 90:3.120–125*il*
    types by, 90:3. 121–123*il*
Twomey, Juliet Spohn, 90:2.76–77
    On Type article (Roman inscriptions), 89:3.134–141*il*
Twowindows Press (Don Gray), 84:3.131–132, 85:2.112
Tyson, Ian, 86:4.200, 203*il*
Tzara, Tristan, 84:3.126–128

U

Udinotti, Agnese, 78:2.41+*il*
Uitgeverij Philip Elchers (fine press), 89:4.185–186+*il*
Underwood, Leon, 88:2.65
Unger, Gerard, 84:1.10, 90:3.121
    FP cover design by, 81:2.71+(cover)
    letter from, 81:1.2–3
    photograph of, 89:1(insert)
    type design by, 80:3.102–103*il*, 88:1.40*il*, 88:3.124, 89:1.29–30+(insert), 89:4.197
Unicorn Press (Alan Brilliant), 76:2.30
University of California – Santa Cruz. *See* Cowell Press
University of Iowa:
    Center for the Book, 85:3.182–183, 86:2.73–74+*il*, 87:3.171
    Center for the Book, *See also* The Windhover Press (Kim K. Merker); university name (in the Subject Index)
University of Kentucky. *See* The King Library Press (University of Kentucky)
university news. *See* specific names (in the Subject Index)
university presses, fine print. *See* specific press names
University of Southern California. *See* Fine Arts Press
University of Texas, Austin, 87:1.6
University of Wales. *See* Gwasg Gregynog Press
Updike, Daniel Berkeley, 77:2.45, 79:1.3, 79:2.41–42, 81:1.23–24, 88:4.159, 89:3.134
    and Stanley Morison, 79:3.72–73, 79:4.130–134, 80:3.96–98, 83:1.18, 86:3.169
Updike, John, 79:4.116, 81:4.130
Uphill Press. *See* Heckscher, August
Upiglio, Giorgio (Grafica Uno; Edizioni Rovio), 85:4.212–215*il*, 86:1.5
Upstairs Press, 78:3.78

V

Váchal, Josef, 87:1.5*il*, 19, 25*il*
Valéry, Paul, 86:4.200, 88:4.176
Van Cleve, Clyde (Image Gallery), 79:2.55–56
Van den Akker, J. A., 87:2.61
van der Vossen, André, 89:4.195+*il*
van der Zee, Sytse, 89:4.186+*il*
Van Dijck, Ger, 81:3.104*il*
van Egten, Henriette, 89:4.185+*il*
Van Krimpen, Huib, 89:4.189–197*il*
Van Krimpen, Jan:
    criticism of his types, 87:4.211
    Greek types by, 85:3.148
    types by, 80:1.28, 81:2.51–56*il*, 81:3.99–102*il*, 82:1.3, 84:4.146, 86:3.149, 86:4.228, 88:3.124, 89:4.190+*il*
van Leeuwen, Jan Storm:
    exhibition reviews by, 87:3.152–154, 88:4.175
    review by, 89:1.22+
Van Niekerk, Sarah, 84:2.68–69
van Noorde, Cornelis, 89:4.198*il*
Van Ostaijen, Paul, 89:2.88
Van Vliet, Claire, 78:1.17, 79:1.14, 81:4.134, 89:3.113
    article by, 77:2.31–32+*il*
    bookbinding by, 89:3.114–118*il*
    FP cover design by, 83:2.43+(cover)
    illustrations by, 87:3.130+*il*
    letter from, 76:1.7
    paperworks by, 77:4.84+*il*, 83:3.106*il*
    photographs of, 77:4.80*il*, 80:4.117*il*, 84:2.77*il*, 85:3.176*il*
    on printing (quotes), 75:2.17, 82:4.137+, 84:1.5
    profiles of, 80:4.115–117*il*, 85:3.177–178
    reviews by, 82:1.34–35, 85:4.232–234
    watermark design, 87:4.183*il*
    See also Janus Press
Vander Weele, Linda Sholund, 75:4.42
Varey, Simon, 87:3.130+
Vernier, Renaul, 85:4.193
Verniere, Laure, 77:1.7+
Veroni, Raúl (Estudio Gráfico), 77:3.65
Vervliet, Hendrik D. L., 83:3.124–125*il*, 85:1.46
Vesalius Andreas, 76:1.2*il*
Vever Collection (Henri de), 89:3.147–150
    See also Collectors and their Collections
Victoria Press (London), 85:2.128
Viking Press, 82:2.53+, 60–61
Villon, François, 81:1.20+*il*
Vincent Fitz Gerald & Co., 85:2.114–116+*il*
Vincent, Stephen, 84:2.69
Vincentino. *See* Arrighi, Ludovico Vincentino degli
Vine Press (John Peters and Peter Foster), 90:1.28–29
Vintage Publications, 79:3.83
Virgil, 83:2.76, 86:2.94–95*il*
Viscomi, Joseph, 82:2.49–50
Visel, Curt, 79:2.55
Visual Studies Workshop, 85:3.167–168
Vlček, Tomáš, 87:1.15, 16–21+*il*, 24
Vogelweide, Walther von der, 86:2.76+*il*
Volk & Huxley, 82:1.6, 9
Volkow, Verónica, 78:1.21, 80:4.122
Voltaire, François Marie Arouet de, 78:4.111, 84:2.62, 88:2.60
von dem Bussche, Wolf (Peter and the Wolf Editions), 88:3.112–113+*il*
von Goethe. *See* Goethe, Johann Wolfgang von
von Hesse, Gudrun. *See* Zapf-von Hesse, Gudrun
von Hofmannswaldau, Christian Hofmann, 76:3.43–44

von Kamphoevener, Elsa Sophia, 86:4.200
von Kritter, Ulrich, 85:2.123–124
von Sichowsky, Richard (Grillen-Presse), 85:2.112–113*il*, 126–127, 86:2.86, 90, 116
Voragine, Jacobus de, 90:3.130–131*il*
Vorst, Benjamin, 86:4.209–211+*il*, 87:2.107–108
Voss, Jan, 89:4.185+*il*
Vrtílek, Ján, 87:1.31*il*
Vyskočil, Josef, 87:1.22

W

Wadsworth, Charles E. (Tidal Press), 79:2.54, 80:4.125+*il*, 85:1.55–56
    press mark, 79:4.109*il*
Wagner, Christian Ulrich, 85:2.79
Wagoner, David, 81:4.129
Wahl, Jean, 75:3.28
Wain, John, 81:2.48
Wakefield, D. R. (Chevington Press), 83:4.171+*il*, 86:3.177–178
Wakoski, Diane, 77:2.35, 78:3.75–76, 83:2.52, 85:1.61–62*il*, 86:1.56, 87:2.68, 89:1.46–48
    See also Penumbra Press (Bonnie O'Connell)
Walker, Edward, 85:4.198–200
Walker, Emery (Doves Press), 78:3.82, 84:3.94–95, 87:2.66–67, 87:4.215–216
Walker, Gay, 84:4.177–178
Walker, Scott, 85:1.11–14
    issue design by, 79:3.71
    Graywolf Press books, 79:1.10–11*il*, 81:4.126, 85:1.11–12, 85:3.136–139, 89:2.86
    profile of, 81:4.116+
Walkup, Kathleen:
    articles by, 81:4.116+, 85:2.100–104*il*, 85:3.177–181*il*
    broadside reviews by, 85:3.140–141, 142–143, 144+
    conference report by, 82:4.136–138+*il*
    Five Trees Press books, 76:4.66, 78:3.74, 78:4.114, 79:2.54, 79:4.115–116
    cover design by, 85:2.128+(cover)
    interview with, 84:2.79–81+*il*
    Matrix Press broadside, 82:1.23–25*il*
    reviews by, 77:3.60, 77:4.88–89, 78:2.42–43, 78:3.75–76, 79:1.11, 79:2.48, 79:3.77–79, 79:4.111, 80:1.16, 80:2.48, 80:4.120, 81:3.89, 81:4.126–127, 82:3.108+
Wallis, L. W., 87:4.206+
Walsdorf, John J., 76:1.9, 85:2.127–128
Walsh, James E., exhibition review by, 81:2.44–45*il*
Walter, Florence, 84:2.79
Walter, Karl Hans, 80:3.101
Walton, Izaak, 82:3.114
Wang Chieh, 90:1.7
Ward, Charlotte, 86:3.163, 86:4.236
Ward, Lynd, 78:4.111
Ward Ritchie Press. *See* Ritchie, Ward
Warde, Beatrice Lamberton (Becker), 80:3.97, 81:4.135, 82:3.90, 86:3.158–159+, 87:2.69–73+*il*, 89:2.75
    Inscription for a Printing Office, 84:3.105–106
    letter from, 84:3.105–106
    photograph of, 86:3.161*il*
Warde, Frederic, 80:1.26, 82:1.3, 86:3.158–161+*il*, 87:2.69–73+*il*, 88:1.9
    archive of, 86:3.158
    letters about, 86:4.236–237
    photograph of, 86:3.161*il*
Wardrop, James, 81:2.62+
Wark, Glenn, 81:2.38
Warwick Press (Carol J. Blinn), 77:2.37, 78:4.113+*il*, 125*il*, 83:2.75*il*, 84:2.71, 85, 87:1.43*il*
    press mark, 79:4.109*il*
Waters, Julian, 85:4.196–198
Waters, Patricia, 83:1.25*il*
Waters, Peter, 79:2.38–39*il*, 80:4.136
Waters, Sheila, 79:2.33–39*il*, 82:1.2
    FP banner by, 79:2.33*il*, 65
    review by, 77:3.66–67
Watson, Andrew C., 83:2.65–66
Watson, James, 89:2.67–69+*il*
Watzl, Anton, 86:4.200, 203*il*
Wawrzyniak, Krzysztof, 90:1.17
Wayzgoose Press (Mike Hudson), 82:3.83, 90:3.112+*il*
Weather Bird Press (Vance Gerry), 80:2.48, 84:3.98+
Webb, Amy, 89:1.35–36
Webb, Sheila, 85:3.142–143
Weber, Renee I., 81:3.87+*il*
Weier, Debra (Emanon Press), 83:3.102–103, 106*il*
Weil, James (Elizabeth Press), 80:1.16+*il*, 82:3.112
Weimann, Christopher:
    article by, 83:4.134–137+*il*
    covers by, 81:3.95+*il*, 83:4.174+*il*
    letter to, 84:2.47
    marbling by, 81:3.78, 81*il*, 86:4.190, 90:1.4
    review by, 89:1.21–22
    works by, 79:1.22–23
    obituary (1946–1988), 89:2.100
Weiss, Emil Rudolf, 77:2.28, 43, 86:2.111, 88:1.9–10*il*
Weisse, Franz, 81:3.86, 84:4.146
Weissenborn, Hellmuth, 76:3.47, 77:4.89–90, 83:4.156–157*il*, 86:4.193–194*il*
Welch, Anthony, 80:2.66+*il*, 80:3.75
Wells, Darius, 83:2.45–46*il*
Wells, Gabriel, 82:4.150
Wells, James M., 86:3.135
    response to, 78:2.35
    reviews by, 77:4.95–96, 85:3.158–159+
Wendt, Allan, 84:2.79
Wentz, Roby, 76:2.32–33, 82:3.83
    article by, 76:4.75–76
Werkman, Hendrik Nicolaas, 79:3.84, 80:4.111, 89:4.177–178+*il*
Werner, Arno, 76:3.41, 81:2.44–45*il*, 83:2.75, 85:2.81
Westreich, Bud (Press of Arden Park), 77:1.14
Weyer, Pat, 90:1.16–17*il*
Weygand, James Lamar (The Indiana Kid), 75:4.42
Whaley, Gould and Charlotte (Still Point Press), 86:4.237, 87:2.90–91
Whalley, Joyce Irene, 76:2.33, 81:3.97–98
Wharton, Edith, 75:4.38–39
Whatman, James, 82:2.52
Wheelock, John Hall, 79:1.15–16
Whirling Dervish Press (Barbara Luck), 78:4.114+*il*, 126*il*, 81:3.95, 88:4.168–170
    broadside from, 85:3.140+*il*
White, Martin, 85:3.136–138
White, Patrick E., 90:1.15–16+*il*
White Rabbit Press (Graham Mackintosh), 86:3.154–156
Whitehouse, Charles (Edition Seefeld), 87:3.122*il*
Whitlock, Alwyn, 86:3.140+*il*
Whitman, Walt, 79:2.50–51+*il*, 81:1.18, 82:2.53+*il*, 59–61+*il*
Whitridge, Thomas (Oyez Press), 76:4.62
Whittier, John Greenleaf, 88:4.181–183+
Whittingham, Charles, 84:4.139, 85:1.73
Whittington Press (John and Rosalind Randle):
    bibliography from, 83:4.156–157*il*
    books from, 76:3.47, 77:4.89–90*il*, 79:1.14–15*il*, 80:2.56–57, 86:4.193–195+*il*, 88:2.58+*il*, 89:2.69–71+*il*, 90:2.80–81*il*
    broadside from, 90:3.108+*il*
    Matrix journal, 82:3.85, 89:1.5–6
    press marks, 79:4.109*il*
Wick, Peter A., 84:3.128–129
Wieck, Roger S. (illustrator), 82:2.43, 84:1.23, 84:3.116–117
    exhibition review by, 83:4.143–145+
Wiegand, Willy (Bremer Presse), 86:2.88, 103–104, 105, 86:4.235–236
Wikstrom, Karin, 88:4.186–188+*il*, 90:1.18*il*

Wilbur, Richard, 87:4.185–187*il*
Wilcox, Michael, 83:1.14–15*il*, 83:4.168–169+*il*, 87:3.152–154
Wild Carrot Letterpress (Daniel Kelleher), 84:2.71
Wild Hare Press (Barton W. McNeil), 78:1.17
Wild Hare Press (Corinne Guiney), 85:2.107*il*
Wilde, Oscar, 76:2.29, 90:2.63*il*
Wiley, William T., 87:3.167+*il*
Wilkes, Walter, 86:2.65, 86:3.150+, 87:1.7+
   article by, 86:2.87–99*il*
   books by, 84:2.82–83, 85:4.196–197, 88:1.6
Wilkins, Cary (Close-Grip Press), 88:3.109–111+*il*
Willberg, Hans Peter, 86:2.65, 100–102
William James Association, 76:4.65–66
Williams, Gerald, 81:1.16
Williams, Graham R. (Florin Press), 81:2.49–50*il*, 85:4.233–234*il*, 86:3.139+*il*, 86:4.223–224+*il*
Williams, Jonathan, 87:2.68, 89:3.130
Williams, Paul Wightman, 78:1.1–3, 11
Williams, Robert:
   article by, 85:2.88–98*il*
   response to, 90:1.49
   reviews by, 82:4.145+, 84:1.16–17, 87:2.102–103, 88:1.17–18, 89:2.88–90, 89:3.143–144
Williams, Tennessee, 77:1.10
Williams, William Carlos, 85:1.54–55
Williamson, Hugh, 82:1.7+, 85:2.127
Willow Press (Susan Allix), 87:2.91–93+*il*, 87:4.181–183, 88:1.5
Wilmot, John, 79:3.73
Wilson, Adrian, 76:1.12, 79:3.85, 85:1.65
   cover and interior design by, 79:4.126+(cover)
   and Jack Stauffacher, 79:1.2–3+*il*, 79:3.85
   letters from, 78:1.30, 86:4.236–237
   quote from, 89:1.6
   review by, 76:4.62–63
   talk by, 80:3.82
   theater programs, book of, 80:3.84–85*il*
   watermark design, 86:3.139+*il*
   obituary (1923–1988), 88:3.104–105
Wilson, Adrian and Joyce Lancaster Wilson, 78:1.11, 30, 81:4.134, 83:2.71–72, 84:4.168+, 86:3.153–154, 88:3.104–105
   See also The Press in Tuscany Alley
Wilson, Joyce Lancaster, 80:4.109–110, 88:2.53
   reviews by, 77:2.32–33, 87:3.129, 88:1.12+, 88:3.109
Wilson, Kim, 88:1.15–16

Wilson, Susan Spring, 78:2.36–37+*il*, 78:3.80
   exhibition review by, 85:3.182–183
   featured bookbinding, 83:1.14–15*il*
   letter from, 77:1.14
   Marquesa Nonpare*il* (pseud.), 79:1.22
   reviews by, 76:1.13–14, 77:1.18–19, 78:4.113, 114, 79:1.17, 80:3.91, 80:4.120
Winans, Robert B., 82:2.50–52
Wind River Press (David Holman), 79:3.73, 84:3.110+*il*
Windell Press (Guy Reading), 90:1.21–22
Windham, Donald, 77:1.10
The Windhover Press (Kim K. Merker):
   books from, 76:3.41, 45, 77:1.11–12, 78:2.43+*il*, 83:3.121–123*il*, 84:4.141–142, 85:1.54–55*il*, 86:3.163–165+*il*, 86:4.228, 88:2.71–72+*il*, 89:1.41–42+*il*, 89:2.84–85
   profile of, 81:4.116+
Windle, John, 79:2.42, 79:3.83
Wineberg, Susan Gosin. *See* Gosin, Susan
Winfield, Rodney, 77:3.65
Winship, Michael, 85:4.198–200
Winter Harbor Press (James Houle), 77:2.45
Wise, Thomas J., 85:1.42–44
Wittock, Michel, 88:4.175
Wolde, Ludwig (Bremer Presse), 86:2.88–89
Wolf, Arne, 83:4.146–147, 87:3.154–156
Wolf, Douglas, 82:4.136
   exhibition review by, 85:2.82–83
   See also Nadja Press
Wolf, Edwin, 2nd, 79:2.60–61
Wolfe, Richard J., 76:4.71, 79:4.110–111, 81:3.78, 86, 90:1.4
Wolff, Eleanor, 79:3.75–77
Wolff, Kurt, 78:2.55
Wollenberg, Leah, 76:2.33
Wolpe, Berthold Ludwig, 77:2.33, 41, 81:1.14–15*il*
   obituary (1905–1989), 89:4.211*il*
Wong, Judy Ling, 80:2.56–57
Wong Moo Chew, 86:4.200+
Woodbine, Paul (Woodbine Press), 79:1.17–18
   letter from, 77:3.73–74
   reply to, 77:4.91
Wooden Rabbit Press (Rik Olson), 87:3.168+*il*, 87:4.200, 90:3.108+*il*
Woodward, David, 88:2.90–91, 89:1.33–34
Woodward, Emily, Private Press of, 82:3.107*il*
Woolf, Virginia, 75:1.4, 78:3.78, 85:2.102–103

   drawing of, 85:2.103*il*
Wordsworth, William, 88:1.23+*il*
Wright, Charles, 78:2.43+*il*, 81:1.20–21, 87:2.97+*il*, 89:1.41+*il*
Wright, John W., 76:4.66
Wright, Scott, 78:2.42–43
Wronker, Lili Cassell, 84:4.162*il*
Wulling, Emerson G. (Sumac Press), 76:1.12, 81:2.39, 83:2.57–58
Wyatt, Leo, 86:4.223–224+*il*
   obituary (1910–1981), 82:3.116–117

Y

Yamada, Kouichi, 81:3.79–81+*il*, 107
Yeats, W. B., 76:1.10, 84:4.141
Yellin, Herb (Lord John Press), 80:2.47, 84:3.107
Yellow Barn Press (Neil Shaver), 87:4.188*il*
   books from, 86:1.28–29*il*, 88:1.23*il*, 89:3.144+
   broadside from, 90:3.110–111*il*
Yolan, Jane, 78:4.111–112
Yolla Bolly Press (James and Carolyn Robertson):
   books from, 84:2.85, 87:4.209–210*il*, 88:4.186–188+*il*, 90:1.18+
   history of, 84:2.57–60+*il*, 86:2.66
Young, Belle McMurtry, 76:2.33
Young, Edward, 82:2.49–50+*il*
Young, Gary, 86:4.226–227*il*
   See also Greenhouse Review Press
Young, Noel (Capra Press), 75:2.13
Yourçenar, Marguerite, 81:2.69*il*, 89:3.124+*il*

Z

Zachreson, Nick (Blackwells Press), 85:2.111
Zahn, Carl, 88:2.84
Zakariya, Mohamed U.:
   article by, 78:4.97–102+*il*
   news of, 80:2.68, 84:4.139
   reviews by, 80:2.66+, 80:3.75
Zanella, Alessandro:
   Edizioni Ampersand, 82:3.82, 88:3.143, 89:2.86
   Plain Wrapper Press, 79:3.81–83+*il*, 81:3.105, 82:3.82
Zanzotto, Andrea, 81:3.104*il*
Zapf, Hermann:
   articles on, 84:4.164–167+*il*, 85:1.35–41*il*
   birthday portfolio for, 89:3.108–109*il*
   books about, 84:3.133, 84:4.146, 85:4.196–198*il*, 88:2.84+*il*
   calligraphic portfolio honoring, 89:3.108–109*il*

calligraphy manual by, 86:2.67
case layout by, 83:2.44
design philosophy of, 84:1.10, 88:2.84+
film on, 78:1.13
cover design by, 85:1.70+(cover)
lectures by, 86:3.132–133, 88:1.25+, 39, 88:2.84
letters from, 86:1.4, 86:2.109, 86:3.179–180
news of, 77:4.91
photograph of, 89:1(insert)
rejoinders to, 86:2.109, 86:3.179–180
type specimen sheets by, 81:4.123–126*il*
typefaces by, 76:1.13, 77:1.12, 77:3.55, 79:1.4, 81:1.32*il*, 86:3.148–149*il*, 87:1.7, 88:2.84+, 89:1.29+(insert), 90:1.20

Zapf-von Hesse, Gudrun, 81:4.124, 88:1.40*il*
   article about, 80:4.134–135*il*
Zauberberg Press (Don von R. Drenner), 89:2.62+*il*
Zauft, Richard (Flatlands Press), 85:3.142–143+*il*, 155, 87:3.120–121+*il*
Zawadiwsky, Christine, 78:4.113
Zdanevitch, Ilia (Iliazd), 87:4.180
   See also Iliazd
Zephyrus Image Press (Holbrook Teter), 88:4.160, 90:3.111
Zimmon, Howard (Seamark Press), 78:2.42–43
Zimnik, Reiner, 86:4.200–203+
Zinn, Nancy, article by, 76:1.5–6+*il*
Zucker, Nancy Ellen, 78:4.114+*il*
Zwang, Christian, 79:4.112, 86:2.116–117*il*
Zwart, Piet, 89:4.178+*il*
Zwicker, Tony, 90:3.143
Zydeck, Fredrick, 86:1.28–29*il*

INDEX BY SUBJECTS

A

abar marbling. *See* marbling, paper
Abbey of St. Gall, 88:4.157–158*il*
abecedaries, 76:3.47–48*il*, 79:2.47–48+*il*, 81:3.93+*il*, 83:4.149–150*il*, 87:4.201–202*il*
  See also letterforms books
abstract art, type as, 86:2.66–67
accents. *See* punctuation and accents
accordion books. *See* bookbinding (history and types)
Addison House, 77:3.56+
advertising art:
  Dutch avant-garde, 89:4.176–179*il*
  old cuts catalogue, 90:3.100–101*il*
aesthetics:
  books as aesthetic objects, 76:4.57–60 (part 1), 77:1.4–6 (part 2)
  of metal type irregularities, 84:1.10
  of paper, 81:2.59, 83:3.92–101+*il*, 88:3.138
  of the printing art (Harry Duncan), 84:2.85
  of the typographic image, 89:2.75–82*il*
  See also artists' books; book design; type design; typography
Alcuin Society (Canada), 76:1.10, 12, 78:2.45, 58*il*, 78:3.77, 85:4.192
alphabet books, illustrated. *See* abecedaries
alphabets, letterform. *See* letterform alphabets; type; type design; writing systems
amate bark-paper, 83:2.50
American Antiquarian Society, 76:3.52–53, 79:3.71, 80:2.68, 80:4.136, 82:2.51, 84:3.134–135, 87:3.116
American Civil Liberties Union (ACLU), 90:3.114–115
American Institute of Graphic Arts (AIGA), 82:2.42, 87:3.116
  critique of, 77:4.93–94
  exhibitions, 75:3.28–29, 76:1.7, 11–12, 76:3.41, 77:2.38, 77:3.66, 77:4.93–94
American Printing History Association (APHA):
  awards, 79:2.46, 84:2.51, 84:3.135, 86:3.135, 87:3.116
  history of, 75:2.10, 77:4.94, 80:1.31, 85:2.129
American Type Founders Co. (ATF), 82:4.146, 83:2.49, 86:3.159, 87:4.215, 89:3.113
  group photograph, 86:3.161*il*
  specimen book, 83:1.29–30*il* (facs. 1896)
  typeface development at, 78:3.91, 78:4.120, 81:4.140–144*il*
American Typecasting Fellowship (ATF), 78:4.115, 79:3.91
  conferences, 80:2.68–69, 83:1.4–5, 85:2.86–87, 86:4.235
Les Amis de la Reliure d'Art (ARA):
  Brussels, 87:3.152–154, 88:2.53, 88:4.175
  Toulouse, 85:3.135–136
Les Amis de la Reliure Originale, 88:2.53
Andrews/Nelson/Whitehead (A/N/W), 76:2.21, 76:3.41, 87:2.60, 87:3.174
  letters from, 76:3.45–47, 83:4.159–161
  paper catalogue, 80:4.136
Anglo-Saxon literature:
  10th century poem, 75:4.39
  medieval poems, 86:3.164–165*il*
  type design and punchcutting for, 86:3.165*il*, 86:4.228–229*il*
animal proverbs books. *See* bestiaries in the Subjects Index
antiquarian booksellers. *See* booktrade and booksellers
Anurakta (Sri Aurobindo Ashram) (papermakers), 76:4.61
APHA. *See* American Printing History Association
apprenticeship. *See* education and teaching, book arts
arabesques. *See* Islamic books and manuscripts; type ornaments
Arabic calligraphers. *See* Islamic books and manuscripts
Arizona State University School of Art. *See* Pyracantha Press (in the Names Index)
Ars Libri, Ltd., 89:1.6
Ars Typographica book series, 78:4.124
Ars Typographica magazine, 80:1.5
Art Institute of Chicago, School of, 84:3.134
The Art of the Printed Book (conference), 81:4.132–135+
artists:
  and book production, 81:1.5–6, 82:3.96–97+, 82:3.103–106*il*
  paper, 83:3.102–103+*il*, 84:1.12, 86:3.145+*il*, 87:2.60, 88:1.11–13*il*
  See also specific individuals (in the Names of Persons and Fine Presses Index)
artists' books:
  altered text page, 88:4.176, 89:1.38–39+*il*
  American, 87:2.79–81, 98–100*il*
  British, 82:4.151–152+*il*, 84:3.133
  conference on, 86:1.18–19
  Dutch contemporary, 89:4.185–186+*il*
  exhibitions, 76:4.68–69, 77:3.66, 82:1.11+, 84:3.133, 85:3.185, 86:4.188, 87:2.79–81, 88:4.176, 89:2.59
  German, 77:2.25–30*il*, 86:2.99, 112, 89:1.38–39+*il*
  multi-disciplinary, 85:3.167–168+*il*
  producers of, 87:2.98, 88:1.11–12+*il*, 89:4.186
  sculptural, 82:1.11+, 85:2.109*il*, 85:3.168+*il*
  the social economy of, 85:1.23–25
  type ornaments, book composed of, 82:2.63*il*
  West German, 79:2.55
  See also book design
Ashkenazi script. *See* Hebrew
Ashling Press and Handmade Papers, 77:2.38, 78:2.35
Asian book arts. *See* names of specific countries
Association Typographique Internationale. *See* ATypI
ATF. *See* American Type Founders Co. (ATF); American Typecasting Fellowship (ATF)
Atheneum, 81:4.116
ATypI (Association Typographique Internationale):
  conference at Stanford University (1983), 84:1.7–10, 84:3.93+, 85:4.192, 88:2.87
  conference in Hamburg (1985), 86:2.113–114
  conference in Lausanne (1977), 78:1.12
  index of typefaces, 82:1.10
  logo, 84:1.7*il*
auctions, book, 75:1.7, 82:2.51–52, 87:4.216
  at Christie's, 78:2.36, 78:4.102+, 82:1.2, 87:4.181, 88:2.55–56, 88:3.148, 89:2.104
  at Sotheby Park Bernet (London), 85:3.135, 87:4.212

at Sotheby Park Bernet (New York), 76:2.23, 77:2.38–39, 88:4.155
See also collectors and their collections
Australia, book arts in, 85:2.80, 85:3.135*il*
authors:
> marks, personal, punchcutting of, 87:4.198–200*il*
> printing apprenticeship for, 88:4.160–162
> publisher relationships with, 80:3.80–81, 81:4.134–135, 88:2.92–93, 88:4.160–162
> signing books, 88:3.118–119
> *See also* Names of Persons and Fine Presses Index

authors of Fine Print articles. *See* Names of Persons and Fine Presses Index; *Fine Print* 1975–1990 Tables of Contents
avant-garde typography. *See* shaped poetry; typography, avant garde or experimental
awards and prizes, book world, 78:2.36
> APHA, 79:2.46, 84:3.135, 86:3.135, 87:3.116
> bookbinding, 79:4.117
> Goudy Award, Frederic W., 76:4.70, 86:1.5
> MacArthur Prize, 82:4.122
> proposed letterpress printing, 86:1.4
> Type Directors' Club, 79:3.72, 88:1.25, 89:1.7

axis of stress. *See* type design

B

Bancroft Library collections, U.C. Berkeley, 79:2.42, 82:1.2, 82:4.129+
Barcham Green & Co. *See* Hayle Paper Mill
Bauhaus School. *See under* type designers; typography, avant garde or experimental
Berliner Typefoundry, 80:4.110–111
Berthold AG types (review), 82:1.6–7
Bertram Rota Ltd. , 78:1.18–19
bestiaries and animal proverbs books, 79:3.74, 79:4.127–128, 82:4.124*il*, 139, 83:4.149–150*il*, 163*il*, 84:1.34–35, 85:3.188*il*, 88:1.12+*il*, 88:2.74–76+*il*
> parody, 89:3.142–143*il*
> *See also* folk and fairy tales; Aesop (in the Names of Persons and Fine Presses Index)

Bettman Photography Archive, 89:2.73*il*
Bibles:
> auction prices of historic, 78:4.105, 88:2.56
> Bremer Presse, 86:2.103*il*, 106–107*il*
> Eliot Indian, 76:2.23
> first from type cast in America, 85:2.122
> first in Hungarian, 84:1.27–29*il*
> Gutenberg, 78:4.102+, 82:4.150+, 83:3.87*il*, 86:4.212–215+*il*, 87:4.180–181, 88:2.56, 89:1.12+
> Gutenberg, types of the 42-line, 86:1.6*il*, 86:4.215+*il*
> watermarks in, 86:4.213, 233*il*
> Oxford Lectern, 79:2.41, 82:1.2, 87:2.65
> and translation from Hebrew, 86:1.7

Biblical literature, 78:4.108–109, 83:2.57–58
> Acts, 84:3.109+*il*
> Ars Memorandi (facsimile), 82:2.43*il*
> The Book of Job 83:1.26 illustrated by V. Angelo
> Canon Tables, 82:2.71–72+*il*
> The Catholicon (incunabulum, 1460) 86:4.232
> glossed books, 82:2.65–67+*il*, 86:4.204*il*, 207–208+*il*, 87:1.51*il*
> Hebrew (letters and type), 86:1.22–24+*il*
> incunabula, 82:2.54+*il*, 90:2.89
> layout of, 81:3.107, 86:4.204–208*il*
> leaf book of, 82:4.150+*il*
> Medieval manuscripts and glossed books, 82:2.65-67+*il*, 86:4.204*il*, 207-8+*il*, 87:1.51*il*
> ornament in medieval, 82:2.64–67+*il*, 70–73
> Postilla Super Totam Bibliam, 82:2.54+*il*
> The Prophet Jonah, 85:2.112–113*il*
> The Psalms, 79:2.51–52+*il*
> The Song of Songs, 76:3.47, 77:4.89–90*il*, 78:3.78, 83:1.26*il*, 85:2.109*il*, 86:2.91*il*
> Speculum humanae salvationis, 86:3.153–154

bibliographies and checklists:
> of bibliomysteries (review), 84:1.17+
> on bookbinding, 77:1.18–19, 87:1.6–7, 87:4.214
> Caslon type, list of books set in, 75:3.22–25*il*
> Century Thumb-Nail Series (stamped leather), 82:1.18+*il*
> collotype printing, 84:3.118–120*il*
> *See also* color printing
> color printing, old techniques, 80:4.112+cover
> fine presswork, 78:4.116
> newspaper-text typeface specimen sheet, 89:1.23+(insert)*il*
> on ornament, 82:2.44–47+*il*, 88:1.9–10*il*
> on paper history, 78:3.81–82
> on paper marbling, 79:1.22, 83:4.165–166, 84:3.120–123
> of printing histories, 76:2.32–33, 89:1.7
> *See also* libraries and collections, book arts

bibliographies of fine presses. *See* catalogues, checklists, and bibliographies of fine presses (by name); press histories; specific press names (in the Names of Persons and Fine Presses Index)
bibliophily. *See* collectors and their collections (by name)
Biblioteca Classense, 90:3.101+*il*
Bibliotheca Bibliographica Breslaueriana, 88:2.53–54
Bibliotheca Palatina, 86:4.189–190*il*
Bibliothèque Nationale (Paris), 85:3.184–185
bilingual editions, 88:3.143, 88:4.152, 89:4.173–174+*il*
> multi-lingual, 86:3.163–165, 90:1.17
> typography of, 80:4.122, 81:1.34, 81:4.121, 83:4.166–167+*il*, 84:2.62*il*, 85:2.115–116+*il*, 86:2.76+*il*, 86:3.147–148, 150+*il*, 87:1.52, 88:3.130–132*il*
> *See also* language

Binny & Ronaldson [typefounders], 81:1.24
The Birdsall Collection (bookbinding tools), 75:3.30
bit maps. *See* digital types and typesetting
black, two-tone. *See* color printing
Blaise Cendrars International Society, 87:3.117
blind stamping. *See* bookbinding techniques and materials
blind text, inked, 85:3.168+*il*, 87:3.127–128
blockbooks, medieval, 86:3.153–154
Boek en Band journal (Netherlands), 87:2.61
book arts conferences. *See* fine printing conferences; specific association names
book arts education. *See* education and teaching, book arts
book arts magazines (1903–1961), 80:1.3+(cover), 4–9
book arts magazines. *See* magazines and journals, book arts; names of specific journals
book arts (regional):
> American 19th century, 77:4.95, 78:2.35, 80:4.113, 82:1.15–18+*il*, 88:3.106, 90:1.8
> American 20th century, 77:4.95–96,

80:2.45–46, 81:4.133–134, 82:4.123, 90:1.8, 90:3.142–143
  in Australia, 85:2.80, 85:3.135
  in Canada, 78:4.107–108, 119, 82:4.123, 83:2.44, 87:3.152–154, 89:2.59
  in the Czech Republic, 87:1.15–39+*il*, 87:2.108
  in East Asia, 90:3.138–140*il*
  in Germany, 77:2.41, 82:3.86–87, 86:2.65, 80–117*il*
  in Italy, 85:4.205–217*il*
  in The Netherlands, 89:4.175–200*il*
  in Poland, 88:4.157, 90:1.17+*il*
  See also names of specific countries
book-breaking. *See* Islamic books and manuscripts; leaf books
book clubs (by name):
  The Book Club of California, 82:3.83, 83:1.39, 83:2.53, 87:4.196
  The Book Club of Texas, 90:2.79–80
  Caxton Club, 77:2.42
  The Double Crown Club, 82:3.96–97+
  Grolier Club, 79:4.119, 80:3.92–94*il*, 82:2.51, 83:3.126–127, 84:4.150–151+*il*, 85:2.82–83, 120–121, 86:3.158
  Konglomerati Foundation, 81:1.24–25*il* (Goudy portrait)
  Limited Editions Club, 77:3.73, 81:1.20+*il*, 82:3.101–102, 83:1.28–29, 86:3.173–175+*il*
  The Pittsburgh Bibliophiles, 78:3.78, 79:1.17
  Rounce and Coffin Club, 79:3.91
  Rowfant Club, 77:3.66
  The Typophiles, 76:1.11, 76:4.75, 82:2.42, 83:2.57, 84:3.105
The Book Collector's Packet monthly review, 80:1.5–6
Book Collector's Quarterly, The Colophon: A, 80:1.6–7
book collectors. *See* collectors and their collections in Index by Names
book conservation. *See* conservation of books
book dealers. *See* booktrade and booksellers
book design:
  aesthetics of, 76:4.57–60, 77:1.4–6, 89:2.87–88*il*
  See also book designers:
  American, 78:3.84–85, 80:3.92–94*il*, 80:4.113+, 81:4.133–134, 88:3.106
  the artist and, 81:1.5–6, 82:3.96–97+
  and book jackets, 81:1.15, 83:1.17–18*il*, 84:4.155–156+*il*
  catchwords, borders, and running titles, 82:2.70–73+*il*, 86:4.208+*il*
  creative collaboration in, 81:1.5–6,
  88:3.116–119+*il*, 137–140+*il*, 89:1.48–49, 89:2.83–86*il*, 96–99+*il*
  Designing Literature, series of articles on, 87:4.196–200*il*, 88:1.26–33*il*, 88:2.92–93, 88:3.116–119*il*, 88:4.160–162, 89:2.83–86*il*
  desktop publishing, 89:1.5
  golden section, using a, 81:2.60*il*, 88:1.22
  in the Czech Republic, 82:4.138, 87:1.15–39+*il*, 87:2.108
  in Germany, 86:2.80–84*il*, 100–102
  legibility, rules of, 82:1.31
  liturgical, 88:3.106
  manuals, 82:1.31+, 88:1.9
  methods (review), 85:2.126
  multilingual, 86:3.163–165+*il*, 90:1.17
  multiple-text, 80:4.120–121+*il*, 86:4.196–198*il*, 87:2.98–100*il*, 87:3.127–128, 88:3.111–112+*il*, 88:4.157–158
  one text with four variations of design, 89:1.48–49
  one text with multiple bookbindings, 83:1.14–15*il*, 88:2.55
  one text with pages of only certain letters, 81:4.121
  one text published by five university presses, 79:2.59–60
  philosophies and principles, 76:3.37–40, 76:4.72, 78:4.106, 79:2.41, 79:3.92–96, 80:3.79–81, 80:4.132, 81:3.106–107, 108–109, 82:2.60, 84:4.150–153*il*, 88:1.9, 88:2.84+, 88:3.105–106, 88:4.168–170*il*
  portfolio, 81:1.24–25, 88:4.178+*il*
  and proportions, 78:1.6
  relation of paper, printing process, and typeface in, 76:3.37–40, 83:4.138–142+*il*
  replicative, 86:3.156
  the social economy of, 85:1.23–25
  as theatre, 88:1.26–33*il*, 90:2.77–78+*il*
  with three-part pages, 82:3.107–108, 86:4.204*il*
  of title pages, 79:2.64*il*, 83:4.153*il*, 84:4.150–151+*il*, 90:3.104–105
  of trade books, 80:3.92–94
  transparency in, 81:1.10–11*il*, 81:4.121, 82:2.61–62+*il*, 85:3.173, 89:4.207+*il*
  of the two-page spread, 80:3.79–80
  typographic plan for a, 85:2.126
  for visual quantitative information, 85:1.48+*il*
  See also bookbinding; format of books; names of specific countries
book design and ornament. *See* ornament in books; type ornaments
book designers. *See also* book design:
  Cover designers, decorative (Boston), 1890–1910. 88:3.106
  exhibitions, 77:4.93–94, 80:4.113+, 81:1.14–15*il*, 83:3.126–127*il*
  monographs on, 78:3.84–85, 80:4.132, 83:4.151–153*il*, 84:4.164–166+*il*, 89:1.18–19*il*, 90:1.34–36*il*, 48–49*il*
  of trade books, 77:4.93–94, 80:3.92–94*il*, 81:3.106–107, 82:3.87–89, 84:3.110+*il*, 87:2.82–86*il*, 88–89*il*, 107, 88:3.105*il*
  and type designers (exhibition of), 81:1.14–15*il*
  See also artists' books; specific individuals (in the Names of Persons and Fine Presses Index)
book formats. *See* format of books
book history. *See* history of the book; history of book publishing
book illustration. *See* illustration, book
book production:
  accounts of, 82:2.49–50, 82:4.150+, 86:3.156, 87:3.151–152+*il*, 88:3.116–119+*il*, 137–140+*il*, 89:1.21–23
  the artist and, 81:1.5–6, 82:3.96–97+
  by relief methods, 80:1.23, 81:2.58–61*il*
  economics and pricing, 76:2.20, 80:3.80–81, 85:3.137, 87:2.88, 87:3.134–137
  essays on, 1920–1925 (London), 87:3.154–156*il*
  Gutenberg Bible, 86:4.212–215+*il*
  medieval, 85:2.107–108*il*
  philosophy and technique, 80:3.76–81, 81:2.58–61*il*, 86:3.156
  print shop rules, 17th century, 89:2.67–68
  relation of paper, printing process, and typeface in, 76:3.37–40, 83:4.138–142+*il*
  small press, contemporary, 76:3.37–40, 81:4.116+, 118–120+
  tracts and composite volume (sammelband), 87:2.68+
  typescript, 81:1.25, 81:3.74–75
  typesetting price, speed, and quality issues, 79:3.81, 85:1.14, 85:3.136–138
  See also artists' books
book reviews about fine press publications. *See* reviews, fine press book
book spines. *See* bookbinding techniques and materials; spines, book
book walls, 83:2.58+*il*, 64–65*il*, 87:2.108, 88:1.34+
book workers guild. *See* Guild of Book Workers (bookbinders)
Book Works gallery, 85:1.69–70

bookbinder exhibitions. *See* bookbinding exhibitions
bookbinder names, individual. *See* Names Index
bookbinders:
    American, 80:2.60–61, 82:1.4–5+, 83:4.162–163+*il*, 87:2.63–64, 87:3.154
    apprenticeships for, 85:1.16, 85:3.136, 87:3.153
    Canadian, 82:4.123, 83:2.44, 87:3.152–154, 89:2.59
    catalogues raisonnés for, 83:4.143, 85:2.124–126, 87:2.64–65
    commissioning a group of, 83:1.14–15*il*, 83:4.171–172+*il*, 88:2.55
    commissioning and patronage of, 79:3.71, 80:2.60–61+*il*, 81:4.135, 82:1.4–5+, 83:2.59, 72+, 83:4.143, 85:1.16+, 85:3.184–185, 88:1.5, 88:4.167–168
    Czech Republic, 87:1.21–24+*il*, 87:2.108
    English, 76:1.1–5*il*, 76:2.24, 77:1.1–4, 78:2.36–37, 78:3.79–80, 79:4.124–126*il*, 128–129, 82:1.21, 82:2.70, 82:3.85–86, 82:4.122–123, 88:1.34+, 88:2.96
    fees of, 81:4.134, 82:1.5
    German, 86:2.116–117*il*
    monographs on, 83:2.75, 87:3.152–154
    photographs of, 80:2.59*il*, 86:2.117*il*
    profiles of, 81:2.44*il*
    the same book done by multiple bookbinders, 83:1.14–15*il*, 88:2.55
    survey and checklist of edition hand bookbinders, 82:1.4–5+, 83:2.60
    Welsh, 78:1.14
    See Fine Print Featured Bookbinders (in the Names Index)
bookbinders in France. *See* France, book arts in
bookbinding collectors. *See* collectors and their collections (in Index by Names)
bookbinding conferences, 85:3.182–183, 184–185, 87:3.169–171
bookbinding exhibitions:
    Australian, 85:2.80
    British, 76:1.13–14, 78:3.79–80, 83:2.59+il, 84:2.48, 86
    Canadian, 89:2.59*il*
    catalogues, list of, 85:1.19
    catalogues of, 78:2.33–34+(catalogue insert), 80:3.94–95+, 83:4.171–172+*il*, 88:2.53–55, 88:4.175, 89:1.22+
    craft history, 79:3.72, 85:3.182–183
    Czechoslovak, Brno Trienále, 87:1.23–24
    European, 85:2.80, 85:3.184–185+, 85:4.193–195, 88:4.175
    Guild of Book Workers (bookbinders), 76:2.33, 82:2.70, 82:4.122–123, 83:4.171–172+*il*, 87:3.171, 88:2.55
    international, 77:1.13–14, 78:1.12, 78:2.33–34+(catalogue insert), 80:2.60–61+*il*, 80:3.94–95+, 85:2.80, 85:3.184–185+, 85:4.193–195, 88:2.53–55
    See also names of specific countries; names of specific institutions
bookbinding (history and types), 85:1.4–5
    accordion and foldout books, 82:3.113, 83:3.103+*il*, 84:3.114–115*il*, 85:2.109*il*, 110–111*il*, 85:3.168+*il*, 85:4.227, 86:2.76–77+*il*, 87:1.14+, 87:2.98–100+*il*, 100–101*il*, 89:2.57, 90:1.10+*il*
    American 20th century, 80:1.31, 80:3.94–95+, 81:4.135, 82:1.4–5+, 82:2.70, 85:2.121–123, 87:3.154, 169–171, 88:1.5
    American pre-20th century, 78:2.36–37, 81:3.83, 85, 82:1.15–18+il, 83:4.162–163+il, 85:2.121–123, 85:4.198–199, 87:2.63–64, 87:3.169–171
    art nouveau and art deco, 90:1.33–34
    bibliographies, 77:1.18–19, 87:1.6–7, 87:4.214
    book walls, 83:2.64–65*il*, 87:2.108, 88:1.34+
    bookseller's catalogues, 84:3.128–129, 88:2.55
    British 20th century, 76:1.13–14, 77:1.1–4, 78:3.79–80, 82:1.2, 83:2.59+il, 86:3.167+, 88:1.34+, 88:2.55
    British pre-20th century, 79:4.128–129, 81:3.83+, 82:1.35, 82:4.129+*il*, 85:1.42, 89:1.22+
    catalogues, bookseller's, 84:3.128–129, 88:2.55
    edition hand bookbinders, 77:1.14–15, 82:1.4–5+, 15–18+il, 83:2.72+, 87:2.75–78+il
    flutter fold, 87:2.100–101il
    fourteen variations of binding on same book, 83:1.14–15il
    French 18th century, 78:4.116–118
    French 20th century, 76:1.5–6+il, 84:3.128–129, 84:4.180il, 85:1.16+, 85:3.183, 184–185, 87:3.171, 88:2.53, 88:4.175, 90:1.33–34
    gift books, 82:1.15–18+il
    Irish and Welsh, 78:1.14
    libraries as supporting, 78:1.14, 80:2.60–61+il, 83:2.59
    trade books, 82:1.35
    trade decorated, 80:1.31, 82:1.15–18+il, 88:3.106
bookbinding manuals, 77:1.18–19, 82:1.35, 83:4.143, 84:4.180oil
bookbinding organizations:
    Hand Bookbinders of California, 75:1.6, 76:2.33, 77:1.13–14, 88:2.55
    Australian, 85:2.80
    European, 85:3.135–136, 87:3.152–154, 88:2.53, 88:4.175
    in the United Kingdom, 77:1.1–4, 78:2.36–37, 82:3.85–86, 83:2.59+il, 88:2.54
bookbinding organizations (by name):
    Les Amis de la Reliure d'Art (ARA), 85:3.135–136, 87:3.152–154, 88:2.53, 88:4.175
    Designer Bookbinders (London), 77:1.1–4, 78:2.36–37, 82:3.85–86, 83:2.59+il, 88:2.54
    Guild of Book Workers, 76:2.33, 76:4.71, 82:2.70, 82:4.122–123, 83:4.171–172+*il*, 87:3.169–171, 88:2.55, 94
    Hand Bookbinders of California, 75:1.6, 77:1.13–14, 88:2.55
bookbinding techniques and materials:
    alum skins, 76:3.41
    American, early, 85:2.121–123, 87:2.63–64
    blind stamping, 82:1.17
    and book spines, 86:1.46*il*, 52, 89:3.115+*il*, 90:1.37–39*il*, 90:2.72
    boxes and containers, 80:2.65, 82:1.12–13*il*, 84:1.20*il*, 23*il*, 85:3.184–185
    brass plate dies, 82:1.17, 83:4.143
    British versus continental, 77:1.1–4
    chemise and slipcase covers, 84:1.15
    cloth, 76:3.38, 82:1.17, 83:4.143
    color stereographic, 85:2.122–123
    concertina spine, 82:4.137, 85:2.110–111*il*, 85:3.168+*il*, 86:2.76–77+*il*
    designs catalogue, 83:4.143
    dictionary of, 84:1.21–23*il*
    embossing, 82:1.24–25*il*, 86:2.116–117*il*
    French 19th century, 78:4.116–118
    French 20th century, 84:4.180*il*, 90:1.37–39*il*
    French medieval and Romanesque, 87:1.51*il*
    gilding, 78:4.117, 86:4.216–217
    gold tooling, 79:3.86+*il*, 82:4.129+, 147*il*
    headbands, 82:2.54, 86:1.49–51*il*, 87:4.214*il*

incunabulum rebinding, 82:2.54+*il*
Japanese, 86:4.217–218+*il*
journal of, 82:3.85–86
leather, 76:3.41, 82:1.15–18+*il*, 24–25*il*, 83:4.143, 86:2.116–117*il*
letterforms in, 90:2.62–63+*il*, 67–68*il*, 72
machine-stamped, 80:1.31, 82:1.15–18+*il*, 85:1.42
metal covers, 82:1.12–13*il*, 19–21, 89:1.8–11*il*
miniature books, 88:2.54
for pages lying flat, 86:1.33, 90:1.37–39*il*
paper covers, 85:1.42
and pricing, 81:4.135, 82:1.5
quire guards for composite volume (sammelband), 87:2.68+
raised onlays, 82:2.70, 88:3.140+*il*
retrospective rebinding, 80:3.94–95+, 82:2.54+*il*, 85:2.107–108*il*
rubbings versus photographs of, 87:2.63–64
sewn, 78:4.119, 86:1.47–52+*il*, 86:4.230, 87:2.75–76, 89:1.8–9*il*, 89:3.114–118*il*
shower-cap, 82:2.61–62+*il*
and signatures, rubrication of, 87:2.104+
simplified binding method, 90:1.37–39*il*
single hinge, 87:3.171, 89:1.8–11*il*
standing books, 83:4.148–149
tools, 75:3.30, 79:3.86, 86:4.217–218+*il*, 87:2.63–64
transparent, 81:1.10–11*il*, 82:2.61–62+*il*
vellum 85:2.107–108*il*
Victorian paper, 85:1.42
visible structure in, 81:1.10–11*il*, 86:1.47–52+*il*
with wood boards, 82:2.54+*il*, 86:1.51–52*il*, 89:3.114–118*il*
See also bookbinders
bookmen. *See* booktrade and booksellers
Bookplate Collectors and Designers, American Society of, 79:3.72
Bookplate Society of England, 84:2.49+
bookplates, 85:2.81
calligraphic, 79:3.72*il*, 82:3.116–117, 82:4.126–127*il*, 86:4.224
books of hours, medieval, 78:1.22–23
Bookslinger Books [distributor], 89:3.130–131
booktrade and booksellers:
American, 77:4.102–103, 82:1.38, 85:2.128–129, 87:2.67–68, 87:4.216, 90:3.142–143
antiquarian, 77:4.92, 88:4.191, 90:1.36+, 90:3.101

British, 79:3.97–98, 85:4.192*il*, 87:4.216, 88:2.56, 90:3.145
European emigré, 88:4.191
of finely printed books, 81:4.119–120, 149–150, 89:3.130–133, 90:3.145
French, 82:2.65–67+*il*, 90:1.34+
French, early, 87:1.51*il*
Irish, 89:1.17–18
and leaf books, 85:4.194, 86:1.4, 88:2.56, 89:3.147–150
profiles of, 77:4.102–103, 79:3.97–98, 89:3.130–133, 90:3.145
See also publishers, commercial; trade books
border designs. *See* book design; type ornaments
Boston Type and Stereotype Foundry, 90:3.100–101*il*
botanical books and catalogues, 80:2.47*il*, 80:3.94–95+, 87:4.212, 89:2.72–73, 89:3.109
See also scientific illustration
botanical illustration, 80:2.47*il*, 83:2.76–77+*il*, 84:3.131–132
Bowne & Co., Stationers (New York), 77:1.12, 88:1.45, 88:4.163–164*il*
boxes, book:
exhibition of containers and, 85:3.184–185
several writing styles in, 80:2.65
for rare books, 84:1.20*il*
solander, 84:1.23*il*
thermoplastic, 87:3.170
Braille letterforms, 82:3.83
brass plate dies. *See* bookbinding techniques and materials
breathing marks. *See* punctuation and accents, and Greek letterforms
Bridwell Library (Southern Methodist University), 82:2.54+, 84:3.94–95, 87:2.66
British Isles, book arts in. *See* United Kingdom, book arts in
The British Library, 78:3.78, 84:1.18, 84:3.116–117
The British Museum, 87:1.5
broadsides:
accordion-fold, 86:2.76–77+*il*
American bicentennial portfolio of, 76:4.65–66
American poetry collection, 82:3.103, 83:1.23–25*il*, 88:1.38–39*il*
broadsheets compared to, 83:2.51–52*il*
classic, 90:3.104–108*il*
a definition of, 87:3.118–119
bicentennial portfolio of, 76:4.65–66
history of, 85:3.139–140, 90:3.104–105
polemical, 90:3.114–117*il*
primitive, 90:3.111–114*il*
typographic, 90:3.109–111*il*

Victorian, 85:3.158*il*
broadsides, reviews of. *See* Fine Print Broadside Round-Up (reviews)
Bryn Mawr College Library, 85:2.121–123
business of books. *See* booktrade and booksellers
business and economics. *See* economics; printing economics

C

California Antiquarian Book Fair, 75:1.6
California Historical Society collections, 76:4.76, 79:3.91
California, University of. *See* University of California
calligrammes, Apollinaire's, 89:2.87–88*il*
calligraphers, 82:1.29, 83:4.146*il*, 87:4.201–202*il*
20th century, 75:3.58, 84:4.155–163
East Asian, 90:3.138–140*il*
and handwriting, 77:3.58
exhibition of (Iceland), 82:4.152, 84:4.155–163+*il* (cover), 86:2.106
monographs on (reviews), 83:4.146–147*il*, 87:4.202*il*
profiles of, 76:4.69–70*il*, 79:1.7–8, 79:2.33–39*il*, 79:3.72, 79:4.118*il*, 82:3.116–117, 82:4.122, 126–127*il*, 132–135*il*, 156, 84:4.158–163+*il*, 86:2.103–107*il*, 86:4.235–236*il*, 87:2.82–86*il*, 87–89*il*
and commercial publishers, 84:4.155–163+*il* (cover)
See also scribes and script; specific individuals (in the Names of Persons and Fine Presses Index)
calligraphers and scribes, societies of:
London, 78:1.12, 78:4.115, 82:4.156, 88:2.90, 88:3.119
New York, 76:2.34, 77:1.21, 77:4.101, 82:1.29, 84:1.5
San Francisco, 75:2.13, 78:4.115
Calligraphers, Society of (pseud., W. A. Dwiggins), 87:2.88
calligraphic books:
alphabets, 89:3.109*il*
design of, 77:3.49–55*il*
reviews of, 78:2.45–46, 79:1.15–16, 79:2.55–56, 80:4.125+, 81:3.94–95, 83:4.146–147+, 88:3.137–140+*il*
scribal influences on, 77:3.52–55*il*
See also calligraphy manuals and sample books
calligraphic manuscripts. *See* manuscripts, illuminated; manuscripts, medieval
calligraphy and writing:
20th century, 77:3.49–52+*il*, 58, 66, 79:2.45, 82:4.132–135*il*

American, 75:3.26, 84:4.155–163+*il*, 183+(cover)
bookplates, 79:3.72*il*, 82:3.116–117, 82:4.126–127*il*, 86:4.224
Chancery cursive, 80:4.132–133*il*, 81:1.26+, 82:4.145+*il*
Chinese, 78:1.11, 90:3.138–140*il*
definitions of, 78:1.30
and drawing, 88:3.119+(cover)
electrostatic printing of, 79:1.15–16
exhibition reviews, 79:2.45, 79:4.119, 81:3.97–98, 82:4.152
French cursive, 77:3.71+*il*
Hebrew, 84:3.106–107, 108+*il*, 111*il*, 86:1.21–27*il*
implements for writing (histories of), 76:2.33, 81:3.97–98
Islamic, 78:4.97–102+*il*, 80:2.66+*il*, 80:3.75, 83:3.124–125*il*, 84:4.139, 85:3.156–158, 86:1.11–17*il*
italic, 78:4.119, 89:2.88–90*il*
Japanese, 77:1.13, 79:1.24*il*
Latin, 86:1.44+
museums, 89:4.198
and ornament, 82:2.64–67+*il*
philosophy of, 79:1.7–8
reproduction of handwriting and, 77:3.58, 85:1.46–48*il*, 87:1.6, 89:4.173–174+*il*
revival and status of, 78:4.118–119, 82:4.132–135*il*, 84:4.155–163+*il*
sho (Japanese), 77:1.13
teaching methods, 76:2.33, 79:1.7–8, 79:2.44–45, 81:1.26+*il*, 82:4.135, 85:3.148–149, 86:3.132, 87:4.202*il*, 88:3.120–121*il*, 89:1.15–17*il*
in type design, 79:4.120–123*il*, 82:1.33, 86:2.103–107*il*, 87:4.201–202*il*
in typographic books, 77:3.49–52+*il*, 52–55*il*, 79:4.120–123*il*, 80:4.125+, 83:2.70–71*il*
See also letterforms; type design
Calligraphy Center, San Francisco, 78:4.115
Calligraphy, Friends of, 75:2.13
calligraphy manuals and sample books, 86:2.67, 87:4.202, 88:2.90*il*, 88:3.120–122*il*, 89:2.88–90*il*
16th century, 81:1.26+, 82:4.145+*il*
gold leaf techniques, 86:4.216–217
penmanship, 82:1.19
See also calligraphic books; manuals (reviews of)
calligraphy societies. *See* calligraphers and scribes, societies of
Camberwell School of Arts and Crafts (England), 84:4.182, 86:1.40, 86:3.145, 147–148+*il*, 88:2.60–61+*il*
Canada, book arts in, bookbinders, 82:4.123, 83:2.44, 87:3.152–154, 89:2.59

Canadian Bookbinders and Book Artists Guild, 89:2.59
Canadian fine books, 78:4.107–108
Cape Dorset, book arts in, 78:3.75, 90–91
Carnegie-Mellon University Libraries, 86:3.132
cartography, 88:2.90–91, 89:1.33–34, 90:1.36*il*
globe gores, 85:1.18*il*,
cast type, metal. *See* metal type production
catalogues, auction house. *See* auctions, book
catalogues, book. *See* booktrade and booksellers
catalogues of exhibitions or collections. *See* names of specific book arts; names of specific institutions; names of specific individuals (in the Names of Persons and Fine Presses Index)
catalogues raisonnés. *See* under bookbinders
catalogues of type. *See* metal type production; type specimen books
catchwords, in medieval manuscripts, 82:2.70
Caxton Club (honoring first printer in England), 77:2.42
Center for Book Arts (New York), 76:1.11, 82:4.146, 90:3.142
catalogues and exhibitions, 82:4.152, 85:2.83–85, 88:4.176, 89:1.7
Center for the Book (national). *See* Library of Congress
Center for Typographic Language (Jack Stauffacher), 80:2.38
centers for book arts:
California, 79:4.117
Iowa, 85:3.182–183, 86:2.73–74+*il*, 87:3.171
Minnesota, 86:3.134–135, 89:3.131, 90:3.129
New York, 76:1.11, 82:4.146, 152, 90:3.142
Chancery. *See* calligraphy; phototypes; typefaces (by name)
chapbooks, 84:2.67–68*il*, 90:2.61
for children, 76:4.75, 90:2.58–59*il*
checklists, fine press. *See* catalogues, checklists, and bibliographies of fine presses (by name)in the Names Index)
Cherokee language, 81:4.134
chiaroscuro color printing. *See* color printing
children, learning handwriting, 78:1.24+
children's books, 76:4.75, 84:1.34–35, 86:4.219+*il*, 88:3.109+*il*, 90:2.58–59*il*
schoolbooks, type for, 81:4.144

See also chapbooks; folk and fairy tales
China, book arts in:
calligraphy, 78:1.11, 90:3.138–140*il*
first printed book, 90:1.7
handmade paper and printing, 83:2.50, 86:1.42–44*il*, 87:3.156+*il*, 90:1.5
Chinook typography, 89:2.81*il*
chromatic wood type, 83:2.46
clubs, book. *See* book clubs (by name); names of specific book clubs
coats of arms. *See* heraldry
codices:
history of, 78:4.114–115, 86:4.205–206+*il*, 90:1.7
St. Gall's (1987), 88:4.157–158*il*
codicology. *See* manuscripts, medieval
collaborations, creative:
author-printer apprenticeship, 88:4.160–162
book design, 81:1.5–6, 88:3.116–119+*il*, 137–140+*il*, 89:1.48–49, 89:2.83–86*il*, 96–99+*il*
bookbinding, 81:1.10–11*il*
custom papermaking, 77:4.77–81*il*
fine press books and trade editions, 81:4.116+, 145, 82:2.53+, 60–61
one text with multiple bookbindings, 83:1.14–15*il*, 88:2.55
collagraphy, 76:2.23
collection catalogues. *See* auctions; collectors and their collections in Index by Names
bookplates, 79:3.72, 84:2.49+
botanical books, 87:4.212
drawings, 89:3.135*il*, 139
hoax, 87:4.203–204
incunabula, 80:2.70–71
Islamic manuscript pages, 89:3.147–150
matrices, 83:2.49, 85:1.45–46*il*, 85:3.138
metal types, 80:3.77, 81:4.140–144*il*, 83:1.5, 83:2.69–70, 84:2.49+, 85:1.45–46*il*, 88:1.6, 45, 89:1.19–20*il*, 89:2.60, 89:4.189–197*il*, 198
paperiana, 78:3.91–92, 82:1.3+, 87:2.62, 107
papermaking, Eastern and Western, 89:2.57+*il*
pressbooks versus artists' books, acceptance of, 85:1.23–25
rare books, 78:1.22, 89:2.56
syllogue (collection), drawings of Roman inscriptions, 89:3.135*il*, 139
watermarks, 87:4.181
wood types, 83:2.43+(cover), 47–49*il*
See also libraries and collections, book arts; museums

collegiate fine presses, conference of, 85:3.153–155
collotype color printing, 80:4.109, 82:2.50
  practicum, 84:3.118–120*il*, 84:4.182
The Colophon: A Book Collector's Quarterly, 80:1.6–7
Colophon Hand Bookbindery, 81:3.78
color printing:
  Ben Day screens, 80:4.110–111
  blurred text (purposely), 84:3.110
  chiaroscuro, 80:4.108, 110
  collotype printing practicum, 84:3.118–120*il*, 84:4.182
  color plate book, first American, 79:4.110–111, 127*il*
  continuous tone, 84:3.101, 103+(insert)
  halftone screen, 80:4.110–111, 81:1.6+, 82:2.49
  history, first color plate book), 79:4.110–111, 81:2.39
  multi-color text, 77:3.58
  paper bookbindings, 85:1.42
  reproducing watercolors (William Blake), 82:2.49–50
  split fountain overprinting, 88:4.176+(cover)
  superannuated, 80:4.108–112+(cover), 127*il*
  theory, 80:4.108–112, 127*il*, 83:4.142
  two-tone black, 88:1.30*il*, 32+*il*
  wood block, 89:2.72–73
  See also illustration, book
color prints. *See* printmaking methods and illustration
Colorgraphics computer, 84:1.1(cover)
Columbus letter (1492), new printings of, 90:2.88–90+*il*
comics:
  a fine press book of, 86:1.39–40*il*
commissions for bookbinding. *See* bookbinders
common wooden presses. *See* hand presses
commonplace books, 86:4.196–198*il*
composition, metal type. *See* metal type composition
Compugraphic Corporation, 82:1.6, 10, 83:2.49
computer technology. *See* digital types and typesetting
concertina-fold books. *See* bookbinding (history and types); spines, book
conservation:
  bindings of parchment and vellum, 86:1.34+*il*
  of paper, 78:2.53–54, 80:1.31, 82:1.3+, 83:2.44
conservation of books, 82:3.85–86, 83:2.44, 87:1.7, 89:2.59
  acid-free paper for, 82:1.3+
  dictionary, 84:1.21–23*il*
  flood emergency, 79:1.8
  insect pests and the, 87:1.50–51*il*
  institutions for, 87:4.181, 88:2.56+
  and over-restoration, 80:1.31
  of paper, 78:2.53–54, 80:1.31, 82:1.3+, 83:2.44
  paper for, 78:2.53–54, 82:1.3+, 82:2.54
  philosophy and principles of, 80:1.31
  and rebinding, 80:3.95+, 82:2.54+*il*, 85:2.107–108*il*
  in secret caves in China, 90:1.7
  training in, 87:4.181
Conservation Department, Harry Ransom Humanities Research Center, 88:2.56+
cooking recipes, portfolio of, 87:3.173
copyright, 78:3.85, 81:4.116
  of graphic design, 78:1.12
  of type designs, 75:1.6, 77:1.12–13, 81:4.124, 82:1.6, 10, 87:3.162, 88:1.40, 88:2.87
costs, book. *See* pricing; printing economics
cover designers. *See* Fine Print cover designers (in Names of Persons and Fine Presses Index)
covers, book. *See* bookbinding techniques and materials
craft printing. *See* fine printing, the art of
CRT typesetting. *See* digital types and typesetting
Cuneo Fine Binding Studio, 79:3.72
Curtis's Botanical Magazine, 89:3.109
custom papermaking. *See* papermakers and papermaking (handmade); papermills
cut-out alphabets, 85:3.168+*il*
Cyrillic and oriental types, 83:3.124–125*il*
Czechoslovakia, book arts in, 87:1.15–39+*il*+cover design by Jan Jiskra
  beginnings, 20th century, 87:1.16–21*il*
  bookbinding, 87:1.21–24+*il*, 87:2.108
  illustration, teaching of, 87:1.32–33*il*
  printmaking, 87:1.5
  type designer profile (Menhart), 87:1.34–39*il*+(cover)
  typography, 87:1.19–21+*il*

D

Dada Archive. *See under* University of Iowa
"The Daily Reader" [fict.] news text specimen sheet, 89:1.23+(insert)
Dard Hunter Paper Museum, 82:1.3+
dating of early books:
  with glosses, 87:1.51*il*
  with watermarks, 86:3.154
deacidification of paper. *See* conservation
Dead Sea Scrolls, 86:1.21–22, 25*il*
Deadstart (journal), 81:4.115
dealers, book. *See* booktrade and booksellers
Deberny & Peignot (type foundry), 78:1.12, 82:2.46
decorated initials. *See* letterforms; manuscripts, medieval; type design; woodtype
demotic script (Greek), 87:1.48
design, book. *See* book design
Designer Bookbinders (London), 77:1.1–4, 78:2.36–37, 82:3.85–86, 83:2.59+*il*, 88:2.54
Designing Literature, series of articles on. *See* Index by Names
desktop publishing, 86:4.188
  books on, 89:1.5, 89:3.111
devices, printer. *See* printers' marks; specific press names (in the Names Index)
The Devil's Artisan: A Journal of the Printing Arts (Canada), 84:1.33
dictionaries and encyclopedia:
  book conservation, 84:1.21–23*il*
  book history, 88:2.88–90
  bookbinding, 84:1.21–23*il*
  bookman's glossary, 84:1.19–20
  Colonial American type ornaments, 76:3.52–53
  Diderot's Encyclopédie, 81:2.61
  Irish 18th century booktrades, 89:1.17–18
  Oxford English Dictionary, editing of, 79:1.19
  printing history, 19th century, 79:1.20–21
  publishing, 84:1.19–20
  See also directories and lists
Didot point system, 90:3.136
dies, brass plate. *See* bookbinding techniques and materials
Dieu Donné Press & Paper, Inc. *See* papermills (by name)
digital foundries (by name):
  Adobe Systems, 88:1.40–41, 88:2.53, 88:3.123–126*il*, 88:4.193, 89:2.60, 90:3.123–125*il*
  Bigelow & Holmes, 80:2.49+*il*, 86:4.238, 88:1.41*il*
  Bitstream, 88:1.40, 90:3.123
  Stone, 88:1.40–41*il*, 88:2.53, 88:3.123–126*il*
  Unger, Gerard, 80:3.102–103*il*
  See also metal typefoundries (by name)
digital types and typesetting:

Adobe Systems, 88:1.40–41, 88:2.53, 88:3.123–126*il*, 88:4.193, 89:2.60, 90:3.123–125*il*
   cathode ray tube (CRT) composition, 79:1.27, 80:3.102–103*il*, 82:1.9–10
   and computerization, 82:3.82, 84:1.7–9*il*, 84:3.93+
   and computerized composition, 77:4.98–100, 82:1.6–10, 84:3.93+, 88:1.24–25+*il*, 88:2.84+, 90:3.124–125
   designing of, 80:3.102–103*il*, 85:3.148–152*il*, 88:2.87–88, 88:3.123–126*il*, 90:1.19–20*il*
   ELF type design program, 84:1.7+
   irregularities in, deliberate, 84:1.9–10
   optical scaling, 89:2.76–77
   TEX + Metafont, 81:1.31–32*il*, 82:3.82, 84:1.8+, 84:3.93+
   See also letterforms; type; type design; typesetting
dingbats, type. *See* type ornaments
directories and lists of fine presses:
   American, 76:2.34, 83:4.151–153*il*, 84:4.172–173, 87:4.181
   British, 78:1.23–24, 81:2.57–58*il*, 84:4.172–173, 87:4.181, 88:2.56–77+ cover, 83, 88:3.140, 89:3.111, 111
   Canadian, 82:4.123+
   German, 82:3.86–87, 89:3.110–111*il*
   See also specific press names (in the Index by Names
   Dutch book arts museums, 89:4.198
   fine presses and other publishers, 86:4.189
   German book arts museums, 86:2.110–112
   hand bookbinders, for editions, 82:1.4–5+, 83:2.60
   hand papermakers, American, 75:4.42
   metal type suppliers, 85:1.22
   Western printing collections, 76:2.32–33
   See also dictionaries and encyclopedias, reviews of; directories of fine presses (reviews and news of)
directors, type. *See* Type Directors' Club
distributors:
   fine press book, 81:4.114, 145, 149, 86:4.189, 89:3.130–133
   paper, 76:2.21–23, 76:3.41, 45–47, 77:1.21, 80:4.136, 83:4.159–161, 87:2.60, 87:3.174
The Dolphin: A Journal of the Making of Books, 80:1.7
The Double Crown Club, 82:3.96–97+
Doves Bindery, 90:2.60
drawing and design of letterforms. *See* calligraphy; letterforms; type design

Drukkerijmuseum van het Grafisch Historisch (Etten-Leur), 89:4.198
Duke University Library, Friends of, 78:4.108–109
Duntog Papermill (The Phillipines), 87:2.60–61
Dutch book arts. *See* Netherlands, The, design and printing in

E

East Asia, book arts in, 90:3.138–140*il*
See also names of specific countries
ebru. *See* marbling, paper
economics:
   formula, book cost and list price, 87:3.137
   of book collecting, 78:1.22, 90:1.34+
   of book distribution, 81:4.114, 145, 149, 89:3.130–133, 90:3.143
   of calligraphy, 82:4.132–135*il*
   of handmade paper, 76:2.20, 76:3.45–47
   and limited–edition pricing, 76:1.11, 79:3.71, 82:1.5, 86:2.102, 87:3.134–137
   small press, 78:1.19, 80:3.80–81, 81:4.116+, 118–120+
   social economy of the book, 85:1.23–25
   typesetting, quality, speed of, 85:1.14, 85:3.136–138
   See also printing economics
editors. *See* specific individuals (in the Names of Persons and Fine Presses Index)
education and teaching, book arts:
   an author's apprenticeship, 88:4.160–162
   bookbinder apprenticeships, 85:1.16, 85:3.136, 87:3.153
   bookbinding, 76:2.33
   calligraphy, 76:2.33, 79:1.7–8, 79:2.44–45, 81:1.26+*il*, 82:4.135, 85:3.148–149, 86:3.132, 87:4.202, 88:3.120–121, 89:1.15–17*il*
   contemporary, 85:1.5–6
   directory of, 76:2.33
   graduate programs, 83:1.2, 84:2.74–77*il*, 78–81*il*, 84:3.134, 85:3.153–154
   illustration (in Prague), 87:1.32–33*il*
   letterforms, German, 86:2.103–107*il*, 113–114, 89:1.15–17
   papermaking, handmade, 76:2.24–25, 90:2.56+
   profiles of teachers, 79:1.7–8, 86:2.103–107*il*
   seminars, reports on, 81:2.66–69*il*, 84:1.7–10, 86:2.113–114, 87:3.169–171, 90:2.56+

   typography, 75:4.33–35, 78:1.3–4, 80:2.38, 85:1.46–48*il*, 88:4.170+, 90:1.8
   workshop versus apprenticeship models of, 85:3.154–155
   See also manuals; names of specific countries; names of specific institutions
Egypt, papyrus-making in, 79:4.117, 81:1.2, 83:2.50
electronic typefaces. *See* digital types and typesetting
electrostatic printing, 79:1.15–16
   and illustration, 82:1.21+*il*, 85:3.142–143+*il*, 86:3.176
encyclopedias. *See* dictionaries and encyclopedias, reviews of
endbands. *See* bookbinding techniques and materials
England. *See* United Kingdom
English Monotype. *See* Monotype Corporation
engravings. *See* printmaking methods and illustration; wood engraving; individual artist names (in the Names of Persons and Fine Presses Index)
Enschedé Foundry:
   borders and ornaments catalogue, 87:2.60*il*
   history and influence of, 89:4.189–197*il*
   and Jan Van Krimpen, 81:2.51–56*il*, 81:3.99–102*il*
   museum, 89:4.198*il*
   typefaces cast by, 77:2.42+*il*, 85:1.36*il*, 86:3.149*il*, 89:4.161+
epigraphy, Latin, 79:4.118*il*, 80:4.126+, 86:1.44+
   sylloge (silloge [*sic*]) collections of, 89:3.135*il*, 139
etching. *See* printmaking methods and illustration
European book arts. *See* names of specific countries
exhibitions (and exhibition catalogues), *See* libraries; museums; also specific names
exhibition reviews. *See* exhibitions under specific book arts; specific reviewer names (in the Names of Persons and Fine Presses Index); *Fine Print* 1975–1990 Tables of Contents
exhibitions of bookbinding. *See* bookbinding exhibitions
exhibitions, press retrospective. *See* specific press names (in the Names of Persons and Fine Presses Index)
experimental papermaking. *See* papermakers and papermaking (handmade)

experimental typography. *See* shaped poetry; typography, avant-garde or experimental

F

Fabriano handmade papers (Italy), 76:2.23–24, 76:3.41, 82:3.114
fabularies. *See* folk and fairy tales
facsimile editions (reviews of), 78:1.29
    Ars Memorandi Biblical literature, 82:2.43*il*
    bookbinding manuals, 19th century, 82:1.35
    calligraphy, 89:2.88–90*il*
    compendium of 19th-century books on printing, 79:1.20–21
    Dada archive (University of Iowa), 84:3.126–128
    Duchamps' notebook, 83:2.71–72, 90:1.6–7
    Fell types (Bishop Fell), 82:4.154*il*
    globe gores, 89:1.33–34
    letterforms book, 88:3.133–135*il*
    medieval alphabet, Italian, 84:1.16–17*il*
    Melville, Herman letter, 87:1.6
    on papermaking, Japanese, 85:1.56–57
    type ornaments, 87:2.60*il*
    type specimen, 1828 English, 87:4.203
    type specimen book, 78:1.29
    writing manuals, Italian 15th century, 82:4.145+*il*
Fairleigh Dickinson University, 81:3.87+*il*, 90:1.6
fairy tale books. *See* folk and fairy tales
Featured Bookbinders. *See* Fine Print Featured Bookbinders (in the Names of Persons and Fine Presses Index)
fees, author. *See* printing economics
"Fifty Books" exhibitions. *See* American Institute of Graphic Arts (AIGA)
Fine Binding and Book Conservation, Institute of, 88:2.56, 94+
fine press directories. *See* directories of fine presses
fine press histories. *See* catalogues, checklists, and bibliographies of fine presses (by name); specific press names (in the Names of Persons and Fine Presses Index)
fine press movement, the, 78:1.19, 85:2.120–121, 89:3.132–133
    in Great Britain, 78:1.23–24, 88:2.57–67*il*
    in the Netherlands, 89:4.187–188
fine press names. *See* the Names of Persons and Fine Presses Index
fine presses, *See also* press histories; specific press names (in the Names of Persons and Fine Presses Index)
fine presses, author relationships with, 80:3.80–81, 81:4.134–135, 88:4.160–162
fine presses as a business, 81:4.118–120+
    and calligraphers, 84:4.155–158+*il*
    commercial publishers, collaboration with, 81:4.116+, 145, 82:2.53+, 60–61
    cost and pricing issues, 76:1.11, 76:2.20, 80:3.92, 81:4.135, 82:1.5, 87:3.134–137
    and distribution, 81:4.114, 145, 149, 89:3.130–133
    marketing strategies for, 81:4.116+*il*, 119
    markets for, 80:3.74, 81:4.116+, 119, 85:1.11–14
    new, 76:4.71, 85:1.32–34
    prospectuses from, 86:3.145, 87:3.136
    publishing by, 79:3.84–85, 91, 80:2.45–46, 80:3.74, 80–81, 81:4.116+*il*, 118–120+, 82:2.53+, 90:1.48–49
    reviews, importance of, 81:4.119–120, 88:4.185–186
    and trade editions, 80:3.92–94*il*, 81:4.116+, 82:2.53+, 85:1.11–14, 89:3.131–133
    value of, 76:3.39–40, 86:2.66
Fine Print Broadside Round-Ups (reviews):
    1984, 84:3.104–113*il*
    1984 Introduction, 84:3.103
    1985, 85:3.140–147*il*, 174–175*il*
    1985 Introduction, 85:3.139–140
    1987, 87:3.119–125*il*, 164–168*il*
    1990 Introductions and groups of reviews, 90:3.104–117*il*
    See also Fine Print 1975–1990 Tables of Contents
Fine Print broadsides and special inserts:
    continuous tone lithograph, 84:3.103+(insert)
    hand bookbinding today: an international art, illustrated color catalogue, 78:2+(insert)
    newspaper type specimen sheet, 89:1.23+(insert)
    original letterpress broadside, 87:3+(insert)
    poetry broadside, 87:3.141–150(color foldout)
Fine Print color covers:
    split fountain overprinting, 88:4.176+*il*
    superannuated color processes, 80:4.108–112+(cover)
    using film positives and media on acetate, 89:2.60+screenless litho cover
Designing Literature articles, 87:4.196–200*il*, 88:1.26–33*il*, 88:2.92–93, 88:3.116–119*il*, 88:4.160–162, 89:2.83–86*il*
Fine Print and Pro Arte Libri (non-profit), 89:4.159–160
Fine Print Special Issues. *See* Fine Print 1975–1990 Tables of Contents
Fine Print Tenth Anniversary issue: 85:1
    acknowledgments, 85:1.73
    commemorative fine printers' designs on theme of "ten", 85:1.1+*il*
    publisher's Decennary Letter, 85:1.3–10
fine printers:
    collegiate, conference of, 85:3.153–155
    contemporary, 79:3.84–85
    exhibition of five California (review) 79:3.84–85
    interviews with American, 87:2.67–68
    Italian contemporary, 85:4.205–217*il*
    maverick, 87:2.67–68
    philosophies of, 77:3.54–55, 78:4.121–123, 79:1.1–6, 80:3.76–81, 80:4.115–117*il*, 81:2.58–61*il*, 81:4.135+, 135, 148, 82:1.27–29, 83:2.56–57*il*, 84:2.71–72, 84:4.174–175, 85:1.11–12, 88:4.164
    on printing poetry, 80:3.76–81
    profiles of, 78:1.1–4+*il*, 4–8*il*, 79:1.1–6*il*, 81:3.85+, 87+*il*, 88:2.92–93, 78:1.4–8*il*, 82:2.53+, 85:3.177–181+*il*, 87:2.67–68
    profiles of, women, 80:4.115–117*il*, 81:3.96–97, 85:2.103, 85:3.177–181*il*, 86:2.103–107*il*, 90:3.120–125*il*
    quotes from, 78:1.4–6, 82:2.52, 86:2.104–106, 89:1.6
fine printers' surveys, *See* directories of fine presses (reviews of)
fine printing:
    and artists' books, acceptance of, 85:1.23–25
    markets and pricing, 85:3.136–138
    Mexico, 83:1.33–35*il*, 83:2.44+, 83:3.87
    on metal type production, 78:4.115, 79:3.91, 83:1.4–5*il*, 85:2.86–87
    on papermaking, 76:2.24–25, 83:4.159–161
    on parchment and vellum, 88:1.5
    on type designers (ATypI), 78:1.12, 84:1.7–10, 84:3.93+, 85:4.192, 86:2.113–114, 88:2.87
    relation of paper, printing process, and typeface in, 76:3.37–40, 83:4.138–142+*il*
    and trade books, 85:1.11–14
fine printing, the art of:

American, 80:3.98
American book arts magazines, 80:1.4–9
American, critique of, 80:3.98
and aesthetics, 76:4.57–60, 77:1.4–6, 84:1.10, 84:2.85
songs and poems on, 85:3.162–163
See also color printing; typography; names of specific countries
fine printing conferences, 82:4.136–138+*il*, 84:1.4–5, 84:3.91–92
on American book arts, 81:4.132–135+, 90:3.142–143
in collegiate presses, 85:3.153–155
and typographers, 83:1.4–5*il*, 84:1.7–10, 85:2.86–87, 88:1.24–25+*il*, 90:1.19–22
Finland, rare books in, 88:2.56
The Fleuron—A Journal of Typography, 80:1.4, 80:4.129*il*, 81:2.51–52, 83:1.17, 86:3.159
fleurons, typographic. *See* type ornaments
foldout books. *See under* bookbinding (history and types)
folk art ornaments, 82:2.46
folk and fairy tales, 79:3.74, 82:2.43*il*, 83:1.22–23*il*, 83:2.54, 83:4.151*il*, 166–167+*il*, 85:4.207*il*, 86:2.69–70*il*, 88:3.109+*il*
and fabularies, 76:2.34, 81:2.49*il*, 64*il*, 82:3.98*il*, 83:1.26*il*, 85:2.123–124*il*, 86:1.29+*il*, 47, 50–52*il*, 89:1.31+*il*
and nursery rhymes, 82:2.58*il*, 84:3.109+*il*, 90:2.58–59*il*
fonts. *See* typefaces
footnotes versus endnotes, merits of, 87:2.91
foreign languages, typography in. *See* bilingual editions; type design
forgeries, identifying literary, 85:1.42–45*il*, 86:3.154
format of bindings. *See* bookbinding (history and types)
format of books:
from scroll to codex, 86:4.205–208+*il*
gift books, Thumb-Nail Series, 82:1.15–18+*il*
miniature books, 82:1.15–18+*il*, 83:2.78, 85:2.107*il*, 88:2.54
and pagination, 86:4.206–207
book portfolio, 81:1.24–25, 88:4.178+*il*
and proportions, 78:1.6, 86:4.206
and shaped paper, 83:3.103+, 88:4.176, 89:2.71+*il*
and signatures, rubrication of, 87:2.104+
and size, 78:1.6, 86:4.205–206, 88:3.116–117
three-part pages, 82:3.107–108, 86:4.204*il*
tracts or composite volume (sammelband), 87:2.68+
two-page spread, 80:3.79–80
See also book design
formats, bilingual. *See* bilingual editions, multilingual
foundry names. *See* metal typefoundries (by name); specific foundry names
Foundry type, American standard height (.918″) type production, 80:2.67–68, 87:4.181, 90:3.136–138*il*
Fourier analysis. *See* letterspacing, optical
France, book arts in:
bookbinding, 20th century, 76:1.5–6+*il*, 77:1.2+, 84:3.128–129, 84:4.180*il*, 85:3.183, 184–185, 88:2.53, 88:4.175, 90:1.33–34
bookbinding, pre-20th century, 78:4.116–118, 87:1.51*il*
booktrade in, 82:2.65–67+*il*, 90:1.34+
fine printing, 20th century, 86:2.80–86+*il*, 87–99+*il*
illustrated books, 84:1.23–24+, 84:3.128, 87:2.60
livres d'artistes, 86:2.111, 87:4.180
papermaking, 76:4.73–74
women printers in, 85:2.103
Franklin Mint Corporation, 78:2.36
freedom of the press (broadside), 90:3.114–115
Friends of Calligraphy, 75:2.13, 83:2.43
Friends of the Earth Foundation, 77:2.35–36
Friends of Paper, 76:2.34

G

gay fine press, 88:3.109–111+*il*
geometric letterforms. *See under* letterforms
geometric patterning. *See* type ornament
Geordie (Northumberland) dialect book, 89:2.67–69*il*
Germany, book arts in, 86:2.65, 80–117*il*
book design, influences on, 86:2.100–102
book illustration in, 77:2.25–30*il*, 41, 82:3.86–87, 85:2.123, 86:2.109, 87:1.43–44+*il*
education, 86:2.88, 105
Expressionist book illustration, 77:2.25–28+*il*, 31–32+*il*
fine presses, 89:3.110–111*il*
fine printing, 20th century, 86:2.80–86+*il*, 87–99+*il*
first illustrated book, 85:2.123
Klingspor Museum, Offenbach, 77:1.13, 77:2.41, 44, 83:1.11–12, 86:2.110–111
printer profiles, 86:2.80–86+*il*, 103–107*il*
typography, 80:3.101–1027, 82:3.87, 85:2.79–80, 86:2.100–102, 103–107*il*
Getty Museum, J. Paul, 90:2.60–61
gilding. *See* bookbinding techniques and materials
glossaries, book arts. *See also* dictionaries and encyclopedias, reviews of
glossed books, 82:2.65–67+*il*, 86:4.204*il*, 207–208+*il*, 87:1.51*il*
See also Biblical literature; manuscripts, medieval
glyphs, Aztec, 83:1.34*il*
Godine, David R. [publisher], 78:4.119, 79:4.102*il*, 80:3.100, 87:2.68
gold leaf techniques. *See* calligraphy manuals and sample books
gold tooling. *See* bookbinding techniques and materials
golden section, imposition by, 81:2.60*il*
graduate programs. *See* education and teaching, book arts
Grafisch Museum Drenthe (Netherlands), 89:4.198
Granary Books [distributors], 89:3.130–132
graphic artists, monographs on, 84:2.54–55*il*, 88:4.168–170*il*, 89:1.5
See also illustrators; specific individuals (in the Names of Persons and Fine Presses Index)
graphic arts, AIGA. *See* American Institute of Graphic Arts (AIGA)
Graphics Philately Association, 76:2.23
graphs, designing (review), 85:1.48+*il*
gravure, flat-plate. *See* printmaking methods and illustration
Great Britain. *See* United Kingdom, book arts in
Greek letters and types, 82:4.154*il*, 86:1.8+, 87:2.108
accents for, script, 87:1.49–50*il*
alphabet, history of, 83:2.66
composite Greco-Roman, 87:4.201*il*
letter about, 87:1.7
press books using, 77:3.57+*il*, 85:1.51, 86:3.147–148+*il*
and type design, 86:3.148–150*il*
used in a bookbinding, 81:2.46–47*il*
Grolier Club (New York), 82:2.51
Grolier Club, exhibition of 100 fine press books, 1978–79 (catalogue), 85:2.121
exhibitions, 79:4.119, 80:3.92–94*il*, 83:3.126–127, 85:2.82–83, 120–121, 86:3.158

title page designs by Bruce Rogers for, 84:4.150–151+*il*
Guild of Book Workers [bookbinders], 76:4.71
   exhibitions, 76:2.33, 82:2.70, 82:4.122–123, 83:4.171–172+*il*, 88:2.55
   Standards Seminars, 87:3.169–171, 88:2.94
Gutenberg Bibles. *See* Bibles
Gutenberg Museum (Mainz), 86:2.110

H

H. Wolff Book Mfg. Co. of New York, 81:3.106–107
Haas Typefoundry, 80:4.106, 82:1.7
halftone screens. *See* color printing
Hallmark Cards, alphabets for, 81:4.124
Hand Bookbinders of California, 75:1.6, 76:2.33, 77:1.13–14, 88:2.55
hand bookbinders. *See* bookbinders; bookbinding organizations
hand bookbinding. *See* bookbinding (history and types); bookbinding techniques and materials
Hand Paper Makers and Paper Artists, International Association of (IAPMA), 86:3.135, 87:2.60
Hand Papermaking journal, 89:3.110
hand papermaking. *See* paper; papermakers and papermaking (handmade)
hand presses. *See* handpresses
handbooks and manuals. *See* calligraphy manuals and sample books; letterforms books; manuals (reviews and news of)
handmade paper. *See* paper; papermakers and papermaking (handmade)
handpresses:
   as agents of change, 80:1.23–25+, 81:2.61
   Albion, 85:1.69
   apprenticeship on, 85:3.154–155
   at British fine presses, 88:2.58–66*il*, 93+(cover)
   Bobcat wooden, 76:2.25, 79:1.21–22*il*, 79:2.43–44
   common wooden, reconstructions of, 76:2.25, 79:1.21–22*il*, 79:2.43–44, 79:3.72, 80:4.136
   creative use of, 81:4.147
   cylinder, La Pedalette, 88:1.43
   first in the Americas [possibly], 83:1.33–35*il*, 83:2.44+
   Har-ma (new handpress), 85:1.32–34*il*
   history of, 82:3.83, 84:2.82–83*il*
   inks and inking, 76:3.38, 80:4.109–112, 82:4.146, 83:4.142+, 88:1.32+*il*
   makeready and presswork, 80:3.78–79
   museums of, 77:1.12, 83:1.33–35*il*, 86:3.132
   printing shop, view of, 80:4.117*il*
   reconstructions of wooden common, 76:2.25, 76:4.70–71, 79:1.21–22*il*, 79:2.43–44, 79:3.72, 80:4.136
handwriting, personal penmanship, 78:1.24+ (italic instruction), 79:2.36*il*, 82:1.19 (formal)
handwritten texts, 77:3.58, 80:4.125+*il*, 85:1.46–48*il*, 87:1.6
   correction annotations, 89:4.173–174+*il*
   See also calligraphy; manuscripts, medieval; scribes and script; writing systems
Har-ma Hand Press, designing new, 85:1.32–34*il*
Harcourt Bindery (Samuel B. Ellenport), 82:1.5, 83:4.143
Harry Ransom Humanities Research Center Conservation Department (University of Texas, Austin), 83:2.59, 60, 88:2.56+, 94+
   catalog, 84:3.129–131
Harvard University, 80:4.107, 85:3.187
   Houghton Library, 82:2.43*il*, 82:4.127, 84:1.23–24+
   Houghton Library exhibitions, 80:2.60, 81:2.44, 88:3.106
Hayle Paper Mill (Barcham Green & Co.), 76:2.22, 83:3.114
   film about, 76:3.49
   history of (1807–1987), 76:2.17–20*il*, 79:3.98, 87:3.173–174
   paper product reports, 76:2.17, 80:4.133, 82:3.114, 87:4.183
   watermark production at, 86:3.136–143*il*
   closing of, 87:3.173–174, 87:4.183+*il*
headbands. *See* bookbinding techniques and materials
Hebrew letters and types:
   and calligraphy, 84:3.106–107, 108+*il*, 111*il*, 86:1.21–27*il*
   Karmelitic, 86:3.133–134
   letterforms, 84:3.106–107, 108+*il*, 86:1.21–24*il*, 86:3.133–134
   type design, 86:1.7*il*, 24+*il*, 87:1.53–54
   wood type, 85:3.147
Helsinki University Library, 88:2.56
heraldry, 78:2.45, 58*il*, 79:3.88+*il*
   See also bookplates; printers' marks; watermarks for handmade papers
Herzog August Bibliothek (Wolfenbüttel), 85:2.123–124, 86:2.65, 111–112
historians:
   paper, 77:4.91–92, 81:1.2, 88:3.143

printing, 75:2.10, 76:4.75–76, 80:1.31, 84:1.25–26+, 85:2.129
histories of fine presses. *See* catalogues, checklists, and bibliographies of fine presses (by name); press histories; specific press names (in the Names of Persons and Fine Presses Index)
histories of printing, 82:4.123, 84:3.105–106
   in America, 76:1.14–15, 76:2.32–33, 76:4.76, 77:4.95–96, 80:4.113, 82:2.50–52, 85:1.64–65, 88:3.106, 90:1.8
   bibliographies of, 76:2.32–33, 89:1.7
   in China, 86:1.42–44*il*
   with collotype, 84:3.118–120*il*
   in color, 80:4.108–112, 127*il*
   in England, 83:3.88–91, 84:3.105–106
   and Gutenberg, 78:4.102+, 82:4.150+, 83:3.87*il*, 86:4.212–215+*il*, 87:4.180–181, 88:2.56, 89:1.12+
   and metal type production, 89:4.189–197*il*
   in San Francisco, 85:1.64–65, 85:2.102, 86:3.154–156
   and social change, 80:1.23–25+
   See also history of book publishing
histories of specific printing collections. *See* collectors and their collections in Index by Names; libraries, book arts museums
history:
   of American book arts magazines, 80:1.1(cover), 4–9
   of book design, 83:2.67
   of broadsides, 85:3.139–140, 90:3.104–105
   of cartography, 88:2.90–91
   of censorship, 90:3.114–115
   of handpresses, 77:1.12, 81:3.96–97*il*, 82:3.83, 83:1.33–35*il*, 83:2.44+, 84:2.82–83*il*
   of medieval scribe curses, 84:3.125
   of metal type production, 89:4.189–197*il*
   of paper, 78:3.81–82, 82:1.3+, 82:3.83, 83:3.104–105+*il*, 86:1.42–44*il*
   of paper marbling, 76:4.71, 81:3.76–78+, 83:4.165–166, 84:3.120–123
   of papermakers (facsimiles), 82:2.52
   of parchment and vellum making, 86:4.209–211+*il*, 87:2.107–108
   of scroll to codex, 78:4.114–115, 86:4.205–208+*il*, 90:1.7
   of writing implements, 76:2.33, 81:3.97, 89:4.198
history of book printing. *See* histories of printing

history of book publishing,
  84:2.50–51
 of Anglican liturgy, 88:3.106
 of book catalogues, 82:2.50–52
 and book design, 80:3.92–94*il*,
  83:2.67, 86:3.153–154, 88:3.106
 of encyclopedia editions, 81:2.61
 and intellectual history, 80:1.23–25+
 and printers' marks, 79:3.88+*il*,
  79:4.102–109*il*, 82:3.119+(cover)
 in the United States, 79:3.91,
  84:2.50–51, 87:3.116
 See also booktrade and booksellers;
  trade books
history of bookbinding. *See* bookbinding (history and types)
history of the book, 79:1.23–26*il*,
  82:4.123, 83:2.67, 86:3.153–154,
  88:3.122+
 American, 87:3.116
 American book arts magazines,
  80:1.4–9
 commonplace books, 86:4.196–198*il*
 contemporary, 81:1.23–24
 dictionaries and encyclopedias (reviews), 79:1.20–21, 88:2.88–90
 earliest complete printed (in China),
  90:1.7
 glossary, 81:1.23–24
 indexes, origin of, 86:4.207
 in Japan, 79:1.23–26*il*
 and leaf books, 82:4.150+*il*
 See also history of book publishing
history of printing. *See* histories of
  printing
history of typography. *See* typography
history of writing. *See* calligraphy; letterforms; writing systems
hoaxes, literary. *See* forgeries, identifying literary; humor and satire
Holiday House publishers, 89:2.100
Holland. *See* The Netherlands, design
  and printing in
Hollander beater, 83:3.95, 100*il*
Houghton Library. *See* Harvard University
hours, books of, 78:1.22–23 (review)
Humanities Research Center [H. R. C.],
  (University of Texas, Austin)
  See Harry Ransome Humanities
  Research Center
humor and satire:
 on Gutenberg's "wife," 87:2.88*il*
 "numismatic" book, 89:2.61*il*
 on paper marbling, 79:1.22
 spoofs and parodies, 78:1.13, 78:2.37,
  84:1.12, 87:4.203–204*il*,
  89:3.142–143*il*
Hunt Institute for Botanical Documentation, 80:3.94–95+

Hunter, Dard, Paper Museum, 82:1.3+
hymns, medieval Latin, 85:3.172–173

I

ideograms, Chinese, 79:1.24, 79:3.87,
  85:4.236–237*il*, 86:1.43
Ikarus digital type design system,
  79:1.30, 84:1.8+*il*
illuminated manuscripts. *See* manuscripts, illuminated
illustration, book:
 American, Colonial, 76:3.52–53
 biblical 15th century, 82:2.43*il*
 botanical, 80:2.47*il*, 83:2.76–77+*il*,
  84:3.131–132
 calligraphy and drawing,
  88:3.119+(cover)
 collaborative, 87:1.44+*il*,
  88:3.137–140+*il*
 color printing techniques,
  80:4.108–112, 127*il*
 computer imagemaking in,
  89:2.96–99+*il*
 and designing literature,
  88:3.116–119+*il*
 Expressionist, 77:2.25–30*il*
 French, 84:1.23–24+, 84:3.128, 87:2.60
 German, 77:2.25–30*il*, 41, 82:3.86–87,
  85:2.123, 86:2.109, 87:1.43–44+*il*
 history of, 76:3.52–53,
  79:3.86+*il*, 82:1.38, 82:2.43*il*,
  83:1.30–31, 83:3.91+, 83:4.143–145*il*
 Japanese, 79:1.23–26*il*
 photographic, 76:1.11, 80:4.109–110
 pochoir techniques for, 78:3.70–73*il*,
  80:4.111, 82:2.50
 pop-ups in, 83:3.102–103+*il*, 87:1.43*il*,
  87:2.100–101, 88:4.157
 silhouettes in, 83:1.11–12*il*
 stenciled, 80:1.18–19+*il*, 87:2.89*il*
 stenciled text and, 89:1.6
 watercolor, 81:1.1(covers, front and
  back), 5.4–8+*il*, 82:2.49–50,
  88:3.137–140+*il*
 See also color printing; printmaking
  methods and illustration
illustration, color. *See* color printing
illustration, wood engraved. *See* under
  wood engraving
illustrators:
 articles on, 83:1.26–29*il*, 87:2.82–86*il*,
  87–89*il*
 catalogues and monographs on,
  81:4.136–138*il*, 82:1.34–35*il*,
  84:2.54–55*il*, 84:3.129–131*il*,
  88:4.168–170*il*, 89:1.4–5*il*
 See also specific individuals in the Index by Names

Imago Handmade Papermill (Robert
  Serpa), 77:4.92, 81:2.38, 82:3.114
incunabula, 82:2.43*il*, 85:1.45, 90:2.88*il*
 Biblical literature, 90:2.89
 collection, 80:2.70–71
 leaf book made from, 82:4.150+*il*
 physical and textual investigation of,
  82:4.150+, 86:4.212–215+*il*
 rebinding, 82:2.54+*il*, 76–77*il*
 See also history of the book
indexes:
 origins of, 11th century, 86:4.207
 thumb, 89:4.178+*il*
India, books and handmade paper in,
  76:4.61, 79:1.20, 80:3.74–75, 84:1.12+*il*
 exhibition review, 84:1.18–19
 and paper marbling, 83:4.134–137+*il*,
  89:2.100
Indian languages. *See* Native American
  languages
indigenous languages. *See* Native American languages
indulgences, printing of 15th century,
  87:2.68+
initials. *See* bookplates; letterforms;
  manuscripts, medieval; type design
ink floating, Japanese (suminagashi),
  77:4.101, 81:3.77, 79–81+*il*, 89:1.21
 See also marbling, paper
inks and inking, printing, 76:3.38,
  80:3.78–79, 82:4.146, 83:4.142+,
  84:4.175
 and blind text, 87:3.127–128
 Gutenberg's, 86:4.214+*il*
 safety and suppliers, 90:3.101
 two-tone black, 88:1.32+*il*
 unimaged plates, 80:4.111
 See also handpresses
inscriptions, Latin, 89:3.135*il*, 139
 Trajan column, 79:4.118*il*, 80:4.126+,
  86:1.44+
insect pests in books, 87:1.50–51*il*
Institute of Fine Binding and Book
  Conservation, 88:2.56, 94+
instruction books. *See* calligraphy manuals and sample books; letterforms
  books; manuals (reviews of)
instruction. *See* education and teaching,
  book arts
International Association of Hand Paper Makers and Paper Artists (IAHPMA), 86:3.135, 87:2.60
International Association of Paper Historians, 77:4.91–92, 88:3.143
International corporate style, typography (Swiss), 84:3.125–126*il*
International Typeface Corp. (ITC),
  80:2.45, 87:4.214–215, 88:2.87
ITC Zapf Chancery (review),
  80:1.26–30*il*

Legacy type, 90:1.19–20*il*, 90:2.71*il*
licensing, 88:1.39–40
interviews. *See* fine printers; specific professions; specific names (in the Names of Persons and Fine Presses Index)
Inuit languages, 78:3.90–91+*il*, 83:2.58*il*
Iowa Center for the Book. *See* University of Iowa
Ireland, book arts in, 78:1.14, 89:1.17–18
   See also United Kingdom, book arts in the
Islamic books and manuscripts:
   and Arabic type, 83:3.124–125*il*, 86:1.9*il*
   calligraphy in, 78:4.97–102+*il*, 80:2.66+*il*, 86:1.11–17*il*
   collections, 83:1.2, 89:3.147–150
   geometric ornament, 82:2.47
   history of, 85:3.156–158
   in India, Hindu and, 84:1.18–19
   Koran, paper for the, 84:4.139
   leaves, selling of, 89:3.148–149
   paper marbling (ebru), 81:3.76–78+, 95+(cover), 83:4.134–137+*il*, 86:4.190+, 89:1.21–22
   See also marbling, paper
Israel:
   Dead Sea Scrolls, 86:1.21–22, 25*il*
   hand papermaking in, 83:2.50–51
italic calligraphy. *See* calligraphy
italic type. *See* type; typefaces (by name)
Italy, book arts in, 79:2.45, 80:1.13+, 85:4.193
   15th century, 82:4.150+
   16th century, 81:1.25, 90:1.34–36*il*
   contemporary fine printers and publishers, 79:4.105*il*, 80:2.44*il*, 82:3.116, 85:4.205–217*il*, 238+
   the Dante types, 85:4.219–222*il*
   medieval alphabet (facsimile), 84:1.16–17*il*
   papermaking, 76:2.23, 76:3.41, 82:3.114
   roman type origins, 89:3.134–141*il*, 90:2.69–71*il*, 76–77
   woodcuts, 15th century, 90:3.101+*il*
ITC. *See* International Typeface Corp. (ITC)

J

jackets. *See under* book design
Japan, book arts in:
   bookbinding techniques, 86:4.217–218+*il*
   calligraphy exhibition, Sho, 77:1.13
   Kanji typography, 86:1.10*il*, 88:3.124*il*
   printing and book illustration, 79:1.23–26*il*
   suminagashi marbling (ink floating), 77:4.101, 81:3.77, 79–81+*il*, 89:1.21
   typographic ornaments, 82:2.45–46
Japan, papermaking in, 77:1.15–16, 78:2.52, 83:3.92–93, 95, 84:1.13*il*
   international paper conference (1983) and, 83:4.159–161
   Kamisuki Chohoki facsimile, 1871, (review), 85:1.56–57
   nagashizuki, 78:3.85, 80:2.39+(cover), 40–44*il*, 53–55*il*, 83:4.159–160, 84:2.53, 86:3.146, 89:2.57+*il*, 90:2.56
   and paper uses, 83:4.159, 84:2.52–53*il*
   shiroishi shifu (paper fabric), 86:3.146–147
   washi, 77:4.100–101, 79:2.57–59*il*, 80:2.40–44*il*, 53–55*il*, 83:4.159, 85:1.56–57, 60–61, 86:3.146–147
   Western history of, 85:1.56–57
John Howell—Books, 85:2.128–129
Journal of Printing History, 89:3.113
journals. *See* magazines and journals, book arts; names of specific journals

K

Kemble Collection, California Historical Society, 76:4.76, 79:3.91
Kew, Royal Gardens of, 89:3.109
Klingspor Foundry, Offenbach, 78:4.121–123, 81:2.67, 83:1.11–12*il*, 86:2.110–111
Klingspor Museum, Offenbach, 77:1.13, 77:2.41, 44, 83:1.11–12, 86:2.110–111
Koran, paper for a, 84:4.139
   See also Islamic books and manuscripts
Kunsthaus Lempertz, 83:1.22–23, 85:2.112–113*il*

L

labor costs. *See* printing economics
laid paper. *See* papermakers and papermaking (handmade)
language:
   and letter frequencies, 89:2.81
   and literacy, 87:1.48–49, 89:1.20–21
   morphemes and phonemes in, 89:2.82
   and non-roman types, 86:1.6–10*il*+cover
   and phonetic types, 83:1.8–9*il*
   and punchcutting, 83:1.8, 86:1.6–10*il*
   written and spoken, 80:4.130–131, 89:1.20–21
   See also bilingual and multilingual editions; dictionaries; literacy; writing systems
Lanston Monotype. *See* Monotype Corporation
laser printing. *See* digital types and typesetting
Lasercomp typesetting, 82:1.7
Latin language:
   epigraphy, 79:4.118*il*, 80:4.126+, 89:3.135*il*, 139
   hymns, medieval, 85:3.172–173
letter frequency and texture, 89:2.81*il*
leaf books, 76:1.8, 77:1.14, 82:4.150+*il*, 87:1.50
   Ottoman, 85:3.135
   Persian and Indian, 89:3.147–150
   the selling of, 82:4.150+*il*, 85:4.194, 86:1.4, 88:2.56, 89:3.147–150
Leaf Papers (papermill), 81:2.38
legibility factors:
   rules (manual), 82:1.31
   typography, 80:2.65–66, 89:1(insert)
   See also reading; type design
letterers. *See* calligraphers; scribes and script
letterform alphabets:
   20th century, 86:2.70+*il*, 87:4.201–202*il*
   broadside, 84:3.104*il*
   calligraphic, uncial, 79:3.86–87
   Druidic, 79:2.47–48+*il*
   Greek, 77:3.57+*il*
   made of human figures, 89:4.198*il*
   made of single graphic, 89:4.166*il*
   medieval Italian (facsimile), 84:1.16–17*il*
   metamorphic, 88:4.177*il*
   pop-up, 85:3.168+*il*
   roman, history of, 88:1.6–8
   "St. Alphabet," 81:3.93+*il*
   wood engraved, 86:4.223–224*il*
   woodcut, 89:4.198*il*
   Zapf, Hermann, calligraphic portfolio honoring, 89:3.108–109*il*
   See also abecedaries; punctuation and accents; type design
letterforms:
   15th century, Greek, 87:1.47–50*il*
   accents for, Greek, 87:1.47–50*il*
   for bookbinding design, 90:2.62–63+*il*, 67–68+*il*
   Braille, 82:3.83
   constructed (geometric), 84:4.174*il*, 85:4.194+(cover)
   drawings for, 76:4.72–73, 78:4.118–119, 82:1.29–31*il*, 85:1.46–48*il*, 86:3.137*il*, 156–157*il*, 88:3.133–135*il*
   Druidic, 79:2.47–48+*il*
   essays on, 87:3.151–152+*il*, 154–156*il*
   geometric construction of, 84:4.174*il*, 85:4.194+(cover)
   Gothic, 84:4.176

Greek, 81:2.46–47*il*, 83:2.66
Greek 15th century, 87:1.47–50*il*
Hallmark Cards, alphabets for, 81:4.124
Hebrew, 84:3.106–107, 108+*il*, 86:1.21–24*il*, 86:3.133–134
history of, avant-garde, 82:4.141–145*il*, 87:3.155–156*il*
histories of, 76:3.50–51, 84:4.175–177*il*, 86:2.66–67, 106, 87:3.154–156*il*, 90:2.76–77
humanist and roman, origins of, 89:3.134–139*il*
inscriptional influences on, 79:4.118*il*, 80:4.126+, 86:1.44+, 53, 89:3.134–141*il*
Islamic, 78:4.97–102+*il*, 80:2.66+*il*, 86:1.11–17*il*
italic 16th century, 89:2.88–90*il*
italic upright, 80:1.28, 81:3.87
and letterspacing, 76:3.38, 77:4.98–100, 80:1.29–30, 87:4.212*il*, 90:2.67–68+*il*
linoleum cut text, 81:2.50+*il*, 63*il*, 84:3.98
non-roman, 86:1.6–17*il*, 21–27*il*
ornamented letters, 85:3.172–173*il*, 90:2.79–80*il*
ornamented letters, medieval, 79:3.86, 82:2.64–67+*il*, 84:1.16–17*il*
roman, 76:3.50–51, 79:4.118*il*, 80:4.126+, 84:4.174*il*, 85:4.194+(cover), 89:3.134–141*il*
roman, constructed, 82:4 (cover), 84:4.174*il*, 85:4.194+(cover)
roman sloped, 81:2.54–55, 89:4.195
signs and symbols, 82:1.29–31*il*, 82:2.43*il*, 47+*il*
spacing of, 76:3.38, 77:4.98–100, 79:1.28–29, 80:1.29–30, 84:1.9, 87:4.212*il*, 90:2.67–68+*il*, 87*il*, 90:3.124
stone-carved, 79:4.118*il*
teaching, 89:1.15–17*il*
Trajan column, 79:4.118*il*, 80:4.126+, 86:1.53, 88:3.139
upright italic, 80:1.28, 81:3.87
versals, 88:2.90*il*
wood-engraved, 78:3.83–84, 86:4.223–224+*il*
woodcut, 79:1.14–15*il*
letterforms books, 76:4.75, 77:2.41, 79:3.86–87, 88:3.133–135*il*
abecedaries, 76:3.47–48*il*, 79:2.47–48+*il*, 81:3.93+*il*, 83:4.149–150*il*, 87:4.201–202*il*
handbooks and manuals, 81:4.136, 88:2.90, 88:3.120–122*il*, 89:2.88–90*il*
medieval Italian (facsimile), 84:1.16–17*il*
Victorian, 85:3.158*il*, 89:1.19–20
letterforms, Greek. *See* Greek letters and types
letterpress printing:
business aspects of, 81:4.118–120+
calligraphers in, 77:3.55
color, 80:4.108–112+(cover), 127*il*
future of, 77:3.50
and offset, uses of, 82:4.146
paper for, 82:2.42, 83:3.110–112, 84:3.99–100
philosophy and techniques, 78:1.4–6, 80:3.76–81, 80:4.111–112, 81:1.2–3
phototype comparison with, 83:4.140–141*il*
safe materials for, 90:3.101
"typographic printmaking" term for, 80:3.76, 81:1.3, 81:2.59, 81:4.115
See also offset printing
letters, published correspondence:
book design for, 87:4.196–200*il*
See also Index by Names
letterspacing, optical, 77:4.98–100, 79:1.28–29, 80:1.29–30, 83:4.139–140, 90:2.67–68+*il*, 90:3.124
Fourier analysis, 77:4.99–100
See also phototypes, digital types
The Lewis Carroll Society of North America, 78:2.42
libraries and collections, book arts, 82:1.3, 83:2.45, 85:3.187, 88:2.56, 89:4.198
as bookbinding patrons, 80:2.60–61+*il*, 83:2.59
in China, secretly preserved, 90:1.7
as fine printing customers, 81:4.119, 149, 88:1.5
German, 86:4.189*il*
Islamic, 85:3.157
Library Company of Philadelphia exhibition, 80:4.113
See also collectors and collections (by category); museums; names of specific institutions
Library of Congress, 80:4.136, 82:1.3, 84:2.86
book history resources, 78:3.91–92, 88:3.122+, 89:1.7
books from, 84:1.20+, 88:2.53, 89:2.73*il*
Center for the Book, 78:1.12–13, 79:2.46, 81:2.38, 85:1.64–65, 87:3.117, 88:1.45–46, 88:3.122+, 89:1.7
collection catalogues, 80:2.71, 83:4.143–145+*il*
DEZ preservation process, 83:2.44
library exhibitions. *See* collectors and their collections in Index by Names; names of specific institutions
library of types, 80:3.77
Librije van de St. Walburgskerk (The Netherlands), 89:4.198
licensing:
of metal type and punchcuts, 86:3.132–133
of type, 88:1.39–40
limited edition bookbinding. *See* bookbinding techniques and materials
Limited Editions Club, 83:1.28–29
books from, 77:3.73, 81:1.20+*il*, 82:3.101–102, 86:3.173–175+*il*
limited editions pricing, 76:1.11, 79:3.71, 82:1.5, 85:1.11–14, 85:3.136–138, 86:2.102, 87:3.134–137
limp vellum. *See* parchment and vellum
line spacing. *See* letterforms; type design
linoleum-cut text, 81:2.50+*il*, 63*il*, 84:3.98
See also printmaking methods and illustration
Linotype Co.:
letter about, 87:1.7
and photocomposition, 88:2.87, 88:4.193
the trade name, 86:4.236
type anthology (review), 88:1.8–9*il*
type specimen book (review), 82:1.7+
typeface development at, 79:1.27–30*il*, 80:1.29–30, 80:2.45, 80:3.83+, 81:1.32, 86:1.9, 89:1.26–27
typefaces, 80:3.75, 82:1.7+, 87:1.7, 88:1.8–9*il*, 88:2.87, 88:4.172–174*il*, 193, 89:4.190+*il*
Linotype (machine):
an author learns the, 88:4.160–162
type sizes and measurement systems for, 89:4.193*il*, 196
linters, cotton. *See* papermakers and papermaking (handmade)
list price formula, limited editions, 87:3.137
literacy, and orality, 78:3.90–91, 81:4.134, 87:1.48, 89:1.20–21
See also language; reading
lithography:
continuous-tone, 84:3.101, 103+(insert)
image and text, 77:2.43*il*
origins of, 79:4.110–111
screenless, 89:1.23+(insert), 89:2.60+*il*
liturgical books, Anglican, 88:3.106
liturgical manuscripts, medieval, 78:1.22–23, 85:4.196
livres d'artistes, French, 86:2.111, 87:4.180
See also artists' books
Logos digital type design system, 84:1.9
logos. *See* printers' marks; watermarks for handmade papers
The London Mercury, 87:3.151–152
loom, paper mould, 83:3.114*il*

loose leaves. *See* leaf books
Ludlow Typograph Company, 87:2.61, 87:4.213+*il*, 90:2.70

M

MacArthur Prize Fellowship, 82:4.122, 88:3.104
machines, typesetting. *See* digital types and typesetting; typesetting machines
Mackenzie-Harris Corp. (typesetter), 81:4.118, 152*il*, 82:2.74*il*
magazines and journals, book arts, 77:2.42
    American (1903–1961), 80:1.1–4+cover, 4–9
    British, 80:4.129*il*, 82:3.85, 89:1.5–6
    Czech, 87:1.18
    European, 89:1.6
    German, 77:2.41
    graphic arts, 79:1.23
    Netherlands, 87:2.61
    paper conservation, 80:1.31
    printing history, 78:4.124, 80:1.31, 85:1.9, 89:3.113
    See also names of specific journals
Maggs Brothers Limited (booksellers), 88:2.55, 89:1.22+
manuals of calligraphy. *See* calligraphy manuals and sample books
manuals:
    18th century bookbinding, facsimiles of, 82:1.35
    on book design, 82:1.31+, 88:1.9
    on bookbinding, 77:1.18–19, 82:1.35, 83:4.143, 84:4.180*il*
    on boxes for books, 84:1.20*il*
    and letterforms books, 81:4.136, 88:2.90, 88:3.120–122*il*, 89:2.88–90*il*
    on safe printmaking, 90:3.101
    on typography, 81:2.59–61*il*, 82:1.31+, 84:3.125–126*il*, 85:1.46–48*il*, 88:4.164*il*, 170+*il*
    See also education and teaching, book arts
manuscripts, codex. *See* codices
manuscripts, illuminated:
    20th century, 88:4.157–158*il*
    humanist, 89:3.138–139*il*
    Ottoman, leaves from, 85:3.135
    renaissance (exhibition), 84:3.116–117
    renaissance, inscriptional style, 89:3.134–141*il*
    See also calligraphic books; scribes and script
manuscripts, medieval:
    collections of, 80:4.136, 84:1.23–24+
    decorated initials in, 79:3.86–87, 82:2.64–67+*il*, 84:1.16–17*il*
    essays on, 83:2.65–66
    European (1350–1525), 84:1.33
    evolution of books from, 86:3.153–154
    French, 84:1.23–24+, 87:2.60
    glossed, 82:2.65–67+*il*, 86:4.204*il*, 207–208+*il*, 87:1.51*il*
    liturgical, types of, 85:4.196
    museum videodisc of, 90:2.60–61
    organization of text in, 86:4.207–208+*il*, 87:1.51*il*
    ornament and layout in (Books of Hours [review]), 82:2.64–67+*il*, 87:1.50*il*
    Books of Hours, 14th- and 15th-century, 78:1.22–23
    production of, 85:2.107–108*il*
    punctuation and accents in, 82:2.64–67*il*, 86:4.207
    scripts in (review), 81:4.136
    See also handwritten texts; letter-forms; manuscripts, illuminated; scribes and script
marbling, paper:
    abar (Indian 17th century), 83:4.134–137+*il*, 174+(cover), 89:2.100
    ebru (Turkish), 81:3.76–78+, 95+(cover), 83:4.134–137+*il*, 86:4.190+, 89:1.21–22
    Fine Print covers using, 81:3.95+(cover), 83:4.174+(cover)
    history and bibliography, 76:4.71, 81:3.76–78+, 83:4.165–166, 84:3.120–123
    ink floating, Japanese (suminagashi), 77:4.101, 81:3.77, 79–81+*il*, 89:1.21
    and printing, 89:1.21–22
    techniques, 78:3.85, 79:1.22–23, 83:4.134–137+*il*, 87:2.80, 88:1.4, 88:2.96, 90:1.4
    See also ink floating, Japanese (suminagashi)
Marder, Luse and Co. typefoundry, 90:3.136–137*il*
Marius-Michel bookbinders, 76:1.5
marketing. *See* economics; fine printing
marks, author's personal, punchcutting of, 87:4.198–200*il*
    See also printers' marks; watermarks for handmade papers
marks, printers. *See* printers' marks; specific press names (in the Names of Persons and Fine Presses Index)
material culture, the book in, 85:1.23–25
matrices. *See* metal type production
Matrix: A Review for Printers and Bibliophiles (journal), 82:3.85, 89:1.5–6
medieval manuscripts, *See* manuscripts, medieval
Mère Cie. paper, 80:3.75
Mergenthaler. *See* Linotype (machine)
Metafont type design, digital program for, 81:1.31–32*il*, 82:3.82, 84:1.8+, 84:3.93+
metafonts, definition of, 84:1.9
metal type composition:
    broadside honoring, 85:3.144*il*
    from slugs, 83:3.87, 86:4.232, 87:4.213*il*
    makeready and presswork, 76:3.38–39, 80:3.78–79
    point system for, 80:2.67–68, 90:3.136–138*il*
    stereotypes, 86:4.232, 90:3.100–101*il*
    sticks, 80:3.73(cover), 83:3.111*il*, 85:3.144*il*, 87:4.213*il*
    typecases, 80:3.73(cover), 81:2.59*il*, 83:2.44, 85:4.216*il*, 86:1.1(cover), 4, 42–43*il*
    See also digital types and typesetting; typesetting machines
metal type design and punchcutting, 78:3.87–90*il*, 84:1.10, 89:3.113, 90:2.58
    Anglo-Saxon characters, 86:1.4+(cover), 6–10*il*, 86:3.165*il*, 86:4.228–229*il*
    Arrighi type (Monotype), 86:3.158–161+*il*
    the craft of, 83:1.5, 86:4.228–229*il*, 236
    Cyrillic and Near Eastern, 83:3.124–125*il*
    history of, 84:1.25–31*il*, 85:1.45–46*il*, 85:4.220–221, 86:1.6–10*il*
    and justification, 85:1.41
    and language, 83:1.8, 86:1.6–10*il*
    licensing of, 86:3.132–133
    Ludlow typograph, 87:4.213*il*
    matrices, pantograph for, 83:2.46*il*, 86:1.9
    museums of, 83:1.5, 83:2.69, 85:1.45–46*il*, 88:1.6, 88:3.143, 89:4.198
    personal marks, 87:4.198–200*il*
    of punctuation and accents, 86:1.6–10*il*
    tools, 86:4.228*il*
metal type production:
    American, 81:4.141–144, 83:1.29–30*il*
    American standard height (.918″), 80:2.67–68, 87:4.181, 90:3.136–138*il*
    and buying type, 80:1.31–32, 86:3.132–133
    collections, 81:4.140–144*il*, 83:1.5, 83:2.69–70, 85:1.45–46*il*, 88:1.6, 45, 89:1.19–20*il*, 89:4.189–197*il*, 198
    conferences on, 78:4.115, 79:3.91, 82:2.42, 83:1.4–5*il*, 85:2.86–87,
    and electrotype duplication, 77:3.67+
    future of, 83:1.4–5, 85:1.20–22, 89:4.196
    history of, 83:1.4–5*il*, 86:1.6–10*il*, 88:1.6, 45, 90:3.136–138*il*, 89:4.189–197*il*

and identification, 81:1.2
international variations in, 80:2.67–68, 90:3.136–138*il*
and language, 83:1.8, 86:1.6–10*il*
letterspacing, 76:3.38, 83:4.139–140, 87:4.212*il*, 90:2.67
manufacturers, 81:4.118, 87:4.181
matrices collection, 83:2.49, 85:1.138
matrices and punches for, 78:3.86–87+*il*
newsletter on, 79:3.91
of non-roman types, 83:3.124–125*il*, 86:1.6–17*il*, 21–27*il*
point system for, 80:2.67, 67–68, 90:3.136–138*il*
and preservation, 86:3.132–133
and private typefaces, 78:2.46–48*il*, 78:3.86–87+*il*
suppliers list, 85:1.22
technology of, 84:3.123–124
and typecasting, 81:1.24, 82:4.146, 85:1.20–22, 41, 86:4.229
See also metal type composition; phototypes; specimen books, type; typesetting machines; specific business names
metal type punches. *See* metal type design and punchcutting
metal type sizes. *See* type sizes and measurement systems
metal typefoundries:
closing of, 78:1.12, 85:1.20, 86:1.4, 86:3.132–133, 88:1.6, 88:3.143
histories of, 83:1.18–19+, 85:2.79, 89:4.189–197*il*
photographs, book of, 88:1.6
silhouettes of activities at, 83:1.11–12*il*
stereotypes, 88:2.91, 90:3.100–101*il*
type design in, 80:4.106, 81:4.140–144*il*, 82:1.6–7+, 84:2.49, 89:4.161–162*il*, 189–197*il*
See also metal type production; specimen books, type; specific foundry names
metal typefoundries (by name):
American Type Founders Co. (ATF), 78:3.91, 78:4.120, 81:4.140–144*il*, 82:4.146, 83:1.29–30*il*, 83:2.49, 86:3.159, 161*il*, 87:4.215, 89:3.113
Enschedé, 77:2.42+*il*, 81:2.51–56*il*, 81:3.99–102*il*, 85:1.36*il*, 86:3.149*il*, 87:2.60*il*, 89:4.161+, 189–197*il*
Haas, 80:4.106, 82:1.7
Klingspor, 78:4.121–123, 81:2.67, 83:1.11–12*il*, 86:2.110–111
Norstedt, 85:1.45–46, 85:3.138
Private Press & Typefoundery (Paul Hayden Duensing), 76:2.29–30, 77:1.13, 79:4.108+*il*
Schriftgiesserei Service Gerstenberg, 89:4.198
Stempel, 80:4.134–135, 82:1.7, 86:2.99, 86:3.149*il*, 88:1.6, 88:2.84+, 88:3.143
Stephenson Blake, 83:1.4, 89:4.195–196*il*
Taylor, E. H. [Pat], 78:3.91, 83:1.5
Tetterode, 89:4.190
See also digital types (by name)
Metropolitan Museum of Art:
exhibitions, 83:4.171–172+*il*, 89:2.59
Museum Press, 86:3.170
Mexico, fine printing in, 81:1.12–13+
first printing press (supposed), 83:1.33–35*il*, 83:2.44+, 83:3.87
and Zapotec writing, 80:4.106, 81:1.12
micrography, Hebrew, 86:1.22–23+*il*
Micronesia, papermaking in, 86:3.146–147
Middleton Collection (Bernard C. Middleton), 84:2.48
Mills College, 78:4.114–115, 83:1.2, 84:2.79–81+*il*, 89:2.56
See also Eucalyptus Press
mills, paper. *See* papermakers and papermaking (handmade); papermills; papermills (by name)
miniature books, 85:2.107*il*, 88:2.54, 89:4.165*il*
Minnesota Center for Book Arts (MCBA), 86:3.134–135, 89:3.131, 90:3.129
mitnaan paper, 83:2.50–51
Mohawk Letterpress paper, 82:2.42, 83:3.110–112, 83:4.130, 84:3.99–100
Monotype Corporation, 80:1.26, 80:3.82–83+, 83:1.4–5, 89:3.113
composition stick, 83:3.111*il*
English, 90:2.70–71*il*
phototype specimens (review), 82:1.7+
recut typefaces, 78:3.86*il*, 86:2.73, 90:2.70–71*il*
reproduction quality of typefaces, 83:4.140+
special and swash characters, 78:2.47, 86:1.9, 88:1.9
specimen books, 78:2.47, 82:1.7+
type designers working with, 77:1.13, 82:3.90–91+*il*, 85:4.219–222*il*, 86:3.158–161*il*, 89:4.195, 90:2.71*il*
typefaces, 81:1.14, 82:1.7+, 85:4.219–222+*il*, 86:2.73, 86:3.158–161*il*, 87:2.69–73+*il*, 108, 88:3.134, 89:4.211, 90:1.26–29*il*, 90:2.70–71*il*
typographers working with, 80:3.96–97, 83:1.17, 29
See also typefaces
Monotype, the trade name, 86:4.236
Mother's Papers (Pondicherry), 80:3.75
moulds, paper. *See* under paper
Mount Tam [printing] Press museum, 86:3.132
movie review, *The Name of the Rose*, 87:2.102–103
multilingual texts, typography of, 86:3.163–165+*il*, 90:1.17
Museo Nacional de Artes Gráficas (Mexico), 83:1.33–35*il*
Museum Enschedé, Stichting (Haarlem), 85:1.45, 89:4.198*il*
Museum für Kunsthandwerk (Frankfurt), 86:2.67
museums:
of 19th century type and ornament specimens, 83:2.49, 88:4.163–164*il*
of antique handpresses, 77:1.12, 83:1.33–35*il*, 86:3.132
in Belgium, 80:3.75, 88:4.192
in Germany, 86:2.110–112
of hand papermaking, 82:1.3+, 87:2.62, 89:2.57+*il*
of metal typefounding, 83:1.5, 83:2.69, 85:1.45–46*il*, 88:1.6, 88:3.143, 89:4.198
of Mexican printing, 83:1.33–35*il*, 83:2.44+, 83:3.87
in the Netherlands, 89:4.198
of printing equipment, 82:2.43, 86:3.132, 88:1.45
of wood engravings, 85:2.81, 89:1.4*il*
See also collectors and their collections in Index by Names
music texts and music:
experimental theater score, 85:3.167–168+*il*
Hungarian songs, 79:1.14
jazz duet, 87:3.127–128
Latin hymns, medieval, 85:3.172–173
Mexican folksong, 81:1.13+
opera (17th-c.), 90:1.12+*il* (foldout binding)
ragtime quotes keepsake, 84:3.95
songs and poems about printing, 85:3.162–163
Muslim calligraphy. *See* Islamic books and manuscripts

N

nagashizuki. *See* Japan; papermakers and papermaking (handmade)
Nahuatl (Aztec language), 83:1.34*il*, 88:3.131–132
The Name of the Rose (movie review), 87:2.102–103
names of fine presses and book arts practitioners. *See* Names of Persons and Fine Presses Index

National Aeronautics and Space Administration (NASA), 83:2.44
Native American languages:
- Aztec glyphs, 83:1.34*il*
- Cherokee, 81:4.134
- Clackamas Chinook, 89:2.81*il*
- Inuit (Eskimo), 78:3.90–91+*il*, 83:2.58*il*
- Nahuatl (Aztec), 88:3.131–132
- and oral literature, 81:1.134, 86:4.198, 88:4.186–188+*il*
- Quiche (Guatemala), 79:3.75–77+*il*
- Washoe Tribe, 80:1.15–16+*il*
- Zapotec, 80:4.106, 81:1.12

near-paper, handmade:
- amate (bark), 83:2.50
- papyrus, 79:4.117, 81:1.2, 83:2.50
- sample books, 83:2.50–51
- *See also* paper; papermakers and papermaking (handmade)

Nederlands Persmuseum (Amsterdam), 89:4.198
Neiman-Marcus, 82:1.22
Netherlands, design and printing in the, 89:4.175–198*il*
- advertising art, 89:4.183+*il*
- avant-garde book designers, 89:4.176–184*il*
- contemporary book designers, 89:4.185–186
- and the Enschedé Foundry, 77:2.42+*il*, 81:2.51–56*il*, 81:3.99–102*il*, 87:2.60*il*, 89:4.161+, 189–197*il*, 198*il*
- medieval xylography and protoypography, 86:3.153–154
- museums, graphic arts, 89:4.198
- overview, 89:4.175
- private presses, 89:4.187–188
- type designers, 80:3.102–103*il*, 89:4.161–162*il*, 189–197*il*

The New Bookbinder annual, 82:3.85–86
New England, private presses in, 82:2.52
New York Central Supply Co., 76:2.22–23, 77:1.21
New York Graphic Society, 80:2.58
New York Public Library:
- collections, 82:4.127, 87:2.62
- exhibitions, 80:2.45–46, 81:3.104–105*il*, 85:2.83–85, 85:4.194

Newberry Library (University of Chicago), 82:4.123, 83:2.44, 86:2.123, 89:1.7
newspapers:
- an old printing office for, 86:1.28*il*
- origins of, 90:3.105
- text types, 79:1.25, 83:1.18, 85:3.143+*il*, 89:1.23–30*il*+(insert)
- type specimens, 89:1.23–30*il*+(insert)

The Next Call journal, 89:4.177–178+*il*

non-roman types (*Fine Print* January 1986 Special Issue), 86:1.6–17*il*, 21–27*il*
Norstedt Collection catalogue, 85:1.45–46, 85:3.138
Northern Illinois University, 79:1.21–22
Northwestern University Library, 79:3.72
"novel," typographic manual as, 88:4.164*il*
numbering methods, text:
- pagination and foliation, 86:4.206–207
- rubrication of signatures, 87:2.104+
- *See also* format of books
numismatic edition, spoof, 89:2.61*il*

O

obituaries. *See* specific individuals (in the Names of Persons and Fine Presses Index)
Offenbach Workshop, 76:4.69–70*il*, 81:2.66–67*il*, 86:2.88
offset printing, 77:3.50, 80:3.99, 81:4.120
- and letterpress, uses of, 82:4.146
- paper for, 83:3.110–111
- *See also* letterpress printing
Ogham (druidic alphabet), 79:2.47–48+*il*
optical letterspacing. *See* letterspacing, optical
oral literature:
- Czech folktales, 84:4.171*il*
- native American, 79:3.75–77+*il*, 80:1.15–16+*il*, 81:4.134, 86:4.198, 88:4.186–188+*il*
- preservation of, 81:1.13+, 81:4.134
- and writing systems, 86:4.207
oral literature, printing of, 81:1.13+, 84:4.171*il*, 88:4.186–188+*il*
orality, and literacy, 78:3.90–91, 81:4.134, 87:1.48, 89:1.20–21
Origin Books (bookshop), 89:3.130–132
ornament:
- bibliographies on, 82:2.44–47+*il*, 88:1.9–10*il*
- from natural forms, 82:2.44–45*il*
- geometric and typographic, 82:2.45*il*
- Japanese, 82:2.45–46
- pattern analysis of, 82:2.47+
- as unnecessary in books, 80:3.80
- *See also* stencil ornament; type ornaments
ornament, medieval. *See* manuscripts, medieval
ornaments, type. *See* type ornaments
Oxford University. *See* Oxford University Press (in the Names of Persons and Fine Presses Index)

P

Pacific Center for the Book Arts (now San Francisco Center for Book Arts), 79:4.117
The Packet magazine, 80:1.5–6
page design. *See* book design
painters' books. *See* artists' books
painting:
- paper pulp, 83:3.102–103+*il*, 84:1.12, 86:3.145+*il*, 88:1.11–13*il*
- Renaissance manuscripts (exhibition), 84:3.116–117
- watercolor illustrations, 81:1.4–8+*il*, 82:2.49–50, 88:3.140+*il*
- *See also* medieval manuscripts, illuminated
paleography, 82:4.154, 83:2.65–66, 84:3.132–133
pantograph devices, 83:2.46*il*, 86:1.9
paper:
- aesthetics of, 78:1.6, 81:2.59, 82:3.114, 83:3.92–101+*il*, 98, 99+, 88:3.138
- Arabic early, 86:4.188
- attributes of, technical, 82:3.114
- bark (amate), 82:2.50
- in China, 83:2.50, 86:1.42–44*il*, 87:3.156+, 90:1.5
- choice of handmade, 76:2.19–20*il*, 21–23, 76:3.38, 80:3.74–75, 80, 81:2.59, 82:4.136–137, 84:1.12, 86:2.120, 88:3.138, 90:1.8–9
- commercial, 80:3.80, 86:2.102
- Mohawk Letterpress, 82:2.42, 83:3.110–112, 84:3.99–100
- conservation of handmade, 78:2.53–55, 80:1.31, 82:1.3+, 83:2.44
- cost of handmade, 76:2.20, 21, 76:3.46, 81:4.118
- cotton linters for, 81:2.41–43
- ethnography of handmade, 83:2.50–51
- for conservation of books, 78:2.53–55, 80:1.31, 82:1.3+, 82:2.54
- in Gutenberg Bible, 86:4.213, 233*il*
- history of, 78:3.81–82, 82:1.3+, 82:3.83, 83:3.104–105+*il*, 86:1.42–44*il*, 87:3.172
- for a Koran, 84:4.139
- kōzo (Japan), 84:1.13*il*
- laid, 81:2.59, 83:3.113–115*il*
- moulds, 80:3.74–75, 80, 83:3.104–105+*il*, 113–115*il*
- paper pulp illustrations, 83:3.103+
- permanence, standards and symbol for, in books, 86:2.66
- plant fibres for, 77:4.100–101, 80:2.53–55*il*, 81:2.40–41, 81:4.114–115, 83:2.50–51, 84:2.52–53, 85:3.136, 86:3.135, 146–147, 87:1.5, 6,

87:2.79–80, 87:3.156+*il*, 172–173, 90:2.56
See also paper, raw materials for
pulp painting, 83:3.102–103+*il*, 84:1.12, 86:3.145+*il*, 88:1.11–13*il*
rag, 79:1.20, 81:2.41–43
raw materials for, 79:1.20, 79:3.73, 81:2.40–43+*il*, 81:4.114–115, 83:2.50–51, 83:3.92–101+*il*
See also paper, plant fibers for
recycled, 81:2.41–43
relation of printing process and typefaces to, 77:3.54, 78:1.5, 83:4.138–142+*il*, 89:1.23–30*il*
shaped, 83:3.103+, 88:4.176, 89:2.71+*il*
shiroishi shifu (paper fabric) 86:3.146–147
sizing, 81:2.43+, 81:4.114, 84:4.139
sorting handmade, 77:2.39–40
standards for permanent paper, 86:2.66
suppliers, 76:2.21–23, 76:3.45–47, 76:4.61, 79:1.19–20, 79:3.88, 80:4.136, 83:3.92–101+*il*, 83:4.159–161, 166, 87:2.60, 88:2.95
uses in Japan, 83:4.159, 84:2.52–53
washi, in Japan, 77:4.100–101, 79:2.57–59*il*, 80:2.40–44*il*, 53–55*il*, 83:4.159, 85:1.56–57, 86:3.146–147
watercolor, 81:1.5
western book paper, 83:3.92–101+*il*
woodpulps for, 81:2.41
See also near-paper; parchment and vellum; July 1983 *Fine Print* Special Issue
Paper and Book Intensive (PBI) seminar, 86:3.147, 90:2.56+
paper bookbindings, Victorian, 85:1.42
paper conservation. *See* conservation
paper distributors, 76:2.21–23, 76:3.41, 45–47, 77:1.21, 80:4.136, 83:4.159–161, 87:2.60, 87:3.174
paper for letterpress and offset, 83:3.110–111
paper handling techniques:
and acid-free standards, 82:1.3
dampening, 76:2.19–20*il*, 76:3.39, 79:4.111
deacidification and preservation, 83:2.44
laboratory tests, 83:3.110–112, 84:3.99–100
See also conservation; papermakers and papermaking (handmade)
Paper Historians, International Association of, 77:4.91–92, 88:3.143
Paper Historians, International Congress of, 81:1.2
Paper Makers and Paper Artists, International Association of (IAPMA), 86:3.135, 87:2.60
paper marbling. *See* marbling, paper
paper mills. *See* papermills (by name); papermills (handmade)
paper museums and collections, 82:1.3+, 87:2.62, 89:2.57+*il*
papermaker trademarks. *See* papermills (by name); watermarks for handmade papers
papermakers and papermaking (handmade), 85:1.5
American, 77:4.77–81*il*, 79:3.88, 83:3.92–101+*il*, 104–105+*il*, 84:4.139, 89:3.110, 90:1.5, 75:4.42
art and technology in, 83:3.92–101+*il*, 119–121*il*
beaters for, 83:3.95, 100*il*, 84:2.52*il*
in Britain, 76:2.17–20*il*, 76:4.71, 82:2.52, 82:3.114, 88:3.143, 89:3.120–121*il*, 90:3.140–141*il*
characteristics of, 83:3.95+
in China, 83:2.50, 87:3.156+
conferences on, 76:2.24–25, 83:4.159–161
contemporary, 77:4.77–81*il*, 79:3.88, 83:3.92–101+*il*, 119–121*il*, 84:1.11–13+*il*, 90:1.5, 90:2.56+
the earliest (China), 87:3.172
experimental and primitive, 77:2.38, 77:4.100–101, 80:2.68, 83:2.50–51, 85:3.136, 86:3.146–147, 90:2.56+
in France, 76:4.73–74
histories of (facsimiles), 82:2.50–52
history collections, 82:1.3+, 87:2.62, 89:2.57+*il*
Hollander beaters for, 83:3.95, 100*il*
in India, 76:4.61, 79:1.20, 80:3.74–75, 84:1.12+*il*
in Israel, 83:2.50–51, 84:1.13*il*
in Italy, 76:2.23, 76:3.41, 82:3.114
in Japan, 77:1.15–16, 78:2.52, 78:3.85, 79:2.57–59*il*, 80:2.39+(cover), 40–44*il*, 53–55*il*, 83:3.92–93, 95, 83:4.159–160, 84:2.52–53*il*, 85:1.56–57, 60*il*, 86:3.146–147, 89:2.59*il*, 90:2.56
for the Koran, 84:4.139
in Micronesia, 86:3.146–147
moulds, wire mesh for, 83:3.114*il*, 86:3.141*il*
museums and collections, 82:1.3+, 87:2.62, 89:2.57+*il*
on space shuttle Columbia, 87:2.61–62
study of, 85:4.193, 90:2.56+
water for, 81:2.43
Western book paper, 83:3.92–101+*il*, 90:1.5
worldwide surveys of (reviews), 84:1.11–13+*il*, 90:1.8–9*il*
See also papermills (by name); watermarks for handmade papers
papermills, handmade (by name):
Ashling Press and Handmade Papers, 77:2.38, 78:2.35
Dieu Donné Press & Paper, 79:3.73, 83:3.98, 88:3.121+*il*
Duntog Papermill, 87:2.60–61
Fabriano, 76:2.23–24, 76:3.41, 82:3.114
Hayle Mill (Barcham Green & Co.), 76:2.17–20*il*, 17, 22, 76:3.49, 79:3.98, 82:3.114, 83:3.114, 86:3.136–143*il*, 87:3.173–174, 87:4.183+*il*
Imago Handmadé Papermill (Robert Serpa), 77:4.92, 81:2.38, 82:3.114, 83:3.117–119+*il*
Leaf Papers, 81:2.38
St. Cuthberts Paper Mill, 76:2.22
Sea Pen Press and Papermill (Suzanne Ferris and Neal Bonham), 88:2.95
books from, 78:3.75–76, 79:3.74, 80:4.123, 83:2.54–55, 85:2.110–111*il*, 87:2.79–80
broadsides from, 81:4.129, 84:3.110, 87:3.121+*il*
press marks, 79:4.108*il*
Siegenthaler Paper Mill, 77:2.38
Sri Aurobindo Ashram, 76:4.61
Twinrocker Handmade Paper, Inc. (Kathryn and Howard Clark), 76:2.22, 77:4.77–81*il*, 84, 82:3.114, 83:3.93–95, 103+*il*, 106*il*, 84:4.139, 86:3.144–145+*il*, 90:1.5
Wookey Hole Paper Mill, 76:4.71
papermills, 76:2.21–23, 76:3.45–47, 79:1.19–20
American, 77:4.77–81*il*, 83:3.93–95, 90:2.61
closing of, 87:3.173–174, 87:4.183+*il*
in England, 76:2.17–20*il*, 76:4.71, 82:2.52, 82:3.114, 87:3.173–174, 88:3.143, 89:3.120–121*il*
histories of, 77:4.77–81*il*, 79:3.98, 83:3.127, 86:3.136–143*il*
water for, 81:2.43
worldwide survey of (review), 84:1.11–13+*il*
See also papermakers and papermaking (handmade); names of specific papermills; names of specific individuals
papyri, photographic archive of, 81:1.2
papyrus-making in Egypt, 79:4.117, 83:2.50
parchment and vellum, 82:2.76–77+*il*, 86:1.47+*il*

books printed on, 20th century, 86:1.34+il, 88:4.157–158
conference on, 88:1.5
conservation bindings of, 86:1.34+il
edition binding of, 87:2.75–78+il
fine press books printed on, 85:2.107–108il, 86:1.34+il
history of, 86:4.209–211+il, 87:2.107–108
indulgence printed on, 15th century, 87:2.68+
making ancient and 20th century, 86:4.209–211+il, 87:2.107–108, 89:4.161
See also bookbinding techniques and materials
parodies. *See* humor and satire
patterns, ornamental. *See* ornament in books; type ornaments
patterns, text. *See* shaped poetry; typography; visual imagery within text
Penguin Books, 76:3.52, 80:1.31, 84:3.110+il, 87:2.107
trademarks, evolution of, 88:3.105il
periodicals. *See* magazines and journals, book arts
Philadelphia Museum of Art, 90:1.6–7
philately, graphics, 76:2.23
Philippines, hand papermaking in (Duntog), 87:2.60–61
philosophy and principles:
of book conservation, 80:1.31
and book production, 80:3.76–81, 81:2.58–61il, 86:3.156
of calligraphy, 79:1.7–8
of craft printing of poetry, 80:3.76–81
of form in seriffed typefaces, 88:4.171–174il
of letterpress printing, 78:1.4–6, 80:3.76–81, 80:4.111–112, 81:1.2–3
in trade book publishing, 85:1.11–14
See also book design; fine printing; specific book arts topics
phonetic typeface. *See* typefaces
photocomposition. *See* typesetting; phototypes
photocopying:
calligraphy, 79:1.15–16
images, 82:1.21+il, 85:3.142–143+il, 86:3.176
photographic illustration, 76:1.11
and color separation, 80:4.109–110
photographs and portraits of book arts practitioners:
book designers, 86:2.108il, 87:2.83il, 87il
book illustrators, 81:4.137il, 82:3.91il, 86:2.108il
bookbinders, 80:2.59il, 86:2.117il
calligraphers, 82:3.91il, 89:1(insert)

cartographer, 81:1.28il
in fine printing shops (groups), 84:2.56il, 85:2.101il, 128+(cover)
hand papermakers, 77:4.80il, 80:2.39+(cover)
men, 78:1.8il, 80:1.20il, 81:4.137il, 82:3.91il, 82:4.147il, 84:2.56il, 77il, 85:1.28il, 85:4.215–217il, 86:2.108il, 117il, 88:2.63–64il, 89:1.23+(newspaper types specimen sheet insert)
printer, fine commercial (Italian), 85:4.217il
scribes, women, 16th and 17th c., 85:2.91il, 100il
setting type, 85:2.101il, 103il
type designers, 81:1.26il, 82:3.91il, 89:1+(insert), 90:3.125il
typographers, 81:4.137il, 86:3.161il
women, 78:1.26il, 80:2.59il, 80:4.117il, 82:4.147il, 84:2.56il, 77il, 78il, 85:2.91il, 100il, 101il, 103il, 85:3.176il, 85:4.216il, 86:2.82il, 88:2.63–64il
working at presses, 84:2.56il, 85:1.33il, 85:2.101il
writing mistresses, 16th–17th century, 85:2.91il, 100il
phototypes:
composition of, 80:1.29–30, 82:1.6–10
designing for, 79:1.27–30il, 80:1.26–30il, 88:2.84+, 89:1.27
Greek types, 87:1.7
Hebrew, 86:1.24+il
letterpress comparison with, 83:4.140–141il
optical scaling of, 89:2.76–77
printing process and calligraphy, 77:3.54
printing processes and paper, relationship to, 83:4.138–142+il
sans serif, 80:3.103il, 88:4.171–172il
seriffed, 88:4.172–174il
specimen books (review), 82:1.6–10+il
typographic "novel" [manual] using, 88:4.164il
Zapf Chancery (ITC), 80:1.26–30il
See also digital types and typesetting
photo-electric spacing of, 77:4.98–100, 79:1.28–29, 80:1.29–30, 90:3.124
phototypesetting, development of, 79:1.30, 80:3.83–84, 100, 86:2.102, 89:1.27
phototypesetting, variations among systems of, 82:1.33
pica system. *See* type sizes and measurement systems
The Pittsburgh Bibliophiles, 78:3.78, 79:1.17

pixels. *See* digital types and typesetting
plant fibres. *See* under papermakers and papermaking
Plantin-Moretus Museum (Antwerp), 80:3.75, 88:4.192
plates. *See* color printing; printmaking methods and illustration
pochoir illustration, 78:3.70–73il, 79:3.84, 80:4.111, 82:2.50, 82:3.92il, 87:2.86+il
See also color printing; illustration
poetry:
about printing, Scottish, 85:3.162–163
Anglo-Saxon, 75:4.39
concrete and visual, 79:2.51, 81:2.59, 88:4.176
craft printing of, 80:3.76–81, 81:2.58–61
Frost, Robert and his printers, 86:3.157+il
Futurist, 86:2.76–77il
Japanese, 79:2.55–56
medieval Latin devotional, 85:3.172–173
Nahuatl (Aztec), 88:3.131–132
shaped poetry, 78:1.15+il, 78:3.80, 78:4.106, 81:1.18, 83:1.12–13+il, 89:2.87–88il
Spanish ancient ballads, 75:4.37il
in two voices, 8:73.127–128
typography of, 80:3.76–81, 98, 80:4.120, 81:3.108, 81:4.121, 82:3.103, 107–108, 83:1.12–13+il, 85:2.116–117il, 88:3.131–132, 89:2.87–88il
women's broadsides, portfolio of, 83:1.23–24+il
See also Fine Print Broadside Roundups
point system. *See* type sizes and measurement systems
Poland, fine printing in, 88:4.157, 90:1.17+il
polemics, freedom of speech (broadside), 90:3.114–115
pop-up alphabets, 85:3.168+il
pop-up paper sculptures. *See* under illustration, book
portfolio formats, 81:1.24–25, 88:4.178+il
posters, silkscreened, 84:2.54–55il
PostScript (Adobe Systems), 88:1.40–41, 88:3.123–126il, 90:3.125
Prague, The Academy of Applied Art in, 87:1.32–33il
preservation, book. *See* conservation of books; museums
preservation of paper. *See* conservation; paper handling techniques
preservation of types. *See* metal type production; museums

221

press book about, and printed on vellum, 86:1.34+*il*
press books versus artists' books, acceptance of, 85:1.23–25
press catalogues and checklists. *See* catalogues, checklists, and bibliographies of fine presses (by name)
press, a handmade. *See* handpresses
press histories:
    76:3.37–40, 76:4.75, 81:2.61–62+*il*, 81:3.104–105+*il*, 81:4.116+*il*, 139+*il*, 82:2.52, 82:3.83, 87–89, 92*il*, 82:4.125+*il*, 83:1.11–12*il*, 84:2.57–60+*il*, 86:2.66, 87:2.65–67*il*, 89:3.152–154, 89:4.165–166*il*
    fine press books 1968–1978 (exhibition), 85:2.120–121
    university presses, 79:2.40–41+*il*, 82:4.154, 83:2.69–70*il*
press marks. *See* printers' marks; specific press names in the Index by Names
press, a handmade. *See* handpresses
presses, collegiate. *See* collegiate fine presses
pressmarks. *See* printers' marks
pricing:
    and book production, 76:2.20, 80:3.80–81, 85:3.137, 87:2.88, 87:3.134–137
    of bookbinding, 81:4.135, 82:1.5
    of limited editions, 76:1.11, 79:3.71, 82:1.5, 86:2.102, 87:3.134–137
    of trade books, 80:3.92, 87:3.135
    See also printing economics
Princeton Graphic Arts Collection, 80:2.60–61+*il*
Print: A Quarterly Journal of the Graphic Arts, 80:1.8
printed facsimiles. *See* facsimile editions (reviews of)
printers' marks, 79:3.88+*il*, 82:3.119+(cover)
    1975–1980 survey of, 79:4.102–109*il*+(cover)
    corrections to survey of, 80:1.9, 80:2.44
    heraldic, 79:3.88+*il*
    spoof (Typographeum Poltronianum), 79:2.52*il*
    See also watermarks for handmade papers
Printing & Graphic Arts (PaGA) journal, 80:1.8–9
The Printing Art magazine, 80:1.4–5
printing arts conferences. *See* fine printing conferences; specific association names
printing economics:
    formula, list-price, 87:3.137
    handmade paper cost, 76:2.20
    labor costs, 81:4.118
    and pricing, 76:2.20, 80:3.92, 87:3.134–137, 90:1.47
    small press, 78:1.19, 80:3.80–81, 81:4.116+, 118–120+, 85:1.11–14
    social acceptance and, 85:1.23–25
    spoof of, 87:2.88
    of trade books, 80:3.92, 87:3.135
    See also economics; pricing
Printing Historical Society (U. K.), 85:1.69
printing history. *See* histories of printing
printing inks. *See* inks and inking, printing
Printing Office, Inscription for a (B. Warde, broadside), 84:3.105–106
printing office, newspaper, 86:1.28*il*
printmaking methods and illustration:
    and book design, 85:1.52–53+*il*
    collagraphy, 76:2.23
    collotype color printing, 80:4.109, 82:2.50, 84:3.118–120*il*, 84:4.182
    color, superannuated processes, 80:4.108–112+(cover), 127*il*
    Czech, 87:1.5*il*
    English 19th-century, 80:1.23
    engraving, copperplate, 82:2.49–50+*il*, 82:3.116–117, 83:4.139*il*
    etching, drypoint, 90:3.100*il*
    etching, intaglio, 88:3.102–103+*il*, 116–119+*il*
    etching, relief, 75:2.16–17
    gravure revival, flat-plate, 82:2.61
    letterpress, 79:3.84
    linoleum cuts, 80:2.39+(cover), 84:3.98, 88:2.93+(cover)
    linoleum-cut text, 81:2.50+*il*, 63*il*
    lithography, 79:4.110–111, 84:3.101, 103+*il*
    metal relief, 80:1.23
    photocopying, 82:1.21+*il*, 85:3.142–143+*il*, 86:3.176
    safety of materials for, 90:3.101
    serigraphs, 84:2.54–55*il*
    silkscreened books, 81:1.19, 84:2.54–55*il*, 85:2.114–115+*il*, 85:3.166–167*il*
    silkscreened posters, 84:2.54–55*il*
    "typographic," 80:3.76, 81:1.3, 81:2.59, 81:4.115, 148
    woodcuts, 85:1.60*il*, 62*il*, 85:2.112–113*il*, 90:3.101+*il*
    woodcuts, reduction, 85:2.113–114+*il*, 88:1.13+*il*
    woodcuts, 77:2.28–30*il*
    See also illustration, book; wood engraving

The Private Libraries Association, 77:2.42, 79:1.26, 81:1.35, 81:2.61–62+*il*
private press catalogues. *See* catalogues, checklists, and bibliographies of fine presses (by name); directories of fine presses (reviews and news of)
private press names. *See* Names of Persons and Fine Presses Index
private presses. *See* fine presses
private typefaces. *See* type; type design
prizes. *See* awards and prizes, book world
Pro Arte Libri and Fine Print, 89:4.159–160
profiles of book arts professionals. *See* specific professions; specific individuals (in the Names of Persons and Fine Presses Index)
profit, press. *See* printing economics
proverbs, books of. *See* bestiaries and animal proverb books; Biblical literature; Aesop (in the Names of Persons and Fine Presses Index)
publication catalogues. *See* catalogues, checklists, and bibliographies of fine presses (by name)
publishers, commercial, 83:2.56–57*il*
    artists' books versus, 85:1.23–25
    in Europe, 85:2.80–81
    fine press collaborations with, 81:4.116+, 119–120+, 82:2.53+, 60–61
    trade editions, 80:3.92–94*il*, 82:2.53+, 85:1.11–14
    See also booktrade and booksellers; trade books; university presses; names of specific institutions
publishers, fine press. *See* fine presses; fine printers
publishing history. *See* history of book publishing
publishing trade. *See* booktrade and booksellers; trade books
pulp painting. *See under* paper
punchcutting and design. *See* metal type design and punchcutting; type design
punctuation and accents:
    and breathing marks, Greek, 87:1.47–50*il*
    Czech type, 87:1.35–37*il*
    ellipsis, 88:4.161
    and Greek letterforms, 87:1.47–50*il*
    in medieval manuscripts, 82:2.64–67*il*, 86:4.207
    punchcutting history of, 86:1.6–10*il*
    for roman letterforms, 88:1.7–8
    and underlining, 87:3.159, 88:1.5+
    use critiques, 81:1.18–19, 81:3.108
    See also letterforms

Q

quarterlies. *See* magazines and journals, book arts

R

rags for paper, 81:2.41–43
Ransome Humanities Research Center Conservation Department, *See* Harry Ransome Humanities Research Center
reading:
   and arrangement of texts, scroll to codex, 86:4.207–208*il*
   artifacts for (exhibition), 86:2.67*il*
   legibility rules (manual), 82:1.31
   medieval glossed literature, 86:4.207
   multi-sensory, 85:3.166+*il*, 167–168+, 89:1.38–39*il*, 89:2.98
   and oral literature, 81:1.13+, 84:4.171*il*, 88:4.186–188+*il*
   orality and literacy, 78:3.90–91, 81:4.134, 87:1.48, 89:1.20–21
   quotes and anecdotes, 89:2.73*il*
   silent, effects of, 86:4.207
   Year of the Reader (Library of Congress, 1987), 87:3.117*il*
rebinding. *See* bookbinding techniques and materials; conservation of books
recipes, portfolio of cooking, 87:3.173
recycled paper, 81:2.41–43
reliure (French), *See* bookbinding (history and types)
Renaissance era:
   manuscripts (exhibition), 84:3.116–117
   manuscripts and type influenced by Roman inscriptions, 89:3.134–141*il*
   printers, 81:1.25
   scribes, 81:1.26+, 82:4.145+*il*
reviews, fine press book:
   audience and critics, 88:4.185–186
   dialogues over controversial, 81:3.75, 108–109, 88:2.78–79+, 88:4.152–154
   importance of, to small press publishers, 81:4.119–120, 87:3.136–137, 88:4.185–186
Rijksmuseum Het Catharijneconvent (Utrecht), 89:4.198
Rijksmuseum Meermanno-Westreenianum (The Hague), 89:4.198
Rochester Institute of Technology, 78:4.120, 80:1.31, 80:4.113+, 81:1.2, 84:2.48, 86:3.170–171*il*
Rounce and Coffin Club of Los Angeles, 79:3.91
Round-Ups, Broadside. *See* Fine Print Broadside Round-Ups (reviews)
The Rowfant Club, 77:3.66
Royal Printing Office, Norstedt Foundry Collection (Stockholm), 85:1.45–46, 85:3.138
rubbings:
   of bookbindings, 87:2.63–64
   of tombstones, 84:2.67–68*il*
rubrication of signatures. *See* under bookbinding techniques and materials
running titles, use of, 82:2.70–73+*il*, 86:4.208+*il*
Russia, book arts in, 82:4.143–144, 89:4.176, 178+*il*, 90:1.31–33*il*

S

St. Bride Printing Library (London), 77:1.13
St. Cuthberts Paper Mill, 76:2.22
St. Gall, Abbey of (modern illuminated manuscript), 88:4.157–158*il*
samizdat books, 82:4.138
samples, type. *See* specimen books, type
San Francisco, fine printing in, 85:1.64–65, 85:2.102, 86:3.154–156
San Francisco Museum of Modern Art, bookbinding exhibitions, 77:1.13–14, 78:2.33–34+(insert: color catalogue)
San Francisco Public Library, Grabhorn Collection, 76:1.14–15
San Francisco State University, 86:1.5
   Tallone printers (Italiian), exhibition of, 85:4.238+
Sangorski and Sutcliffe bookbinders, 82:2.70, 82:4.122–123
Sans Serriffe, book arts in [imaginary] Republic of, 79:1.22, 89:2.61*il*
satire. *See* humor and satire
schools. *See* education and teaching, book arts
Schriftgiesserei Service Gerstenberg (typefoundry), 88:3.143
Schriftmuseum J. A. Dortmond (Amsterdam), 89:4.198
scientific illustration, 79:4.110–111, 83:2.76–77+*il*, 84:3.131–132
   See also botanical illustration
Scotland, poems from, 85:3.162–163*il*
   See also United Kingdom, book arts in
screens, halftone, 81:1.6–8*il*
Scribes and Illuminators, Society of (London), 78:1.12, 82:4.156, 88:2.90
scribes, modern. *See* calligraphers; calligraphy
scribes and script:
   20th century, 88:4.157–158*il*
   Carolingian, 88:3.123*il*, 89:3.137
   and codices, 86:4.205–208+*il*
   essays on, 83:2.65–66
   Hebrew, 86:1.21–27*il*
   history of, 77:3.52–55*il*, 78:1.30, 81:1.26+*il*, 81:3.97–98, 86:4.205–208+*il*, 89:3.134–137*il*
   implements used by, 81:3.97
   italic writing, 16th century, 89:2.88–90*il*
   manual, medieval, 81:4.136
   medieval, 79:2.61–62, 81:4.136, 83:2.65–66, 84:3.125, 89:3.137
   in a movie, 87:2.102–103
   in Muslim society, 80:2.66+*il*, 86:1.11–17*il*
   Renaissance, 81:1.26+*il*, 82:4.145+*il*
   Roman inscriptions, influence of, 89:3.134–141*il*
   and type design, 77:3.52–55*il*, 71*il*, 82:2.64–67+*il*, 70–73, 82:4.145+*il*
   writing mistresses, 16th–17th century, 85:2.88–98(*il*)
   See also incunabula; manuscripts, medieval; writing systems
scrolls:
   earliest complete printed, 90:1.7
   to codex, change from, 78:4.114–115, 86:4.205–208+*il*
Scryption museum (Netherlands), 89:4.198
sculptural books. *See* artists' books
Sefardic script. *See* Hebrew letters and types
sellers of books. *See* booktrade and booksellers; distributors
serigraph. *See* silkscreen
sewing structures. *See* bookbinding techniques and materials
shaped paper. *See* altered pages in books; paper
shaped poetry, 78:1.15+*il*, 78:3.80, 78:4.106, 81:1.18, 83:1.12–13+*il*, 89:2.87–88*il*
shops, book. *See* booktrade and booksellers
shops, printing (images of), 84:2.56*il*, 85:1.33*il*, 85:2.101*il*, 128+(cover)
Siegenthaler Paper Mill, 77:2.38
signs. *See* symbols and signs; type ornaments; writing systems
silhouettes as illustration, 83:1.11–12*il*
silkscreen printing:
   of book text, 85:2.114–115+*il*, 85:3.166–167+*il*
   of images, 81:1.19, 84:2.54–55*il*, 85:3.166–167+*il*
silloge [sic] (drawings of Roman inscriptions). 89:3.135*il*, 139
   See epigraphy, Latin
simulacrum. *See* facsimile editions
simultaneous book, the first, 87:3.139–140+*il*

size of books. *See* format of books

sizes, type. *See* type sizes and measurement systems

sizing. *See* papermakers and papermaking (handmade)

slugs, printing from:
- 15th century, 83:3.87, 86:4.232
- Ludlow machine using, 87:4.213*il*
- *See also* metal type composition; typesetting

Smithsonian Institution, 81:4.141, 82:3.83
- Ben Franklin press, 79:1.21–22*il*
- collections, 78:3.91, 83:2.49, 89:3.147–150

Society of Calligraphers (pseud., W. A. Dwiggins), 87:2.88

Society of Scribes and Illuminators (London), 78:1.12, 78:4.115, 82:4.156, 88:2.90, 88:3.119

Society of Scribes of New York, 76:2.34, 77:1.21, 77:4.101, 82:1.29, 84:1.5

The Society of Typographic Arts, 82:4.156, 85:4.204, 88:2.84+

software, type design. *See* digital types and typesetting

songs and poems about printing, 85:3.162–163, 87:3 (insert)

sorts, lead. *See* metal type design and punchcutting; type ornaments

space shuttle, papermaking on Columbia, 87:2.61–62

Spain, ancient ballads of, 75:4.37*il*

specimen books, type:
- American, 76:3.42–43, 52–53, 78:1.29, 83:1.29–30*il*, 84:2.49, 90:3.100–101*il*, 137*il*
- British, 86:2.67+, 87:4.203, 90:2.75+*il*, 81–82*il*
- collection of, 82:4.127
- digital typefaces, 82:1.6–7+
- German, 85:2.78
- Monotype "specials," 78:2.47
- ornamental type, 78:2.47, 81:4.152*il*, 82:2.45, 74*il*, 83:1.29–30*il*, 87:2.60*il*, 88:1.9–10*il*, 88:4.163–164*il*
- phototypes, critical review of, 82:1.6–7+
- writing systems, world, 83:2.58*il*
- *See also* metal type production; metal typefoundries

specimen sheets:
- broadsides illustrating, 87:3.122*il*, 168+*il*
- decorative and display type, 87:3.168+*il*, 77:3.67–68, 88:1.1(cover)
- digital type, 81:4.123–126*il*
- metal type, 81:4.123–124+*il*, 83:1.4
- newspaper types, 89:1.23–30*il*+(insert)
- wood type, 76:3.42–43, 83:2.45–49+*il*, 84:2.70*il*, 88:4.163–164, 90:2.75–76*il*

spines, book:
- concertina format, 82:4.137+, 85:2.110–111*il*, 85:3.168+*il*, 86:2.76–77+*il*
- exposed, 89:3.115+*il*
- "floating" title piece, 90:1.37–39*il*
- letterforms on, 90:2.72
- removable, 86:1.46*il*, 52
- *See also* bookbinding techniques and materials

spoofs and parodies. *See* humor and satire

Stanford University, 76:1.10, 84:1.7–10, 84:3.93+
- Library, 79:1.8

State University of New York at Purchase, 84:3.134

statistics, pictorial presentation of, 85:1.48+*il*

Stempel Typefoundry, 80:4.134–135, 82:1.7, 86:2.99, 86:3.149*il*, 88:2.84+
- closing of, 88:1.6, 88:3.143

stencil ornament, 80:1.18–19+*il*, 82:2.46, 87:2.89*il*
- on *Fine Print* covers, 83:4.174+(cover), 87:2.62+(cover)
- and pochoir illustration, 78:3.70–73*il*, 80:4.111, 82:2.50, 82:3.92*il*, 87:2.86+*il*
- *See also* marbling, paper; type ornaments

Stephenson Blake (typefoundry), 83:1.4, 89:4.195–196*il*

sticks, composition. *See under* metal type composition; typesetting

stores, book. *See* booktrade and booksellers

suminagashi. *See under* marbling, paper

suppliers, paper. *See under* distributors, paper; paper; papermills

surveys. *See* directories of fine presses (reviews and news of); directories and lists (reviews and news of)

syllogue (drawings of Roman inscriptions), 89:3.135*il*, 139
- *See* silloge

symbols and logos. *See* printers' marks; watermarks for handmade papers

symbols and signs:
- Aztec glyphs, 83:1.34*il*
- design of, 80:4.131–132*il*
- letterform signs, 82:1.29–31*il*, 82:2.43*il*, 47+*il*
- for permanent paper, 86:2.66
- *See also* punctuation and accents; type ornaments; writing systems

T

teachers and teaching. *See* education and teaching, book arts; names of specific book arts

Technical Association of the Pulp and Paper Industry (TAPPI), 84:3.99, 87:4.181

Technische Hochschule Darmstadt, 86:3.150+*il*

teletypesetting (TTS) for news text, 89:1.27–28

Tetterode typefoundry (Nicolaas Tetterode), 89:4.190

TEX computer text layout language, 81:1.31–32, 84:3.93+

texture in typography. *See* typography

Thames and Hudson [typography manual], 90:1.8–9

theatre, the book as, 88:1.26–33*il*, 90:2.77–78+*il*

Thumb-Nail Series (Century Company, stamped leather bindings), 82:1.15–18+*il*

title pages, 80:4.129*il*, 84:4.150–151+*il*
- design of, 79:2.64*il*
- early, 90:3.104–105

titles, running, 82:2.70–73+*il*, 86:4.208+*il*

tombstone rubbings, 84:2.67–68*il*

tools, bookbinding. *See* bookbinding techniques and materials

tracts or composite volume (sammelband), 87:2.68+

trade books, 85:1.11–14, 87:4.216, 89:3.130–133
- book designers of, 77:4.93–94, 80:3.92–94*il*, 81:3.106–107, 82:3.87–89, 84:3.110+*il*, 87:2.82–86*il*, 88–89*il*, 107, 88:3.105*il*
- decorative cloth bindings for, 88:3.106
- exhibitions of, 77:4.93–94, 80:3.92–94*il*
- fine press books published as, 81:4.116+, 145, 82:2.53+, 60–61
- fine press relationships to, 81:4.116+, 82:2.53+, 60–61, 84:2.60, 89:3.133
- in Germany, 86:2.100–102
- leather stamped bindings for, 82:1.15–18+*il*
- price, speed, and quality issues, 85:1.14, 85:3.136–138, 87:3.135
- and prices, 87:3.135
- publisher interview, 87:2.67–68
- spoof of, 87:2.88*il*
- trade press profiles, 82:3.87–89, 84:3.110+*il*
- typographers and, 82:3.96–97+, 85:3.136–138
- *See also* publishers, commercial

trademarks. *See* printers' marks; watermarks for handmade papers
Trajan column inscription, 79:4.118*il*, 80:4.126+, 86:1.53
transparency, book designs using, 81:1.10–11*il*, 81:4.121, 82:2.61–62+*il*, 85:3.173, 89:4.207+*il*
Twinrocker Handmade Paper, Inc. (Kathryn and Howard Clark), 76:2.22, 77:4.84, 82:3.114, 83:3.103+*il*, 106*il*, 84:4.139, 86:3.144–145+*il*
    book from, 85:1.51
    expansion news, 90:1.5
    profiles of, 77:4.77–81*il*, 83:3.93–95
type :
    16th century, 89:2.88–90*il*, 90:1.49
    as abstract art, 86:2.66–67
    accents and points for, 86:1.6–10*il*
    American metal, 20th century, 87:4.214–215
    Anglo-Saxon, 86:3.165*il*, 86:4.228–229*il*
    antiquing of, 84:1.9–10
    Arabic, 86:1.9*il*
    banning of Gothic, 86:2.100
    calligraphic influence on, 77:3.54–55
    choosing for a fine press, 80:3.76–78
    classification catalogue (review), 85:4.202–204*il*
    cloning of, 82:1.6, 10
    collections of, 80:3.77, 81:4.140–144*il*, 83:1.5, 83:2.69–70, 84:2.49+, 85:1.45–46*il*, 88:1.6, 45, 89:1.19–20*il*, 89:2.60, 89:4.189–197*il*, 198
    copyright for, 75:1.6, 77:1.12–13, 81:4.124, 82:1.6, 10, 88:2.87
    cover designs using mixed, 80:1.1(cover), 86:1.1(cover), 88:1.1(cover)
    critiques of, 78:1.5–6, 87:4.204–206+
    Czech, 87:1.34–39*il*
    decorative and display(reviews), 77:3.67–68, 87:3.168
    digital, 80:3.102–103*il*, 82:3.82
    digital (Stone), 88:3.123–126*il*
    digital, transition of traditional to, 81:1.2–3, 31–32*il*, 82:1.6–7+, 10, 84:3.93+, 88:1.24–25+*il*, 88:3.123–126*il*, 89:1.19
    Gothic (blackletter), 84:4.176, 86:2.100, 87:3.159
    Hebrew, 85:3.147, 86:1.21–27*il*, 87:1.53–54
    identification of, 82:1.6–7+, 10, 85:4.202–204*il*
    identification of literary forgeries by, 85:1.42–45*il*
    irregularities in, deliberate, 84:1.10
    italic, 80:1.28, 80:3.101–102*il*, 81:2.53–55*il*, 81:3.100*il*, 89:2.88–90*il*, 90:1.49
    for maps, 88:2.91
    Monotype Corporation, 81:1.14, 82:1.7+, 83:4.140+, 86:2.73, 86:3.149*il*, 87:1.35–36*il*, 87:2.69–73+*il*, 108, 88:3.134, 89:4.211, 90:1.26–29*il*, 90:2.70–71*il*
    newspaper type specimens, 89:1.23–30*il*+(insert)
    non-roman, production of, 83:3.124–125*il*, 86:1.6–17*il*, 21–27*il*
    for period settings, 80:3.78
    phonetic, 83:1.8–9*il*
    phototype, development of, 80:1.29–30*il*
    private design, 78:2.46–48*il*, 78:3.86–87+*il*
    protection of designs, 78:1.12
    public signage system, 80:3.103*il*
    roman, 79:1.4–5*il*, 79:4.118*il*, 80:3.78, 97, 80:4.126+, 81:3.102*il*, 83:4.140–141*il*, 84:4.175–177*il*, 85:4.194+*il*, 87:4.204–206+, 88:1.6–8, 88:4.193, 90:2.71*il*
    roman minuscules, slab serif, 88:3.120*il*
    roman, origin of, 89:3.134–141*il*
    roman sloped, 81:2.54–55, 89:4.195
    sans serif, 76:1.13, 79:4.120–123*il*, 81:3.101*il*, 88:4.171–172*il*
    for school books, 81:4.144
    seriffed, 81:3.101*il*, 88:3.120*il*, 88:4.171–174*il*, 89:3.138–140*il*
    signage system, 88:4.171*il*
    sloped roman, 81:2.54–55, 89:4.195
    small caps, use of, 80:3.97, 101, 84:4.153*il*
    typewriter, 81:1.25, 85:3.166–167+*il*, 89:4.200–201*il*
    uncials by Victor Hammer, 78:4.121–123*il*, 87:4.193–195+*il*
    upright italic, 80:1.28
    Victorian, ornamented, 85:3.158*il*, 89:1.19–20*il*
    wood-engraved or woodcut, 78:3.83–84, 81:3.87, 86:4.223–224+*il*
    wooden type, 76:3.42–43, 83:2.45–49+*il*+(cover)
    See also letterforms; specimen books, type; type ornaments
type collections. *See* collectors and collections (by category)
type composition. *See* metal type composition
type design:
    20th century, critique of, 87:4.204–206+
    Anglo-Saxon characters, 86:3.165*il*, 86:4.228–229*il*
    and antiquing digital types, 84:1.9–10
    axis of stress in, 89:1(insert)
    calendar of, 89:3.108
    calligraphy in, 79:4.120–123*il*, 82:1.33, 86:2.103–107*il*, 87:4.201–202*il*
    Chinook, 89:2.81*il*
    computer programs for, 81:1.31–32*il*, 82:3.82, 84:1.7–9*il*, 84:3.93+
    conferences on, 86:2.113–114, 88:1.24–25+*il*
    creation process, 85:1.35–42*il*, 85:3.148–152*il*, 85:4.219–222+*il*, 89:1.24–26
    criticism of, 78:1.5–6, 87:4.204–206+
    Cyrillic and oriental, 83:3.124–125*il*
    Czech, 87:1.24+(cover), 87:1.19–21+*il*, 34–39*il*
    digital programs for, 81:1.31–32*il*
    drawings for, 78:4.118–119, 80:2.45, 80:3.102–103*il*, 88:3.123–126*il*
    essays on, 83:1.18–19+, 87:3.151–152+*il*, 154–156*il*
    families, 81:4.140–144*il*, 85:1.35–41*il*, 88:3.123–126*il*, 90:3.120–125*il*
    Fell types collection, 79:2.40+*il*, 81:4.134–135, 82:4.154*il*
    Hebrew, 86:1.7*il*, 24+*il*, 87:1.53–54
    history of, 82:4.154, 83:1.17–19+*il*, 84:4.175–177*il*, 86:2.106, 87:4.204–206+
    interpolation program for, 84:1.9*il*
    Metafont computer program for, 81:1.31–32*il*, 82:3.82, 84:1.8+, 84:3.93+
    for new technologies, 88:2.87
    for newspapers, 89:1.23–30*il*+(insert)
    non-roman, 86:1.6–17*il*, 21–27*il*+(cover)
    ornamented type, 82:2.45*il*
    phonetic type, 83:1.8–9*il*
    of private typefaces, 78:2.46–48*il*, 78:3.86–87+*il*
    and readability, 80:2.65–66, 89:1(insert)
    sans serif, 79:4.120–123*il*
    scribal influences on, 77:3.71*il*, 80:1.26–30*il*
type classification catalogue (review), 85:4.202–204*il*
    in typefoundries, 80:4.106, 89:4.189–197*il*
    uncials, 78:4.121–123*il*, 87:1.38+*il*, 87:4.193–195+*il*
    wood type, 76:3.42–43, 83:2.43+(cover), 45–49+*il*, 85:3.158*il*
    wood types, pantograph for cutting, 83:2.46*il*, 86:1.9
type designers:
    Bauhaus School, 85:4.200–201*il*

See also typography, avant garde or experimental
  contemporary (since 1970), 87:4.204–206+
  copyright for work of, 75:1.6, 77:1.12–13, 81:4.124, 82:1.6, 10, 88:2.87
  group exhibition, 80:2.45
  Kis and Janson, 84:1.25–31*il*, 84:4.178–180, 86:4.202*il*, 89:3.134–141, 90:2.69–71*il*
  monographs on (reviewed), 76:2.29–30, 78:3.81, 82:1.29–31*il*, 83:2.56–57*il*, 83:3.124–125*il*, 85:3.158–159+*il*, 85:4.196–198*il*, 204+, 90:2.73–75*il*
  in the Netherlands, 89:4.189–197*il*
  for newspapers, 89:1.23–30*il*+(insert)
  philosophies of, 76:4.69–70*il*, 78:4.121–123, 82:1.29–31*il*, 83:2.56–57*il*, 85:4.200–201*il*, 87:1.38+*il*, 88:4.171–174*il*
  piracy of work by, 81:4.124, 82:1.6, 10, 87:3.162, 88:1.40, 88:2.87
  profiles of, 79:4.120–123*il*, 87:1.34–39*il*, 90:1.25–29*il*, 90:3.120–125*il*
  in typefoundries, 81:4.140–144*il*, 82:1.6–7+, 89:4.161–162*il*, 189–197*il*
  women, 80:4.134–135*il*, 86:2.103–109*il*, 90:3.120–125*il*
  See also typographers; Names of Persons and Fine Presses Index
type designers association. *See* ATypI (Association Typographique Internationale)
Type Directors' Club:
  awards, 79:3.72, 88:1.25, 89:1.7
  conference, 88:1.24–25+*il*
type manufacturers. *See* metal typefoundries
type manufacturing. *See* metal type production
type manufacturing standards. *See* type sizes and measurement systems
type ornaments, 76:4.74–75*il*, 78:2.37, 80:2.45*il*, 82:2.48*il*, 83:1.22
  19th century, 77:3.67–68
  American 19th century, 88:4.163–164*il*, 89:1.19–20*il*
  American Colonial, dictionary of, 76:3.52–53
  banner of Fine Print featuring, 76:3.37
  bibliographies, 88:1.9–10*il*
  book composed of, 82:2.63*il*
  and borders (Enschedé), 87:2.60*il*, 89:4.163*il*
  calendar book of, 88:4.152*il*
  covers of Fine Print featuring, 76:3.37(banner), 82:1.1(cover), 82:2.73(cover)
  "December" (Troyer), 76:1.15*il*, 76:2.25
  designing with, 80:3.80, 80:4.125, 82:2.63*il*, 84:3.104
  Dutch avant-garde design with, 89:4.176–179*il*
  facsimile book, 87:2.60*il*
  first lead-cast, 82:1.3
  geometric and typographic, 82:2.45*il*, 46*il*, 89:4.211*il*
  images composed of, 82:2.63*il*, 84:3.104, 88:4.163*il*
  ivy leaf, 75:4.42
  Ludlow Typograph, 87:4.213+*il*
  Monotype (John Peters), 90:1.28*il*
  specimen books, 78:2.47, 81:4.152*il*, 82:2.45, 74*il*, 83:1.29–30*il*, 87:2.60*il*, 88:1.9–10*il*, 88:4.163–164*il*
  stencil, 80:1.18–19+*il*, 87:2.62+(cover), 82–86*il*, 87–89*il*
  typewriter type, 89:4.200–201*il*
  See also ornament in books; stencil ornament
type, photographic. *See* phototypes
type production. *See* digital types and typesetting; metal type design and punchcutting; metal type production
type sizes and measurement systems:
  American standard height (.918"), 80:2.67–68, 87:4.181, 90:3.136–138*il*
  font x-height, 80:2.67–68, 87:1.49–50, 87:4.181, 89:2.77, 90:3.136–138*il*
  and Fourier analysis of letterspacing, 77:4.98–100
  and letterspacing, 80:1.29–30, 87:4.212*il*
  for Linotype machines, 89:4.193*il*, 196
  optical scaling, 89:2.76–77
  origins of, 90:3.136–138*il*
  pica system, 90:3.136–137
  Picco scale, 15th century, 87:1.49
  point system, 80:2.67, 90:3.136–138*il*
  teletypesetting (TTS) for news text, 89:1.27–28
  units per em, 80:1.29–30
  variations in, 80:2.67–68, 82:1.6–10, 89:2.75–78*il*, 90:3.136–138*il*
  See also metal type production
type specimens. *See* specimen books, type; specimen sheets
type specimens illustrated in *Fine Print*. *See* typefaces (by name)
typecases, 83:2.44, 85:4.216*il*, 86:1.4
  Chinese, 86:1.42–43*il*
  Fine Print cover images of, 80:3.73(cover), 85:2.77(cover), 86:1.1(cover)
  layout of, 81:2.59*il*
Typecasting Fellowship. *See* American Typecasting Fellowship (ATF)
typefaces (by name):
  Abrams Venetian, 90:2.71*il*, 76–77
  Albertus, 81:1.14–15*il*, 89:4.211*il*
  Aldine Greek, 87:1.47–50*il*
  Aldine Roman, 88:4.193
  American Uncial, 78:4.123+*il*, 87:4.193–195+*il*
  Amerigo, 88:1.40*il*
  Andreas-Schrift, 89:2.56*il*
  Andromaque, 78:4.123+*il*, 87:4.193–195+*il*
  Angelus (Monotype), 90:1.28*il*
  Antigone, 81:2.47+*il*, 53*il*, 89:4.195+*il*
  Antigua (Bremer Presse), 86:2.88–89
  Antiqua, 76:4.70*il*, 77:2.42+*il*, 79:1.5*il*, 79:4.120–123*il*
  Ariadne initials, 80:4.134–135*il*
  Arrighi, 80:1.26, 83:1.8*il*, 86:3.158–161+*il*, 86:4.236–237, 87:2.69–73+*il*, 101*il*
  Arrighi-Vincenza, 78:2.57*il*
  Augustin (Kis), 86:4.202*il*
  Augustin Roman 2, 77:2.42+
  Basilia, 89:3.108*il*
  Baskerville, 86:2.69
  bastarda, 77:3.71, 78:1.23, 81:3.101*il*
  Bell (Mountjoye), 82:4.129
  Bell (Scotch roman), 79:1.3, 79:2.41–42, 84:3.110*il*, 86:2.68–69
  Bembo roman, 80:3.78, 83:4.140–141*il*, 84:1.9*il*, 90:2.71*il*
  Blado (Monotype), 80:1.26, 83:1.9*il*
  Block Condensed, 90:3.143+(cover)
  Bodoni, 78:2.55–56, 79:4.121*il*, 86:3.149*il*, 89:1(insert)
  Bremer (press) Bible, 86:2.106–107*il*
  Bremer (press) Greek, 86:2.105*il*
  Breughel, 88:4.173–174*il*
  Caledonia (Linotype), 87:2.82, 87–89
  Cancelleresca Bastarda, 80:1.28, 81:2.55*il*, 81:3.101*il*, 89:4.195
  Carmina Light, 88:1.40*il*
  Carolus, 84:3.109*il*
  Caslon (Adobe), 75:3.22–25*il*, 77:4.86–87, 80:3.78, 82:4.128*il*, 84:4.152, 90:3.121–125*il*
  Castellar, 87:4.177(cover), 210, 90:1.25
  Catfish, 83:4.154*il*
  Centaur, 90:2.70*il*
  Century, 81:4.140–144*il*, 89:1.23+(insert)
  Chancery (Zapf), 80:1.26–30*il*
  Charlemagne, 90:3.124*il*
  Charter, 88:1.40*il*
  Civilité, 77:3.71–73*il*, 78:1.30, 85:1.35–41*il*
  Claudius, 76:4.70*il*, 81:1.15
  Cloister Old Style, 90:2.70*il*

Contura open, 89:4.161*il*
Corona, 89:1.24+(insert)
Cushing, 81:4.142
Dante, 78:2.56, 57*il*, 81:4.147, 85:4.219–222+*il*, 86:2.104*il*
David, 86:1.24*il*
Delphin, 85:3.144*il*
Demos, 80:3.102–103*il*, 89:4.197
Diotima, 80:4.134–135*il*, 81:4.124
Dow text, 89:1.28+(insert)
Eboracum, 90:2.75*il*
Edison, 89:1.29+(insert)
Emergo, 89:4.194*il*, 196
Emerson, 83:2.56*il*, 86:4.236
Erasmus, 89:4.190–191*il*
Excelsior, 89:1.24+(insert)
Experimental No. 223, 89:1(insert)
Fairfield (Linotype), 88:1.9*il*
Figural (Menhart), 87:1.35+*il*
Fleischman Antiqua, 77:2.42+*il*
Frutiger (Roissy), 82:1.30, 88:4.171–172*il*
Futura, 87:3.155*il*
Galliard, 79:1.27–30*il*, 80:3.75, 81:1.20, 82:1.34, 84:1.9
Garamond, 77:3.57, 79:4.131–132, 80:3.78, 89:1.34+(cover), 89:2.60
Gill Sans, 77:1.13, 77:2.40–41, 82:3.95, 119+*il*, 86:3.149*il*, 88:3.134
Golden Type, 90:2.70*il*
Goudy Greek, 76:4.67–68
Goudy Newstyle, 82:2.60, 68
Goudy Scripps Oldstyle, 77:1.23*il*, 80:2.38
Goudy Thirty, 82:3.99*il*
Granjon, 80:3.75, 88:1.10
Griffo, 77:3.57+*il*, 78:2.56, 57*il*, 86:3.149*il*
Grimaldi, 83:1.30*il*
Grotius (now Nassau), 89:4.190+*il*
Harvard (Kestrel), 80:3.83, 88:4.193
Helvetica, 80:4.106, 84:1.9*il*
Hiero-Rhode Italic, 80:3.101–102*il*
Hollandse Medieval, 89:4.191*il*
Hollar (Menhart), 87:1.35+*il*
Houtsneeletter, 89:4.195+*il*
Hunt Roman (Zapf), 79:1.4–5*il*
Icone, 88:4.172–173*il*
Imperial, stencil, 87:2.62+(cover)
Imprint Old Style, 78:3.82, 82:3.93
Inkunabula, 77:4.83
Ionic No. 5, 89:1.24*il*+(insert)
Iridium, 88:4.172*il*
Isadora, 80:3.73(cover), 85:3.148–152*il*
Jenson, 89:3.134–141, 90:2.69–71*il*
Jessenschrift, 76:4.70*il*
Joanna (Monotype), 76:3.37–38, 82:3.97+, 119+*il*
Jubilee, 89:1.26–27+(insert)
Juliana, 89:4.193*il*, 196

Karmelitic Hebrew, 86:3.133–134
Kelmscott, versions of, 78:3.85, 95
Kennerley Old Style, 87:4.216
Kestrel (Harvard), 80:3.83, 88:4.193
Kis (Janson sic), 79:1.5*il*, 84:1.25–31*il*, 84:4.178–180, 86:4.202*il*, 90:2.69–71*il*
Koch Antiqua, 76:4.70*il*
Koren, 86:1.24
Kursiv (Menhart), 87:1.36*il*
Legacy (ITC), 90:1.19–20*il*, 90:2.71*il*
Leviathan, 80:2.49+*il*
Linotype Modern, 89:1.27*il*+(insert)
Lithos, 90:3.120–122+*il*
Lucida, 85:1.70, 86:3.150*il*, 88:1.41*il*, 89:2.75–82*il*
Lucida Greek, 86:3.150, 87:3.162*il*
Lutetia, 81:2.51–52*il*, 89:4.190+*il*
Manuscript (Menhart), 87:1.35+*il*
Marconi, 88:2.87
Menhart Roman and Italic, 87:1.34–36*il*
Menhart Series 397 (Monotype), 87:1.15, 34–35+*il*
Méridien, 88:4.171*il*
Mikado, 83:1.30*il*
Mirarae, 90:3.123*il*
Modern No. 7, 89:1(insert)
Molé Foliated Capitals, 89:4.196
Monument (Menhart), 87:1.37*il*–38
Mountjoye (Scotch Roman, Bell), 79:1.3, 79:2.41–42, 82:4.129, 84:3.110*il*, 86:2.68–69
Nassau (Grotius), 89:4.190+*il*
Neuland, 76:4.70*il*
Nimrod, 89:1.29*il*+(insert)
Olympian, 89:1.28*il*+(insert)
Optima, 81:4.124, 82:2.62–63, 88:2.87
Optima Greek, 87:1.7
Oxford, 81:1.24
Pacioli, 78:2.56
Palatino, 84:3.109+*il*
Parlament (Menhart), 87:1.38+*il*
Pegasus, 81:1.14–15*il*
Pellucida, 86:3.150, 86:4.185(cover), 238
Penman Script, 78:1.29
Perpetua, 77:1.13, 77:2.40–41, 82:3.90–91+*il*, 93–95*il*, 119+*il*, 87:2.108, 89:1(insert)
Perpetua Titling, 84:3.105–106
Pindar Uncial, 78:4.122–123
Plantin, 82:3.93, 89:1.29+(insert)
Poliphilus, 86:2.73
Poliphilus Roman, 90:2.71*il*
Praxis, 80:3.103*il*
Roissy-Frutiger, 88:4.171–172*il*
Romanée, 81:2.53–54*il*, 86:4.228–229*il*
Romanée Antigua and Kursive, 87:3.122*il*

Romanée Italic, 81:2.53–54*il*, 81:3.100*il*, 89:4.195
Romulus, 81:2.54–56*il*, 89:4.175–198*il*
Romulus Greek and Roman, 81:3.102*il*, 89:4.195
Romulus Sans Serif, 81:3.101*il*
Samson Uncial, 78:4.122*il*
Scotch Roman (Bell), 79:1.3, 79:2.41–42, 84:3.110*il*, 86:2.68–69
Scripps Old Style, 77:1.23*il*, 80:2.38
Sheldon, 81:3.99–100*il*
Smaragd, 80:4.134–135*il*
Spectrum, 81:3.99, 87:4.177(cover), 210, 89:4.195
Stone Informal, 88:1.41*il*, 88:2.53, 88:3.124–125*il*
Subiaco, 87:2.66*il*
Swift, 89:1.23–31*il*+(insert)
Syntax-Antiqua, 79:4.120–123*il*, 89:2.81*il*
Tallone, 80:1.21, 85:4.206*il*
Textura, 89:2.77*il*
Times Europa, 89:1.28–29*il*+(insert)
Times New Roman and Italic, 80:3.97, 83:4.140–141*il*, 89:1.24–25+(insert)
Times Roman, 84:3.107*il*
Trajan, 90:3.124+*il*
Trajanus, 84:2.65*il*, 90:2.70*il*
Traveller (Monotype), 90:1.26–28*il*
Trinité, 84:1.9+*il*, 89:4.194*il*, 195*il*
Unciala (Menhart), 87:1.38+*il*
Uncials (Hammer), 78:4.121–123*il*, 87:4.193–195+
Univers, 82:1.30, 88:4.177
Viennese style, 83:4.152*il*
Weiss, 88:1.9–10*il*
Wilhelm Klingsporschrift, 76:4.70*il*, 84:2.65*il*
Zeno, 78:2.56, 57*il*
typefaces, electronic. *See* digital types and typesetting
typefaces, Greek (by name):
    Aldine 15th century, 87:1.47–50*il*
    Antigone, 81:2.47+*il*, 53*il*, 89:4.195+*il*
    Bremer, 86:2.105*il*
    Gill Sans Upright, 86:1.9*il*
    Goudy, 76:4.67–68
    Granjon, 82:4.145*il*
    Lucida digital, 87:3.162*il*
    Optima, 87:1.7
typefaces, names of specific. *See* under typefaces (by name)
typefaces, ornamental. *See* type ornaments
typefounding, metal type production; phototypes
    See digital types and typesetting;
typefoundries. *See* metal typefoundries; metal typefoundries (by name)

typesetting:
- 15th century, 83:3.87
- an author learns, 88:4.160–162
- for bookbinding, 90:2.67–68+*il*
- by hand, 76:3.38–39, 77:3.54–55, 80:3.78–79
- Chinese, 79:1.25
- and desktop publishing, 89:3.111
- teletypesetting (TTS), 89:1.27–28
- *See also* digital types and typesetting; metal type composition

typesetting, digital. *See* digital types and typesetting

typesetting machines:
- Linotype (Mergenthaler), 88:4.160–162
- Ludlow Typograph, 87:2.61, 87:4.213*il*
- Monotype, 88:4.160–162
- typewriter, 81:1.25, 89:4.200–201*il*
- *See also* digital types and typesetting; metal type production

typesetting measurements. *See* type sizes and measurement systems

typewriter typefaces, 81:1.25, 85:3.166–167+*il*, 89:4.200–201*il*

Typocrafters Annual Meeting (1989), 90:1.19–22

typographers:
- 19th century, encyclopedia of, 79:1.20–21
- awards to, 79:3.72, 89:1.7
- conferences of, 83:1.4–5*il*, 84:1.7–10, 85:2.86–87, 86:2.113–114, 88:1.24–25+*il*, 90:1.19–22
- corporate consultant, 85:4.200–201*il*
- monographs on, 83:4.151–153*il*, 88:1.4, 88:3.105, 89:1.18–20*il*, 89:4.201–203*il*, 90:2.73–75*il*
- philosophies of, 79:3.92–96, 84:4.164–167+*il*, 90:2.87–88*il*

Type Directors' Club, 79:3.72, 88:1.24–25+*il*, 89:1.7
- *See also* type designers; specific individuals (in the Names of Persons and Fine Presses Index)

typographic image, elements of, 89:2.75–82*il*
- *See also* visual imagery within text

typographic manual as "novel," 88:4.164*il*

typographic ornaments. *See* type ornaments

"typographic printmaking," 80:3.76, 81:1.3, 81:2.59, 81:4.115, 148

Typographica magazine anthology (review), 89:2.87–89*il*

typography:
- text in all Caslon capitals, 77:4.86–87
- as an art, 76:4.57–60, 77:1.4–6, 78:1.5–6, 80:3.76–81, 81:1.2–3, 82:4.141–145*il*
- Anglo-Saxon, 75:4.39, 86:3.165*il*, 86:4.228–229*il*
- avant-garde or experimental, 76:1.13, 78:1.15+*il*, 79:2.50–51+*il*, 81:4.123–126*il*, 82:4.141–145*il*, 83:1.12–13+*il*, 84:3.110, 85:4.200–201*il*, 86:2.99, 87:3.155–156*il*, 89:2.71+*il*, 87–88*il*, 89:4.200–201*il*, 90:1.32
- of bi- and multi-lingual texts, 80:4.122, 81:1.13+, 81:4.121, 83:4.166–167+*il*, 86:3.150+*il*, 163–165+*il*, 88:3.130–132*il*, 90:1.17
- blurred text, purposely, 84:3.110
- and book design, 77:3.49–55*il*, 85:2.126
- in bookbinding, 90:2.62–68+*il*
- broadside specimens, single sheet, 81:4.123–126*il*
- and calligraphy, 77:3.49–55*il*
- criticism of, 81:1.18
- Dada, 84:3.126–128*il*
- desktop publishing, 89:1.5
- digital programs for, 81:1.31–32*il*
- elements of, 89:2.75–78*il*
- form and pattern issues in, 78:4.106, 80:3.98, 88:4.188, 89:2.78–79*il*
- and Fourier analysis, 77:4.99–100
- functional, 79:3.92–96
- legibility factors, 80:2.65–66, 89:1(insert)
- and letter frequencies, 89:2.81*il*
- manuals, 81:2.59–61*il*, 82:1.31+, 84:3.125–126*il*, 85:1.46–48*il*, 88:4.164*il*, 170+*il*
- mixing typefaces, 86:2.100–101, 88:1.1(cover)
- and optical letterspacing, 79:1.28–29, 81:1.31–32*il*
- and oral literature, 81:1.13+, 81:4.134, 88:4.186–188
- pattern in, 78:3.80, 78:4.106, 89:2.79–80*il*, 89:4.200–201*il*
- and poetry, 80:3.79–81, 87+*il*, 98, 80:4.120, 81:3.108, 81:4.121, 82:3.103, 107–108, 85:2.116–117*il*, 88:3.131–132
- and poetry, shaped, 78:1.15+*il*, 78:3.80, 78:4.106, 83:1.12–13+*il*, 89:2.87–88*il*
- relation of paper and printing process to, 78:1.6, 83:4.138–142+*il*
- satire in, 82:2.63*il*
- teaching of, 75:4.33–35, 78:1.3–4, 80:2.38, 85:1.46–48*il*, 88:4.170+, 90:1.8
- texture in, 89:2.75–82*il*, 80–81
- theories of, 76:3.51–52, 78:3.81, 87:3.151–152+*il*, 89:2.75–82*il*, 90:2.87–88*il*
- with typewriter types, 81:1.25, 85:3.166–167+*il*, 89:4.200–201*il*
- typographic image, elements of, 89:2.75–82*il*
- *See also* fine printing; metal type production; writing systems

typography, bilingual. *See* bilingual editions

typography computerization. *See* digital types and typesetting

typography measurement systems. *See* type sizes and measurement systems

The Typophiles, 76:1.11, 76:4.75, 82:2.42, 83:2.57

U

underlining. *See* punctuation and accents; type ornaments

unimaged plates, printing from, 80:4.111

United Kingdom, book arts in the, 82:1.21, 88:2.96
- artists' books, 82:4.151–152+*il*, 84:3.133
- bookbinding, 20th century, 76:1.13–14, 77:1.1–4, 78:1.14, 78:3.79–80, 83:2.59+*il*, 86:3.167+, 88:1.34+, 88:2.55
- bookbinding conference in, 85:3.184–185
- bookbinding organizations in, 77:1.1–4, 78:2.36–37, 82:3.85–86, 83:2.59+*il*, 88:2.54
- bookbinding, pre-20th century, 79:4.128–129, 81:3.83+, 82:4.129+*il*, 85:1.42, 89:1.22+
- booksellers, 76:2.24, 79:3.97–98, 85:4.192*il*, 87:4.216, 90:3.145*il*
- collectors and collections, 78:2.36, 84:2.49+, 85:1.42–45
- exhibitions, 78:2.36, 78:3.79–80, 85:2.80, 85:3.184–185
- fine press directories, 78:1.23–24, 81:2.57–58, 88:2.66–67+, 88:3.140, 89:3.111
- fine presses, 76:1.7, 78:1.23–24, 79:4.109*il*, 81:2.61–62+*il*, 82:3.87–89, 85:2.81, 88:2.57–67+*il*, 89:3.111
- and Ireland, 78:1.14, 89:1.17–18
- magazines and journals, 80:4.129*il*, 82:3.85, 89:1.5–6
- medieval scribes and manuscripts, 83:2.65–66
- papermaking and paper mills, 76:2.17–20*il*, 76:4.71, 82:2.52, 82:3.114, 89:3.120–121*il*, 90:3.140–141*il*

photographs and portraits of fine printers, 82:3.92*il*, 88:2.63–64*il*
poet of World War I, 89:2.57
printing history, 79:3.90, 80:3.74*il*, 83:1.4–5*il*, 83:3.88–91, 85:2.102–103, 87:4.203, 88:3.106
and Scotland, 85:3.162–163*il*, 89:2.67–69+*il*
type specimen books, 86:2.67+, 87:4.203, 90:2.75+*il*
typefounding in, 83:1.4–5*il*, 11–12*il*, 89:4.195–196
and Wales, 78:1.14, 79:4.129–130, 81:2.50+*il*, 61–62+*il*, 84:2.68–69, 88:2.78+*il*, 88:4.152–154
watermarks, 76:2.18*il*, 89:3.120–121*il*
wood engraving, 81:2.49*il*, 88:2.65, 96–97, 90:2.58–59*il*, 80–81*il*
wood type, 90:2.75–76*il*
United States bookbinding. *See* bookbinding (history and types)
University of Alabama:
collegiate presses conference at, 85:3.153–155
graduate book arts program, 84:2.74–77*il*, 89:1.7
University of California–Berkeley, Bancroft Library, 79:2.42, 82:1.2, 82:4.129+, 89:2.56
University of California–Los Angeles, 82:3.82–83, 85:1.69
University of California–Santa Cruz (Cowell Press). *See* Names of Persons and Fine Presses Index
University of Chicago, Newberry Library, 82:4.123, 83:2.44, 86:2.123, 89:1.7
University of Delaware, 89:2.57+
University of Georgia, 85:4.193
University of Heidelberg, 86:4.189–190
University of Illinois at Chicago, 87:2.61
University of Illinois at Urbana, 81:1.2
University of Iowa:
Center for the Book, 85:3.182–183, 86:2.73–74+*il*, 87:3.171
Cummington Press at, 78:1.3
Dada Archive, 84:3.126–128
Typography Laboratory, 81:1.20–21, 90:1.48–49
University of Iowa, Windhover Press. *See* Names of Persons and Fine Presses Index
University of Kentucky, King Library Press. *See* Names of Persons and Fine Presses Index
University of Nebraska at Omaha, Abattoir Editions. *See* Names of Persons and Fine Presses Index
university presses:
collegiate conference of, 85:3.153–155

comparative study of book design in, 79:2.59–60
University Publishing (journal), 81:3.75
University of Southern California Fine Arts Press. *See* Names of Persons and Fine Presses Index
University of Texas, Austin (Humanities Research Center), 83:2.59, 60, 84:3.129–131

V

"vanity publishing," 80:3.80–81
vellum. *See* parchment and vellum
Victoria & Albert Museum, 81:1.14–15
Victorian era:
broadsides, 85:3.158*il*
color printer, 89:2.72–73
paper bookbindings, 85:1.42
typefaces collection, 89:1.19–20*il*
wood type, 85:3.158*il*
Visible Language (journal), 85:4.192, 88:4.152
visual display of quantitative information, 85:1.48+*il*
visual editing of text, 85:1.46–48*il*
and legibility rules, 82:1.31
visual imagery within text, 85:3.166–167+*il*, 167–168+*il*, 86:2.66–67, 89:1.38–39*il*
patterns of typewriter type, 89:4.200–201*il*
See also type ornaments, images composed of

W

Wales, book arts in:
bookbinding in, 78:1.14
fine printing in, 79:4.129–130, 81:2.50+*il*, 61–62+*il*, 84:2.68–69, 88:2.78+*il*, 88:4.152–154
See also United Kingdom, book arts in
walls, book. *See* book walls
washi. *See* paper, washi, in Japan
water for papermaking, 81:2.43
watercolor book illustrations:
drawing, 81:1.1(cover), 4–8+*il*, 88:3.140+*il*
reproducing, 82:2.49–50
See also color printing; painting
watermarks for handmade papers, 83:3.95+, 115*il*, 84:1.12
collection of, 87:4.181
early American, 83:3.104–105+*il*
English, 76:2.18*il*, 86:3.136–143*il*, 87:4.183*il*, 89:3.120–121*il*
European, 86:4.213, 233*il*, 90:1.9*il*
forgery identification using, 86:3.154

Gutenberg Bible, 86:4.213, 233*il*
wiremarking methods for, 86:3.136–143*il*
See also papermakers and papermaking (handmade); papermills (handmade)
West Coast Print Center, 84:3.101
white pop-up alphabets (uninked), 85:3.168+*il*
White Water Paper Institute, 76:2.23
William James Association. *See* names Index, 76:4.65–66
wiremarking moulds. *See* under papermakers and papermaking (handmade)
H. Wolff Book Mfg. Co. of New York (obituary of Ernst Reichl), 81:3.106–107
women in book arts:
artists' books by, 82:4.151–152+*il*, 85:2.109*il* and many other entries
Arts & Crafts movement, 80:4.126
bookbinders and book cover designers, 79:1.18+*il*, 79:2.33–39*il*, 80:1.10–11*il*, 80:2.58–59*il*, 80:4.118–119+*il*, 81:2.46–47*il*, 81:3.82–83+*il*, 82:1.17–18, 83:1.14–15*il*, 83:3.108–109*il*, 84:1.15+*il*, 84:3.114–115+*il*, 86:1.47–52*il*, 87:2.75–78+*il*, 89:3.114–118*il*
calligraphers, 79:2.33–36+*il*+(banner), 80:4.134–135*il*, 81:1.26+, 86:2.88, 103–107, 86:4.235–236, 88:3.119+(cover)
fine printers, 79:4.119, 85:2.100–104*il*, 85:4.207–209+*il*
fine printers, profiles of, 80:4.115–117*il*, 83:1.23–25*il*, 85:3.177–181+*il*
hand papermakers, 77:4.77–81*il*, 83:3.95
photographs of, 78:1.26*il*, 80:2.59*il*, 80:4.117*il*, 82:4.147*il*, 84:2.56*il*, 77*il*, 78*il*, 85:3.176*il*, 85:4.216*il*, 86:2.82*il*, 88:2.63–64*il*
poetry broadsides portfolio by, 83:1.23–24+*il*
portraits or drawings of women in printing, 85:2.91*il*, 103*il*
printing, in, 85:2.100–104*i*
profiles and interviews of, 81:3.96–97, 86:2.103–107*il*, 86:4.235–236, 90:3.120–125*il*
type designers, 80:4.134–135*il*, 81:4.124, 84:4.166, 85:1.70, 85:3.148–152*il*, 86:2.103–109*il*, 86:3.150*il*, 86:4.235–236, 238, 87:3.162*il*, 88:1.41*il*, 90:3.120–125*il*

wood engravers, 83:2.76–77*il*, 85:4.233–234*il*, 86:4.193–195*il*
writing mistresses, 16th and 17th century, 85:2.88–98*il*
wood engravers (articles and reviews on):
  Bewick, Thomas, 79:3.87
  Eichenberg, Fritz, 78:2.50–51*il*, 88:4.159*il*, 90:1.43–45*il*
  Fawcett, Benjamin, 89:2.72–73
  Gill, Eric, 84:3.129–131*il*
  Kalashnikov, Anatolii, 85:4.232–233*il*
  Morgan, Gwenda, 86:4.193–195*il*
  Moser, Barry, 78:3.65–69*il*
  O'Connor, John, 90:2.80–81*il*
  Poole, Monica, 85:4.234*il*
  Smith, Richard Shirley, 85:4.233*il*
  Stone, Reynolds, 78:3.83–84, 82:2.43
  Weissenborn, Hellmuth, 86:4.193–194*il*
  Wyatt, Leo, 82:3.116–117
  See also wood engraving
wood engraving, 77:3.52*il*, 78:3.65–69*il*, 82:2.57
  alphabets, 86:4.223–224+*il*, 89:4.198*il*
  English, 81:2.49*il*, 85:4.204, 233–234*il*, 86:4.223–224+*il*, 88:2.65, 96–97, 90:2.58–59*il*, 80–81*il*
  on Fine Print cover, 84:3(cover), 135*il*
  German, 86:2.109+*il*
  and illustration, 78:3.65–69*il*, 84:1.34–35, 38–41*il*, 84:2.64–66, 85:4.233–234*il*, 86:2.109+*il*, 121–122*il*
  letterforms in, 86:4.223–224+*il*
  museums, 85:2.81, 89:1.4*il*
  printing techniques, 77:1.19+*il*, 78:3.65–69*il*, 81:2.50, 85:4.204, 233–234*il*, 234, 86:1.29+*il*, 88:1.32+*il*, 88:2.72–73+*il*
  scientific illustration, 83:2.76–77+*il*, 84:3.131–132
  See also printmaking methods and illustration
wood type:
  19th century ornamented, 85:3.158*il*
  American, 83:2.43+(cover), 45–49+*il*, 84:2.70*il*, 85:3.158*il*
  British, 90:2.75–76*il*
  chromatic, 83:2.46
  on Fine Print cover, 83:2.43+(cover)
  Hebrew, 85:3.147
  specimen books of, 76:3.42–43, 83:2.43+*il*, 84:2.70*il*, 88:4.163–164*il*, 90:2.75–76*il*
  Victorian era, 85:3.158*il*
  white on black, 90:2.75*il*
woodcuts:
  black on black, 88:1.32+*il*
  blind embossed, 79:2.55–56+*il*
  illustrations, 84:1.36–37*il*, 84:2.69*il*, 88:1.26–33*il*, 89:1.38–39*il*
  Italian 15th century, 82:2.43+*il*, 82:4.150+*il*, 90:3.101+*il*
  letterforms in, 76:3.47*il*, 79:1.14–15*il*, 89:4.198*il*
  See also printmaking methods and illustration; individual artist names (in the Names Index)
wooden book boards. *See* bookbinding techniques and materials
wooden presses. *See* handpresses
woodpulp. *See* paper
Wookey Hole Paper Mill, 76:4.71
writing implements, history of, 76:2.33, 89:4.198
writing mistresses, 16th–17th century, 81:1.26+*il*, 85:2.88–98*il*
writing systems:
  Aztec glyphs, 83:1.34*il*
  Braille, 82:3.83
  chancery, 82:4.145+*il*
  children's, 78:1.24+
  Chinese ideograms, 79:1.25, 79:3.87, 85:4.236–237*il*, 86:1.43
  Chinook, 89:2.81*il*
  Cyrillic and oriental, 83:3.124–125*il*
  Czech, 87:1.19–21+*il*
  European 16th century, 81:1.26+, 89:2.88–90*il*
  Hebrew, 86:1.7*il*, 21–27*il*, 86:3.133–134, 87:1.53–54
  hieroglyphic, 80:4.106, 81:1.2, 12, 85:3.165*il*, 86:1.8*il*
  Inuit, 83:2.58*il*
  italic, 78:4.119, 79:2.44–45, 82:4.145+*il*
  Karmelitic Hebrew, 86:3.133–134
  Latin language, 79:4.118*il*, 80:4.126+, 86:1.44+
  medieval, 81:4.136
  museums of, 89:4.198
  Ogham (druidic alphabet), 79:2.47–48+*il*
  oral traditions and, 81:1.13+, 81:4.134, 86:4.207, 88:4.186–188
  Roman era, 79:4.118*il*, 80:4.126+, 88:1.6–8, 89:3.135*il*
  from Summarian clay symbols, 78:3.78–79*il*
  surveys of world, 80:4.131–132, 81:3.97–98, 83:2.58–59*il*
  teaching and learning, 78:1.24+, 80:2.68
  theory of, 78:3.78–79*il*
  and typography, 79:4.120–123*il*, 90:2.61
  Zapotec, 80:4.106, 81:1.12
  See also language; letterforms; reading; type design

X

x-height, font, 80:2.67–68, 87:4.181, 89:2.77, 90:3.136–138*il*
xeroxing. *See* electrostatic printing
xylographic books, 15th century, 86:3.153–154

Y

Yale University, Rollins Symposium on type and typography, 80:3.82–83+
Year of the Reader, 1987, (Library of Congress), 87:3.117*il*